DATE DUE

JUL 0 1 1998		
NOV 2 9 1999		
APR 3 0 2001		
NOV 2 6 2001		
APR 23 '03		

DEMCO 38-297

SOCIAL MOVEMENTS PAST AND PRESENT

Robert D. Benford, Editor

PROFILES IN POWER

The Antinuclear Movement and the Dawn of the Solar Age

Jerry Brown, Ph.D., and Rinaldo Brutoco, J.D.

Twayne Publishers
An Imprint of Simon & Schuster Macmillan
New York

Prentice Hall International
London Mexico City New Delhi Singapore Sydney Toronto

Profiles in Power: The Antinuclear Movement and the Dawn of the Solar Age
Jerry Brown and Rinaldo Brutoco

Twayne Publishers
An Imprint of Simon & Schuster Macmillan
1633 Broadway
New York, NY 10019

Library of Congress Cataloging-in-Publication Data

Brown, Jerry, 1942–
    Profiles in power : the antinuclear movement and the dawn of the
solar age / Jerry Brown and Rinaldo Brutoco.
        p.   cm. — (Social movements past and present)
    Includes bibliographical references and index.
    ISBN 0-8057-3879-7 (hc : alk. paper)
    1. Nuclear engineering—Safety measures—Public opinion—United
States. 2. Antinuclear movement—United States. 3. Nuclear
industry—United States. 4. Energy industries—United States.
5. Energy policy—United States. 6. Nuclear energy—Public opinion—
United States. 7. Solar energy—Public opinion—United States.
8. Social change—United States.   I. Brutoco, Rinaldo.   II. Series.
TK9152.B76   1997
333.792'415'0973—dc21   97-26458
                                                                       CIP

The paper used in this publication meets the minimum requirements of American National Standard for Information Sciences—Permanence of Paper for Printed Library Materials, ANSI Z39.48-1984. ∞™

10 9 8 7 6 5 4 3 2 1
Printed in the United States of America

For Marion, Julie, Michael, and Elliot
and
for Krishna, Dana, Orion, and Darya
and
for their children's children for a thousand years

Contents

Foreword

Those on the ramparts of initiatory democratic movements are so focused on the demands of the injustices they are trying to prevent or diminish that they rarely have the time to reflect on what they have accomplished together and what lessons there are for the future. Jerry Brown and Rinaldo Brutoco demonstrate in their book, *Profiles in Power: The Antinuclear Movement and the Dawn of the Solar Age,* just how valuable such a reflection can be.

In their chapters, they remind us just how much bad science, gravely wrong projections, and industrial arrogance composed the corporate state that an aroused citizenry had to challenge. From the assurance in the 1950s that atomic energy would be "too cheap to meter," that it would propel our motor vehicles, and that 1,000 nuclear plants would be operating in the United States by the year 2000 (including 100 in California alone, up and down the Pacific coast), the party line dominated. Then there was the axiomatic assertion by leading economists that there is an inexorable connection between economic growth and growth in energy consumption, an assertion that left little room for energy efficiency. The most grotesque myth of all was that nuclear power was clean and safe for the environment and the planet.

There was clearly a corporate-government ideology that controlled energy policy, selecting highly capitalized, centralized energy technologies, regularly subsidized by taxpayers, over decentralized, renewable, and efficient technologies, starting with household and consumer products and extending to buildings, transportation, industry, commerce, and other uses. Thrift was out; waste was in because it was more profitable to companies whose sales grew in direct proportion to the amount of energy consumed in the economy.

The first citizen breakthrough, for those of us who had been involved in the pursuit of efficient, renewable energy since the sixties, was accurate and challenging information to counteract the energy propagandists. Today's energy activists, overwhelmed with supporting data and achievements for their cause, would find it hard to believe there was such severe secrecy, suppression, and intimidation over information that should have been public and over the few whistle-blowers who spoke up for the right to know and for independently reviewed scientific analysis.

Our mass convocations in Washington—the Critical Mass Conferences—were largely information seminars for the thousands who attended, who took home with them not only information but also the early civic strategies that the speakers found workable. Indeed, information was the currency of energy democracy. Those who attended the seminars returned home and, in community after community where nuclear plants were operating or under construction, led the struggle that this book depicts. The authors show that autocratic technologies, like nuclear power, supported and subsidized by the corporate state of business and government, are not allowed to fail. Certainly, the utility industry's current legislative drive, occurring in many states, is designed to trade acceptance of deregulation for bailing out their nuclear power plant lemons on the backs of taxpayers and ratepayers. The governmental guarantees for nuclear power continue even when the plants are no longer competitive because they are so costly to operate and maintain. The civic struggle continues as well.

The profiles of citizen courage and foresight in this book are representative of many other citizen stalwarts, each of whom deserves similar depiction. The opponents who emerged to fight nuclear power in Oklahoma, Pennsylvania, Ohio, Massachusetts, Tennessee Valley, Oregon, Texas, and Maine come to mind. Someday these stalwarts should be treated with similar attentiveness by contemporary historians who write about social change and the redistribution of decisional power.

Profiles in Power is more than a history of opposition; it promotes replacement energy of the renewable and efficient kind. It is truly remarkable that, notwithstanding the abundant data behind the "soft path" of renewable energy and energy conservation, with its numerous benefits, our government remains unwilling to make a major transformation in this direction. Nuclear power still receives large government subsidies, and the coal, oil, and nuclear lobbies are still decisive in Washington. It seems that what has been happening in our country toward the "soft path" is the cumulative effect of many human energies and entrepreneurial-inventive initiatives that prove the case but are obstructed from diffusing it more rapidly. There are too many nontechnical obstacles, too many nonlevel playing fields from local to national to overcome.

When John Abbotts and I wrote our book, *The Menace of Atomic Energy,* Jimmy Carter was president. The previous five years were full of ferment for energy independence, motor vehicle fuel economy, energy conservation standards, and prospects of solar power. Then Reagan became president and down went Washington's interest in "soft path" energy, down went the tax credit for renewables that would have made for a more level playing field, and down went government research and development. Efficiency standards were frozen or rolled back. Under Reagan and Bush, oil imports climbed to record levels. Under Clinton, the lip service changed but little else changed. Given Gore's professed interest in environmentally benign energy, the protracted lull was especially disappointing. No major statement on energy has come from the president or vice president.

Brown and Brutoco give readers encouraging material to press forward more assertively and effectively. The opponents of nuclear power faced more imposing obstacles at the outset than the proponents of solar and efficient energy do today. We should not have to wait for another catastrophic energy accident, or long lines at gas stations, to arouse the public consciousness and to forge the public policies and marketplace clarities necessary to make the transition to the solar age. This is a transition for which the rest of the world will one day thank us, as a nation that came to grips with the serious global side effects of fossil fuel and nuclear power and accorded crucial respect for future generations.

Ralph Nader
Washington, D.C.
August 1997

Preface

Mark Oncavage never planned to wage an "energy war" on the U.S. Nuclear Regulatory Commission and Florida Power and Light Company (FPL).

In 1979, Oncavage was living a quiet life as a sixth-grade music teacher in Miami, Florida. He did not realize that by blowing the whistle on the $500 million breakdown of the steam generators at FPL's nuclear power plants, he would be drawn into the political cyclotron of the antinuclear movement. Yet he inevitably was.

Ralph Nader made FPL a cause célèbre by calling steam generator corrosion "the largest product failure in the history of American industry." Congressman Edward Markey (D-Mass.) convened public hearings on the endemic radiation and tube leaks that plagued most aging American pressurized water reactors (PWRs). FPL sued Westinghouse, the major manufacturer of PWRs, for supplying FPL with defective steam generators. A *Miami Herald* cover story, "The Trouble at Turkey Point," polled readers on who should pay to resolve the problem of the "green grunge" that was corroding the nuclear power plants—the consumers or the utility?

In the process, Mark Oncavage emerged as a "profile in power."

This book presents 10 "profiles in power." It is about people who have been touched and transformed by "power" in two ways. First, their pivotal confrontations with the energy establishment have significantly impacted the divisive national policy debate that has historically pitted nuclear power against renewable energy and utilities against environmentalists in an imperative search for the cornerstone on which to build America's energy future. Second, they have experienced the political power of Gandhi's *satyagraha* (truth force), which transformed them from *private* citizens into *public* antinuclear activists or solar crusaders in the energy battles of the past two decades.

Sociologist Jerome Price has described the antinuclear movement as "one of the most significant social movements to emerge in the twentieth century." The U.S. antinuclear movement first received national attention in 1977, when 2,000 nonviolent protesters were arrested by the National Guard for occupying a reactor construction site in Seabrook, New Hampshire. Two years later, in 1979, public support for nuclear power began to plummet after a bizarre synchronicity in which the Three Mile Island accident occurred only two weeks after the release of *The China Syndrome,* a film about a reactor meltdown.

Today, after more than 20 years of faulty economics and relentless protest, the nuclear power industry has collapsed in the United States. Activist attention has now focused on the fallout of the nuclear industry—bailout costs for abandoned reactors, monitoring of aging and unsafe plants, and public opposition to radioactive waste storage dumps.

"The 1990s will not see the demise of the antinuclear movement," Price observed in the conclusion to *The Antinuclear Movement.* We concur.

The late 1990s and the beginning of the twenty-first century will witness an ongoing campaign to resurrect nuclear power in the United States. The rebirth of the nuclear option has already set the stage for a renewed clash between the nuclear industry and the antinuclear movement. The energy conflicts of the 1970s and 1980s portend a deepening schism that will test the limits of citizen activism and influence the energy future of the nation into the next century. Concomitantly, the energy crises of the past two decades have produced a new generation of energy activists—*green* utility executives, free-market regulators, independent power producers, demand-side efficiency experts, renewable-energy innovators, and solar technology entrepreneurs—who are establishing an alternative energy paradigm for the United States.

These environmental and entrepreneurial activists in the energy policy drama have played key roles in facilitating the nuclear power stalemate, the conservation revolution, the emergence of a viable renewable-energy industry, and the dawn of the solar age.

During the late 1990s, this renewed energy debate will be exacerbated by new calls for energy independence in the wake of the Gulf War; growing environmental concerns over radioactive waste and acid rain; a spreading consumer rebellion against the $100 billion "bailout bill" for the initial collapse of the nuclear industry; predictions of electrical shortages by the end of the decade; the dramatic international loss of confidence in the "friendly atom," shattered by the Chernobyl disaster; and, most recently, growing worldwide concerns about crop failures, property destruction, and rising sea levels, caused by increasing temperatures and global climate change resulting from the burning of fossil fuels.

Furthermore, the threats of nuclear proliferation, nuclear terrorism, and the nuclear power–nuclear weapons connection have broadened the nuclear power issue from a domestic debate over energy policy into a global question of national security. In the post–Cold War era, apprehension has grown that terrorists may use fissionable materials stolen from former Soviet nuclear power and weapons facilities, where security is in a shambles, to fashion crude but deadly atomic weapons. Already, "rogue nations" such as Iran, Iraq, and North Korea have attempted to use commercial reactor facilities as clandestine bases for nuclear weapons research and production. The potential breakdown of the international nuclear nonproliferation structure may emerge as the defining crisis of the post–Cold War period.

Profiles in Power is a unique work for several reasons. First, through dramatic case studies, it documents the safety, technical, and economic issues that motivated the development of a grassroots antinuclear movement—a movement that accelerated the mercurial meltdown of the nuclear power industry in the United States.

Second, it shows how forward-thinking utility executives and regulatory commissioners implemented a "conservation revolution" as an alternative to building new base-load nuclear or coal plants and to depending further on foreign oil.

Third, it examines the economic, entrepreneurial, and environmental dynamics that are bringing about the new energy paradigm and the dawn of the solar age.

Last, it suggests that an aggressive national program to fully implement energy conservation and the transition to a solar and hydrogen economy can positively address many of America's most pressing energy problems. Among these are the needs to

- reduce the country's rapidly growing oil trade deficit;
- minimize the economic and political threats of continued and increased dependence on Middle Eastern oil supplies;

- limit and eventually prevent further increases in greenhouse gases, thereby reducing pollution and stabilizing the global climate;
- capture a large share of the enormous potential industry for advanced energy and environmental technologies, which could provide one of the largest international markets for high-tech, high-wage jobs in the next century, with annual sales estimated to exceed $800 billion; and
- increase national security by reducing the risks of nuclear theft, sabotage, proliferation, and terrorism.

"Energy is eternal delight," wrote the poet Milton. "And eternal opportunity," John D. Rockefeller might have added. Much as Rockefeller did in the twentieth century with "rock oil," today's entrepreneurs look at the energy and environmental crises as a historic opportunity to create the new power industries and ecological enterprises of the twenty-first century.

"Our mission is simple. We want to replace Exxon," states David Freeman, former head of the Tennessee Valley Authority, in describing his efforts to build "America's premier conservation power plant" in California. The stakes in the energy debate are enormous. To paraphrase historian Daniel Yergin, author of *The Prize: The Epic Quest for Oil, Money, and Power,* the winners in this quest will possess nothing less than the holy grail of perpetual power and mastery of the twenty-first century.

Profiles in Power is an original study based on historical research and field interviews with key actors in the energy drama: private citizens who became antinuclear activists, renewable-energy advocates, and solar power entrepreneurs. In this context, these profiles are not meant to be definitive biographies. Rather, they focus on how these citizens impacted the energy policy debate by challenging energy choices at major utilities and by implementing innovative energy technologies.

Much like the eight U.S. statesmen so eloquently described in President John F. Kennedy's *Profiles in Courage,* our "profiles in power" document the struggles of people who have enriched our public life by displaying that "most admirable of human virtues—courage."

Writing in 1956, President Kennedy observed: "Today the challenge of political courage looms larger than ever before. For our everyday life is becoming so saturated with the tremendous power of mass communications that any unpopular or unorthodox course arouses a storm of protest." But what happens when professional politicians can no longer be counted on to display the political courage required to protect the public health and welfare? When government itself distorts candor and honesty in becoming the chief promoter of the atomic industry?

The fate of the nation then rests on the shoulders of individuals, working often at great personal risk and sacrifice, who challenge the atomic industrial establishment's vision of a nuclear future for America. These individuals are the backbone of the antinuclear movement, the modern Horatios who defend the nation against the plutonium economy, and the profiles in power who serve as midwives for the birth of the coming solar age.

Acknowledgments

Since the birth of the Atomic Age more than 50 years ago, citizens, entrepreneurs, and scientists have been drawn in to the nuclear debate for many different reasons. Initially, for physicists, it was a dual quest for the ultimate nuclear weapon and unlimited electric power. For arms control experts, it was the intrigue of pilfered plutonium, stolen perhaps by Israel, or Iraq, or Pakistan, for clandestine weapons programs. Health physicists have stalked invisible but deadly radioactive isotopes to find the cause of increased cancer rates among American soldiers, Western farmers, nuclear shipyard workers, Three Mile Island residents, and breast cancer patients, all of whom were exposed to high doses of radioactivity. And members of the worldwide medical community have rallied to aid the survivors of Hiroshima and Nagasaki and, more recently, to save the children of Chernobyl.

The nuclear era has also spawned decades of international protest against both nuclear weapons and nuclear power. Across the United States, citizens have demonstrated, lobbied, voted, and gone to court to stop the construction of nuclear power plants. Over the past two decades, a unique coalition of business executives, consumers, environmentalists, labor leaders, and legislators have brought about a veritable conservation revolution at some of the nation's largest and most progressive electric utility companies. At the same time, a new generation of energy entrepreneurs and solar scientists have sought alternatives to nuclear power and have demonstrated the potential to transform the global energy system through clean, renewable-energy technologies, such as solar electric power systems, lightweight electric cars, superefficient lightbulbs, and giant wind farms. Today, a handful of innovators are hoping to lead humanity out of the nuclear and fossil fuel era by seeking the holy grail of infinite energy described in Jules Verne's vision of a hydrogen-powered future.

Our atomic odyssey began with a more prosaic first step, involving a plumbing problem.

The press called it the "green grunge." Technically, it was steam generator corrosion at Florida Power and Light Company's Turkey Point nuclear power reactors 3 and 4, located near Miami. As we became involved in a legal intervention to stop the $500 million cost of the Turkey Point steam generator repairs from being passed on to consumers, we began searching for effective strategies both to stop future nuclear power construction and to promote safe and renewable sources of energy. In the process, we met citizen activists and solar scientists from around the country who were grappling with the same problems.

We have had a long-standing interest in the processes by which private citizens and business executives can affect public policy through public-interest organizations and social movements. As people interested in the process of citizen power, we realized that the leaders of the antinuclear and pro-solar movements were developing successful strategies for stalemating nuclear power and promoting renewable energy. As social scientists, we observed that energy activists and entrepreneurs were creating a powerful social movement that was significantly impacting the national energy debate from the grassroots level. The story of their power struggles needed to be documented. Thus, we initiated the Strategies for Safe Energy research project. *Profiles in Power* presents the findings of our research.

Between 1983 and 1995, we interviewed 33 activists, economists, entrepreneurs, regulators, scientists, and utility executives involved with energy and energy policy in 12 states and the District of Columbia. Our research took us from Florida to Maine, from New York to California. The information and observations presented in this book are based primarily on the research and interviews conducted as part of the Strategies for Safe Energy project.

Our primary debt of gratitude goes to each and every one of those people who so graciously gave of their time for our interviews and questions. Their names and organizational affiliations appear on the list of interviews that follows these acknowledgments. To all of these pioneers who are helping America blaze a trail into the solar age, we offer both our thanks and our apologies, for surely we have not been able to present all of the thoughts and insights they have offered.

Our ability to carry out this study for more than a decade has been facilitated by the generous support of several foundations and individuals. These are the Ark Foundation; the Friedson family, especially Barbara, Belvin, and Lucille; the Omega Point Institute; Rockefeller Family Associates; Margy Stewart; Marion Weber; and Richard B. Wolf. We thank them not only for their financial contributions but also for their intellectual conviction and moral support, which kept us going even in times of greatest difficulty.

Grateful acknowledgment is due to a number of institutions and publishers for their permission to use the materials presented in several illustrations for this book. Figure 5, "SMUD Photovoltaic Electric Vehicle Charging Station," is used by permission of the Sacramento Municipal Utility District. Figure 6, "Energy Partners' Hydrogen 'Gas Station': Using Hydrogen as the Energy Currency of Tomorrow," is used by permission of John H. Perry Jr., chairman of the board, Energy Partners. Figure 7, "Energy Strategy: The Hard Path and the Soft Path," which was compiled from Amory B. Lovins, "Energy Strategy: The Road Not Taken?" is reprinted by permission of *Foreign Affairs*, 1976, copyright 1976 by the Council on Foreign Relations, Inc. Figure 8, "World Energy Use and Carbon Emissions, 1989, with Goals for 2030," is reprinted by permission of the Worldwatch Institute.

We owe sincere thanks to several people who contributed their special skills to the creation and production of this book. To Marion Brown and Ron Meyerson, for their research assistance and insightful comments on the early drafts of the manuscript. To Michael Kraemer, whose fastidious editorial and grammatical talents have made this book more concise and readable. To the editorial staff at Impressions Book and Journal Services, Inc., who made innumerable contributions to the production of a lucid publication. To Anne Davidson, our editor at Twayne Publishers, for her patient encouragement in helping this study reach its full potential.

Last, we want to express our deepest gratitude to Robert D. Benford, the series editor for Twayne Publishers' Social Movements Past and Present. From the beginning of our efforts to publish *Profiles in Power,* he has enthusiastically supported our multiple case study approach as a sound basis for analyzing the dynamics of the new energy paradigm and as a way to bring to life in a concrete and human fashion a topic that might often seem to the lay reader to be abstract and impersonal. Professor Benford has generously shared with us his own research on social movements, nuclear politics, and environmental controversies as a framework for bringing the issue of individual action in the antinuclear movement to center stage while providing readers with a backstage tour of the contentious world of energy policy development. We have been blessed and privileged to be able to bring this work to fruition under his guidance.

Interviews

Phil Amadon and Rich Anderson (Zimmer), Ohio.
Bill Appel, Dan Leahy, Mark Reis (WPPSS), Washington.*
Nora Bredes (Shoreham), New York.*
John Bryson (Southern California Edison), California.*
Roger Carlton, Community Action Research Group, Iowa.
Alvin Duskin, Northwind, Inc., California.
Christopher Flavin, Worldwatch Institute, Washington, D.C.*
David Freeman (Sacramento Municipal Utility District), California.*
John Gofman (TMI and Chernobyl), California*
Amy Goldsmith, Massachusetts Nuclear Referendum Committee, Massachusetts.
David Goldstein, Natural Resources Defense Council, California.
Anna Gyorgy, Critical Mass Energy Project, Washington, D.C.
Jim Harding, Friends of the Earth, California.
Dick Hubbard, MHB Associates, California.
Jim and Ann Hurst, People against Nuclear Power (TMI), Pennsylvania.
Tim Johnson, Citizens for a Prosperous Georgia, Georgia.
Charles Komanoff, Komanoff Energy Associates, New York.
Kermit Kubritz, PG&E, California.
Hunter and Amory Lovins, Rocky Mountain Institute, Colorado.*
Ralph Nader, Critical Mass Energy Project, Washington, D.C.
Mark Oncavage, Floridians United for Safe Energy (Turkey Point), Florida.*
John Perry, Energy Partners, Inc., Florida.*
David Roe, Environmental Defense Fund (PG&E), California.
John Ruoff, Palmetto Alliance, South Carolina.
John Schaeffer, Real Goods Trading Corporation, California.*

*Interview used as basis for case study (profile in power) in this book.

Rusty Schweikert, California Energy Commission, California.
Sandy Silver, Mothers for Peace (Diablo Canyon), California.
Kirk Stone, Citizens for Ratepayers Rights (Seabrook), New Hampshire.
John Stutz, Energy Systems Research Group, Massachusetts.
Kathy Welch, New York Public Interest Research Group (Indian Point), New
    York.

Figures

Chapter One

Profiles in Power

By the year 2000, we should see the reemergence of nuclear energy as the most promising power source for generating electricity. Cheaper than gas and safer than coal, with a near-infinite fuel supply, nuclear power's time has come. Again.
　　　—Albert B. Reynolds, professor of nuclear engineering, 1993

Nineteen ninety-five marked the 50th anniversary of the Atomic Age.

In fact, 1995 was a special year for 50th anniversaries: the liberation of the Holocaust survivors from the death camps of Germany and the Allied victory over Hitler. But, unlike these others, the "golden anniversary" of the dropping of atomic bombs by the United States on the Japanese cities of Hiroshima and Nagasaki was met with a mixture of pride and shame, of patriotic celebration and national self-flagellation.[1]

At zero hour on July 16, 1945, the United States exploded the first atomic bomb in history at 05:29:45 in a remote corner of the New Mexico desert, splitting history and giving birth to the Atomic Age with what James Conant described as a "white light like the end of the world." Scientist Robert Oppenheimer, who coordinated the building of the bomb at Los Alamos, watched the mushroom cloud's brilliant column of fire rise 10,000 feet and thought of the lines from ancient Hindu scripture: "Now I am become Death, the destroyer of worlds."

The first and to date the *last* use of nuclear weapons in warfare occurred on August 6 and 9, 1945, when American B-29 bombers dropped A-bombs on Hiroshima and Nagasaki. According to Japanese estimates, approximately 210,000 people died within three months of the attacks, and about 220,000 more died later from radiation poisoning. As Robert Lewis, the copilot of the *Enola Gay,* the B-29 that dropped the first bomb, looked down on what was left of Hiroshima, he wrote in his diary, "My God! What have we done?"

It seemed as if Prometheus, not content to have snatched fire from the gods, had returned to the heavens again, disguised as Einstein and armed with the knowledge that $E = mc^2$, to steal the primary force of the universe. With the unleashing of the atomic genie, a Faustian battle for the soul of humanity had begun, giving rise to the antinuclear movement—one of the most important social movements of the twentieth century. The stakes were monumental. At times, the "fate of the earth" hung in the balance.[2] With the splitting of the atom, it seemed as if technology had spun out of control and threatened to end history itself.

Although atomic weapons abruptly ended the era of conventional warfare, they simultaneously ushered in another era—the Atomic Age—and along with it the Cold War, the proliferation of nuclear weapons, and the development of commercial nuclear power. In the late 1980s, the world witnessed the crumbling of the Soviet Union, the end of the Cold War, the first international initiatives to physically dismantle intercontinental warheads, and a retreat from the threat of nuclear Armageddon that had dominated international relations for nearly half a century. But, as shown by the Gulf War with Iraq, the tensions with North Korea over nuclear plant inspections, and the crumbling security at nuclear plants and weapons stockpiles in the former Soviet Union, the link between nuclear power and nuclear weapons remains a major concern in the post–Cold War world.

Thus, 50 years into the Atomic Age, the world was haunted by the dual specters of nuclear terrorism and rogue nuclear nations. Only a half century ago, in a more innocent time, it seemed as if the nuclear genie unleashed by World War II could be stuffed back into its bottle and tamed to serve humanity.

In 1953, in the atmosphere of national guilt over dropping the bombs on Japan, President Eisenhower made his famous "Atoms for Peace" address to the United Nations. The United States, he declared, would beat its atomic weapons into nuclear plowshares, harness the power of the "friendly atom," and—borrowing a phrase that would come back to haunt the nuclear industry—generate electricity "too cheap to meter." Two decades later, as the nation reeled from the recession and oil shock caused by the rise of OPEC and the first Arab oil embargo of the 1970s, President Nixon could still praise nuclear power as the key to Project Independence, which would free the United States from the Arab choke hold on the oil that flowed through the Gulf of Oman to the "free world." "Let us pledge that by 1980, under Project Independence, we shall be able to meet America's energy needs from America's own energy resources," he proclaimed.

Today that grand vision of a vigorous U.S. nuclear industry lies in shambles. As of 1995, 17 years have passed since a nuclear reactor has been ordered in the United States, and 22 years (dating back to 1973) since a new plant was ordered and not later canceled.[3] Indeed, between 1972 and 1994, 123 nuclear plants, representing 135,677 megawatts of generating capacity, were canceled by utilities. These cancellations represent more power than the 1994 U.S. total nuclear capacity of 99,000 megawatts at 109 licensed reactors. The cancellations include nearly completed plants whose operating licenses were revoked for safety reasons, such as Zimmer in Ohio; completed plants not granted permission to go on line for lack of an acceptable evacuation plan, such as Shoreham in New York; and dozens of nuclear white elephants that have simply been abandoned at various stages of construction owing mainly to enormous cost overruns.

Stalemated by a combination of domestic and international forces, "nuclear power has suffered one of the most dramatic declines of any industrial sector in the United States in recent history."[4] What happened?

This book traces the impact of the antinuclear movement on the collapse of the nuclear power industry and the dawning of the solar age that is emerging as a viable alternative to a nuclear future.

The End of the Petroleum Era

The petroleum era will end in the twenty-first century. By nearly every expert's assessment, the fossil fuel economy, which rose with the transition from wood to coal in the late 1700s, will end in the near future, geologically speaking. At present rates of demand, and assuming no further backlash from environmental concerns over global warming, the world has enough oil in known and economically viable reserves to last for more than 40 years, enough gas for more than 60 years, and enough coal for more than 230 years. One day in the not-too-distant twenty-first century, a global oil crisis will occur as the spigot to the oil patch runs dry, caused purely by supply and economic considerations. As that watershed approaches, fossil fuel prices will rise, making alternative forms of energy even more economically competitive than they are today.

We live in the midst of a unique period in human history—a time in which the explosive growth of population and civilization has been fueled by the long dead fossils of the age of dinosaurs. Carbon-based energy resources, which were developed over tens of millions of years, are being consumed in what amounts to a fraction of a second if measured by the "cosmic calendar" of the five-billion-year history of our planet.

With the advent of the Industrial Revolution, we entered a period in human history when first coal and later petroleum and natural gas provided energy sources vastly more convenient, less expensive, and easier to control than the muscle power of humans and animals—the power on which past civilizations were built.[5] For centuries, these passive-solar civilizations relied on the burning of wood and animal dung to fuel the fires of the pre-Industrial Age.

The current petroleum era will peak around the year 2000 and face its sunset years by the middle of the twenty-first century. Indeed, there will be "a critical oil shortage impending within our lifetimes."[6] Today we are about to enter the final quarter of the 200-year period from 1850 to 2050 when oil was the world's key natural resource and commodity.

Viewed from a geological time perspective, the world has experienced a global oil feeding frenzy in which we have short-circuited in 200 years an atmospheric-carbon and terrestrial-fuel cycle that took some 70 million years to create. This represents a drunken oil binge, which to future generations will seem like a brief aberration in world energy history. As with any drunken binge, it has been driven by addiction and has been incredibly destructive.

For these reasons, oil sits center stage in power and politics in the twentieth century. In *The Prize: The Epic Quest for Oil, Money, and Power,* author Daniel Yergin finds three central themes in "the century of oil."[7] First is the rise and development of capitalism and modern business, with oil being the world's biggest and most pervasive business and the engine that drives the other key segments of the industrial economy. Second is that oil as a commodity has been intimately intertwined with national strategies and global politics and power—and with the rise and fall of the great powers. Third is that we have become a "Hydrocarbon Society."

Oil defines how we live, where we live, and how we travel. More fundamentally, oil provides the essential components in the fertilizer on which modern agribusiness depends; oil makes it possible to transport food from the countryside to the cities; and petroleum by-products provide the plastics, chemicals, and many drugs that are the building blocks of contemporary civilization.

There is little doubt that as petroleum becomes critically scarce and expensive, humanity will come to a major crossroads. Our very way of life and standard of living will be threatened. We must decrease our dependence on fossil fuels, particularly oil, or as world population and industrialization increase, we will face a dramatic decline in global living standards and the possibility of a major population crash, similar to that originally forecasted by the Club of Rome's study entitled *The Limits of Growth* and later reaffirmed in *Beyond the Limits*.[8]

Certainly, what has been called the "American way of life" would be at stake. Today Americans own more than 190 million cars and trucks and consume 17 million barrels of oil each day. That represents 25 percent of the world's oil, half of which comes from overseas, leaving the United States vulnerable to oil shocks, petroleum cutoffs, recessions, and—as Desert Storm proved—even war.

In fact, the United States has already experienced three major oil shocks and oil-driven recessions. The first two, in 1973 to 1974 and in 1979, were caused by the Arab-led OPEC embargo and the Iranian Revolution, respectively. The last one was caused by Saddam Hussein's seizure of Kuwaiti oil fields and the threat he posed to Saudi Arabia, thereby placing two-thirds of the world's known oil reserves at risk.

But the Gulf War only underscored a national reluctance to give up our addiction to cheap oil. "We have an energy policy today. We will go to war to keep the oil flowing from the Middle East. That's the Bush strategy," observed David Freeman, former director of the Tennessee Valley Authority.[9]

On the eve of the Gulf War, congressional leaders and the defense establishment at the Pentagon converged in their views that energy was both a vital economic commodity and a national security issue. As Senator J. Bennett Johnston (D-La.) put it: "Well, their [the Pentagon's] concerns were the same as mine, that is, that we were fighting a war over energy, in order to protect our supplies of crude from the Middle East, and that they wanted an effective policy, as I did, to get our energy in America rather than having to import it."[10]

However, with a half million troops pouring into the Gulf, option after option supported by the Defense and State Departments to conserve energy in the United States was opposed by President Bush's economic advisers. Among these options were higher fuel efficiency standards for cars, a higher gasoline tax, and a small tax on oil to increase the United States' strategic petroleum reserves. According to sources who attended the key policy meetings, national security adviser General Brent Scowcroft, who sided with the Pentagon view, listened in disbelief as one conservation measure after another was rejected. Finally he asked, "What are we fighting this war for anyway?"[11]

Although oil-driven industrialization has almost universally been viewed as beneficial, during the past 25 years, public awareness of the negative environmental consequences of using fossil fuels has moved to center stage. The releasing of carbon dioxide into the environment has already begun to modify the world's climate and accelerate the greenhouse effect. According to the 1995 assessment of the United Nations Intergovernmental Panel on Climate Change, these trends will cause an average global temperature increase of 1.8 to 6.3°F over the next 100 years, with a potential increase in world sea levels of one-half foot to more than three feet due to melting polar caps.[12] Other negative impacts of fossil fuels include acid rain, early deaths caused by sulfur dioxide air pollution, smog and ozone pollution in our cities, and the thermal pollution of lakes and rivers.

In addition, gasoline-powered cars have led to the destruction of our civil rail transportation system, which now must be rebuilt from the ground up. It is a great irony that the nation that used railroads to forge itself into a single political entity after the Civil War is today the least advanced among industrial nations in the use of municipal and long-distance trains.

Obviously, although the benefits of fossil fuels have been great, the costs have been high—and will continue to grow higher. At the same time, there is no escaping the geological reality that there will be no significant increases in the world's fossil fuel inventory over the next millennium, or even over many millennia. Although energy conservation may delay or mitigate the transition from fossil fuels, the only viable long-term and permanent solution is developing other sources of energy. The choices are limited to two: nuclear power (fission and fusion) and renewable energy in various forms (solar, wind, geothermal, hydroelectric, tidal, and eventually hydrogen-powered fuel cells).[13]

Because of the approaching end of the petroleum era, we are faced with a fundamental, although not necessarily mutually exclusive, choice between two forms of energy—nuclear and renewable—as the basis for the energy system of the twenty-first century and beyond.

The Nuclear Industry Meltdown, 1970s–1980s

To date, the nuclear choice has failed to fulfill its potential. Over the past 20 years, commercial nuclear power has experienced an unprecedented industrial meltdown in the United States.

The prognosis for nuclear power has shifted dramatically from Weinberg's "nuclear energy revolution" (1963) to Bupp's "nuclear stalemate" (1979) to Campbell's postmortem on the "collapse of an industry" (1988).[14] The rapid drop in nuclear power plant orders in 1975, right after the Arab oil embargo of 1973 to 1974, was followed by a complete cessation of new reactor orders from 1979—not surprising given that 1979 was the year of the accident at Three Mile Island—portending nothing less than a crash of the domestic reactor market.[15]

The nuclear power industry roared into the 1970s with all the brashness of a Prometheus unbound. By the end of the decade, Prometheus was not only bound but on his deathbed. As Jasper points out in his review of "the triumph of technological enthusiasm" for the U.S. commercial reactor program, the early demise of nuclear power was unexpected.[16] During the forties, after the atomic bombing of Hiroshima and Nagasaki ended World War II, scientists endorsed nuclear power as a positive use for the "friendly atom." Throughout the fifties, the nuclear power boosters at the Atomic Energy Commission (AEC) eagerly responded to President Eisenhower's call for an "Atoms for Peace" program and developed the light water reactor for commercialization. They set up the AEC's Power Reactor Demonstration Program in 1955, which took a quantum leap forward when two industrial giants, General Electric and Westinghouse, entered the reactor market as manufacturers of nuclear steam supply systems (NSSS).

With the federal government assuming almost complete economic liability for nuclear accidents under the Price Anderson Act of 1957, the last major hurdle to commercialization was to convince reluctant utilities that nuclear power was cost-competitive with coal. In December 1963, General Electric overcame this obstacle by signing a contract to build a 650-megawatt light water reactor for Jersey Central Power and Light. After experiencing several years of "cheap, loss-leader, turnkey" power reactors, provided by manufacturers that made claims of significantly lower costs in the future, the utilities leapt onto the "great bandwagon market" of the late sixties and early seventies. In the first half of the seventies, utilities bought more operating capacity from nuclear manufacturers than they did from oil- and coal-fired plant builders combined.

However, during the reactor market crash that followed, the utilities canceled orders for over 100 nuclear power plants between 1974 and 1982, many of which were well under construction. Of the second wave of nuclear power plants, the 50-plus reactors approved for construction or licensing after 1982, no more than a handful will ever produce electricity. The bulk have been canceled, abandoned, or delayed. The year 1984 alone produced a "winter of discontent" for nuclear power in the United States. The Nuclear Regulatory Commission (NRC) denied Illinois Commonwealth Edison an operating license for the $3.4 billion Byron 1 atomic power plant. Public Service of Indiana abandoned work on two Marble Hill units, nearly 50 percent complete, at a loss of $2.5 billion. Michigan's Consumers Power Company halted construction on its two Midland nuclear units. The history of nuclear power in the eighties was one of "cancellation, frustration, and litigation." As a result, the industry melted down with the speed of a superheated reactor core.

The collapse of the nuclear industry is remarkable. The effort to establish a commercial nuclear power industry in the United States was one of the most ambitious and capital-intensive ventures ever undertaken. It was initially endorsed by the federal government, the atomic industry, Wall Street, the utilities, many corporations and local governments, and key unions. The conventional wisdom was that the development of nuclear power was essential for the United States energy supply, and therefore economically necessary and politically inevitable.

Why did the United States' nuclear power industry collapse? How could such a major miscalculation in public policy occur in a nation noted for efficient capital allocation and technological achievement?

The answers to these questions are complex and multidimensional, involving technical, economic, and social variables. To technical critics, nuclear power was a premature, mismanaged technology that finally crashed under its own weight.[17] On one hand, the federal Office of Technology Assessment blames utility executives and construction managers, unfamiliar with nuclear technology, for errors in judgment that created runaway costs. Others point to an inherent conflict of interest in the NRC's dual mandate of both promoting and regulating nuclear power, leading ultimately to a combination of lax federal regulation and industry-wide ineptitude that allowed unresolved technical and safety problems to fester.[18] Still others condemn federal regulators (first in the Atomic Energy Commission and later in the NRC) for consistently permitting the industry to compromise safety in order to cut costs.[19] Thus a combination of "premature deployment, poor utility management, financing difficulties, and hands-off regulation" became and remained widespread industry weaknesses.[20]

To energy economists critical of nuclear power, the industry's downfall can be traced to "malpractice of nuclear economics" that resulted in a tremendous escalation in nuclear power plant costs over time. For example, nuclear plants completed in 1971 cost an average of $430 per kilowatt of generating capacity, whereas those expected to be completed in 1987 would have cost $1,880 per kilowatt—a fourfold increase.[21] Critics argue that key industry cost assumptions—the level of capital investment, relative advantages over fossil fuel plants, benefits to consumers, and projected growth in electric demand—have been consistently and grossly miscalculated.

Taking the economic argument one step further, Charles Komanoff, a leading authority on nuclear power costs, believes that the financial fragility of nuclear power was increased by three "events external to the industry."[22] First, the oil embargo actually damaged nuclear prospects by igniting hyper-inflation and high interest rates. These in turn raised reactor capital costs and dampened economic growth and electricity demand, so that after 1974 projected electric growth rates dropped from 7 percent to 2 percent annually, leaving many utilities with too much reserve capacity. It was precisely at this point that utilities began to cancel nuclear plant orders. Second, tight federal monetary policy and record high "real" interest rates in the early 1980s undermined nuclear power's initial competitiveness with less capital-intensive alternatives such as coal.

Third, the publication in *Foreign Affairs* of Amory Lovins's seminal article "Energy Strategy: The Road Not Taken?" in 1976 reframed the energy problem from a moralistic pronuclear-antinuclear debate into an objective economic choice between "hard energy" (nuclear and coal) and "soft energy" (conservation and renewables).[23] Lovins's work breached the atomic establishment's perceived monopoly on technical sophistication and gave nuclear opponents and regulatory officials the conceptual tools with which to conduct cost-benefit analysis on alternatives to "base-load" plants (plants that are typically centralized, large scale, and coal or nuclear powered).

Social critics emphasize the moral crusade of the antinuclear movement, which became a prairie fire fueled by the cries of "Harrisburg is everywhere" after the Three Mile Island accident of 1979 and "No more Chernobyls" after the Soviet disaster of 1986.[24] To social scientists and political observers, public opposition to nuclear power has been effective because the movement has not been a single-issue phenomenon.[25] Rather, it has been a classic social movement—and to some a new social movement—embracing a wide range of issues. In their study of antinuclear movements in France and Germany, Nelkin and Pollack found that activists were concerned with more than the risk of nuclear accidents. The European movement, as well as its U.S. counterpart, has

> focused on the social and political properties of this technology, its effect on the forms of authority and power, the concepts of freedom and order, the distribution of political and economic resources, the very fabric of political life.[26]

There is a tendency in public-policy explanation for each observer, whether engineer, economist, or social scientist, to view his or her perspective as the critical one. Looking at the nuclear industry from the interdisciplinary perspective of anthropology, we can appreciate that each viewpoint—technical, economic, and social—addresses a significant part of the puzzle. All these factors had some impact on the industry's demise.[27]

The Second Coming of Nuclear Power

The opening of the twenty-first century will witness the attempted rebirth of commercial nuclear power in the United States and its continued expansion abroad, particularly in Asia. "By the year 2000, we should see the reemergence of nuclear energy as the most promising power source for generating electricity. Cheaper than gas and safer than coal, with a near-infinite fuel supply, nuclear power's time has come. Again," claims Albert B. Reynolds, professor of nuclear engineering at the University of Virginia.[28]

The campaign to resurrect nuclear power has already set the stage for a renewed clash between the nuclear industry and the antinuclear movement. The "energy wars" of the 1970s and 1980s portend a deepening conflict throughout the 1990s that will determine the energy future of the United States in the twenty-first century.

Domestically, this coming conflict will be exacerbated by renewed calls for energy independence in the wake of the Gulf War; deepening environmental concerns over radioactive waste, acid rain, and the greenhouse effect; a spreading consumer rebellion against the $100 billion "damage bill" for the initial collapse of nuclear power; electrical shortages predicted by the end of the decade; and the international loss of public confidence in the "friendly atom," shattered by the Chernobyl disaster. Internationally, the nuclear power–nuclear weapons connection will focus the debate on nuclear proliferation and nuclear terrorism as the national security issue of the post–Cold War period.

Under the banner of "energy independence," most utility executives foresaw an "energy transition" to an "energy secure future for America" that involved switching from oil to an increased reliance on nuclear and coal plants. Articulating this vision in the mid-eighties, NRC commissioner Lando Zech stated that "If the electrical growth in the United States is between two and three percent annually, nearly two hundred new 1,000-megawatt plants will be needed by the year 2000. This means at least one new large power plant, either coal or nuclear, will be needed in our country each month for the next fifteen years." If undertaken, this massive construction program could require an investment of up to one trillion dollars.

The nuclear industry has developed a three-stage strategy for the revival of nuclear power and the eventual centralization of nuclear power generation under federal control. The first, economic stage involves restoring investor confidence in nuclear utilities by passing the $100 billion "damage bill" of prior nuclear plant cost overruns and cancellations on to customers.

The second, technical phase seeks to restore public confidence in nuclear power plant safety and reliability by introducing a new generation of standardized, "inherently safe," advanced reactor designs; providing a perpetual federal disposal site for high-level radioactive spent fuel rods at Yucca Mountain, Nevada; and establishing a series of low-level radioactive waste storage sites around the nation.

The final stage involves a comprehensive legislative agenda that will limit the participation of private citizens and local officials in the regulatory processes for both nuclear plant licensing and electric utility rate setting. Under this agenda, the electric industry seeks to amend the Atomic Energy Act of 1954 and to revise NRC rule making in order to restrict citizen intervention and accelerate the nuclear power plant construction process through "one-stop licensing and site approval" of advanced-design, standardized light water reactors.

Most significantly, the industry seeks to revise the Public Utilities Holding Companies Act (PUHCA) of 1935 to allow the formation of new electric power holding companies that would separate power generation from transmission and distribution. This proposed revision would allow regional holding companies to develop nuclear industrial parks, which would come under *federal,* rather than *state,* regulation. With the exception of passing the utilities' $100 billion "stranded costs" for nuclear plants on to consumers, most of this agenda was incorporated into President Bush's Energy Policy Act, which was passed by Congress in 1992.

In the 1990 annual report of the U.S. Council for Energy Awareness, the nuclear industry stated its case for nuclear energy by stressing four messages:[29]

1. *Nuclear Energy and the Environment.* Nuclear energy is one of the cleanest sources of electricity, since nuclear power plants do not burn anything and therefore do not pollute the environment in the manner that fossil fuel plants do.

2. *Nuclear Power and Energy Independence.* Nuclear power is partly responsible for the dramatic reduction in oil use by electric utilities over the last 18 years. In 1973, oil represented 17 percent of the U.S. electric supply, nuclear energy about 5 percent. Today oil represents only about 4 percent of the U.S. electric supply, and nuclear energy over 20 percent.

3. *Electricity and Economic Growth.* New electric generating capacity will be needed if the United States is to sustain economic growth. All energy resources—coal, oil, natural gas, renewables, efficiency, and nuclear power—have a role to play in supplying electricity.

4. *Nuclear Energy as Insurance for the Future.* In attempting to meet growing demands for electric power, U.S. utilities face major uncertainties. They include uncertainties about energy

conservation (demand-side management and efficiency programs), uncertainties about the price of natural gas, uncertainties about the impact of the 1990 Clean Air Act amendments on existing coal-fired plants, and uncertainties about global warming and the possibility of increasingly stringent restrictions on fossil fuels.

In this context, the report finds that "Nuclear energy represents prudent, strategic insurance against the uncertainty facing the utility industry and the nation in the 1990s and the early years of the 21st century."[30]

There is, however, a central economic flaw in this nuclear cheerleading. By the mid-1990s, it was clear that nuclear power had emerged as the *most expensive* form of conventional energy. On average, nuclear power plants have produced electricity at a higher cost per kilowatt-hour than have conventional power plants. High construction and operating expenses, along with poor plant operating performance, have contributed to the high average costs for nuclear reactors. Thus, between 1968 and 1990, nuclear-generated electricity cost an average of 8.8¢ per kilowatt-hour, or *twice* the comparable cost of electric power generated from coal, oil, or gas during that same period.[31]

Primarily due to nuclear power's dismal economics, nuclear energy has lost its former luster for the elite decision makers in the White House, on Wall Street, and even in the utility industry, whose support is necessary for nuclear energy's resurrection. At her 1993 confirmation hearing, then energy secretary Hazel R. O'Leary, a former utility executive, testified that "The costs of nuclear power, if you include new construction, are not competitive. Moreover, the long term waste storage problems are daunting. . . . For now, we must look to energy conservation and efficiency options."

Most of Wall Street concurred with a 1993 report by Moody's Investor Service, one of the nation's premier stock-rating services, in its pessimistic view about the technology's renewal. "Moody's could not agree more with [Secretary O'Leary's] assessment. Indeed as noted in our September 1992 Electric Utility Industry Outlook, the decade of the 1980s was fraught with difficult times for many nuclear operators as evidenced by the multitude and magnitude of rating downgrades."[32] In October 1993, the Wall Street credit-rating firm Standard and Poor's reclassified most utilities with nuclear power ownership down to a below average rating.

Dan Scotto, an electric utility analyst with Bear Stearns, put it bluntly by stating, "I think the technology has for all intents and purposes become obsolete. . . . Other fuel types are considerably less expensive, when you throw in the capital costs that are associated with nuclear power." Reflecting the growing cynicism of Wall Street, Scotto predicted that the next nuclear power plant would be built in the United States "when Jimmy Hoffa is found alive and well."[33]

In the emerging 1990s climate of utility deregulation and "retail wheeling" of electricity, nuclear power has become a liability for many utilities. Under the Energy Policy Act of 1992, utilities may compete with each other for electricity sales. In this more competitive environment, nuclear power is proving to be a financial burden. *Nucleonics Week* reports that nuclear utilities are not competing so much with each other as with other forms of generation in their power pools. In terms of cost, only 25 percent of nuclear power plants are in a competitive range with replacement power.[34]

As a result, over time utility executives have turned away from the nuclear option. The Washington International Energy Group (WIEG), which analyzes the U.S. energy market from a global perspective, has conducted an annual survey of utility executives since 1968. In the WIEG's 1995 survey, only 31 percent of utility leaders believed that there will be a resurgence of nuclear power. This compares with 42 percent in 1993 and 70 percent in 1992. When asked whether their utility would ever order another nuclear plant, nearly three quarters (74 percent) of utility operators said "no" in the 1995 survey.[35]

Despite these historic setbacks, the nuclear industry declared that 1990 was a "watershed year" for the revival of commercial nuclear power in the United States. In 1990, citing a "growing awareness of the environmental advantages of nuclear power" and the impact of the Gulf War on the need for "secure, domestic sources of energy, such as nuclear power," James J. O'Connor, chairman of Commonwealth Edison Company and the U.S. Council for Energy Awareness, stated

> I am confident that future generations will mark last year as the beginning of a renaissance for nuclear energy in America—a time when the American people and their political leaders awakened to the great benefits of this energy source. . . . In many ways, supplying electric power has become more than just a business. It is a crusade, a daily struggle to provide the electricity America needs to sustain its economic growth.[36]

Nuclear Terrorism

During the 1990s, the renewed threats of nuclear proliferation and terrorism have broadened the nuclear power question from an energy policy debate into a national security issue. In the post–Cold War era, concern has grown that terrorists may use plutonium stolen from former Soviet nuclear power and weapons facilities to fashion crude but deadly atomic weapons while "rogue nations" such as Iran, Iraq, and North Korea may use commercial fuel rods and reactors as a base for nuclear weapons research and production. It would take only about 56 pounds of uranium or plutonium to manufacture a 500-kiloton bomb, powerful enough to devastate a major city.

These concerns are prompted by the diffusion of nuclear power technology worldwide, which has continued to grow—even while nuclear power has stalled in the United States. In 1990, worldwide, the nuclear power produced at 418 operational plants generated approximately 17 percent of all electricity. Of the 25 countries that have nuclear plants, 13—or more than half—generated more than 25 percent of their electricity with nuclear energy. France led the list, generating 74.5 percent of its electricity with nuclear power; Japan was last with 26.2 percent.

Apprehension about domestic terrorism in the United States was ignited by the bombing of the federal building in Oklahoma City in 1995. Such concern was heightened by revelations that a Japanese doomsday cult shopped for nuclear, chemical, and biological weapons in the United States and Russia. United States and Japanese intelligence agencies had largely ignored the threat of the Aum Shinri Kyo cult until an odorless, colorless gas planted by its agents at four Tokyo subway trains killed 12 people and injured close to 5,500 in March 1995. At a U.S. Senate hearing on the global proliferation of weapons of mass destruction, Senator Richard Lugar stated that "Americans have every reason to expect a nuclear, biological or chemical attack before the decade is over."

With the collapse of the former Soviet Union, the espionage thriller theme that has foreign smugglers endangering millions by smuggling plutonium, the highly radioactive ingredient used to manufacture nuclear weapons, is no longer mere fiction. Already German foreign minister Klaus Kinkel has been moved to warn that "traveling salesmen with nuclear suitcases pose new atomic dangers." This 1994 warning was prompted by the capture of four groups of German and foreign traffickers who were caught smuggling hundreds of millions of dollars worth of plutonium into Germany.

The Germans blame the contraband on lax security at nuclear installations in Russia and other former Soviet republics. This confirms a 1992 *Business Week* study that found "the former Soviet Union's vast nuclear industry teetering near disaster."[37] The study found that nuclear regulatory agencies were in disarray and that safety inspections have become much less frequent. Nuclear operators and other experts are taking better-paying jobs in other industries. Security is also in a shambles, leaving nuclear power plants with few security guards, who now make only cursory checks. This is a quantum decline from the Soviet era, when nuclear plants were surrounded by layers of electrified barbed wire and three separate teams of KGB agents stood watch at each plant, aided by networks of plant informants.

These nuclear safety concerns led to a high-level Moscow summit in the spring of 1996, at which Russian president Boris Yeltsin met with the heads of the major industrial democracies to discuss the problems of nuclear material security and nuclear power safety. The meeting was prompted by expert reports claiming that Russia is "a giant, unstable nuclear heap," with hundreds of facilities harboring at least 200 tons of plutonium and up to 1,200 tons of highly enriched uranium spread across thousands of miles of the former Soviet Union. The goal of the summits was to explore how Russia could secure these far-flung facilities against theft, accident, and sabotage.

In *Brittle Power: Energy Strategy for National Security,* Amory Lovins and Hunter Lovins found that "low-level attacks on nuclear facilities have in fact become so common, and the level of violence escalating so steadily, that it seems only a matter of time before a major attack is successfully attempted."[38] In their study, the Lovinses describe possible scenarios for armed attacks and bomb explosions, sabotage by insiders, breaches of security at nuclear facilities, nuclear thefts, and malicious use of nuclear materials.

Potentially far more dangerous than individual economic opportunists or terrorists are "rogue nations," such as Iraq, Iran, and most recently North Korea, led by dictators immune to economic sanctions, that are using nuclear power technology to knock at the back door of the world's exclusive "nuclear club." In the early 1990s, the CIA told President Clinton that North Korea probably had one or two nuclear bombs and that the agency regarded North Korea as the most dangerous potential nuclear power. North Korea operates two reactors and a plutonium plant, manufactures Scud missiles, and has refused to permit international inspection of its nuclear program. To many international observers, North Korea's dash to manufacture nuclear weapons for its ballistic missiles, and probably for export, may be the decisive event of the twenty-first century. If North Korea causes the entire nuclear nonproliferation structure to collapse, the next century may be even more dangerously anarchic than this one has been.

These events, coming on the heels of the Gulf War and the discovery by the West that Hussein was only a year away from having nuclear bombs, have alarmed world military leaders and security experts. But Iraq's nuclear capability should come as no surprise, because for nearly 15 years before the Gulf War, 450 Western companies helped build Hussein's nuclear machine. In September 1975, Hussein called an agreement he had signed with France to purchase a plutonium breeder reactor "the first concrete step toward the production of an Arab atomic weapon." In June 1981, Israeli F-16s took out the Osirak bomb plant in a surgical strike. The world's anger focused on Israel and neglected the cause of the raid, Iraq's atomic bomb, while Iraq literally took its nuclear program underground, creating what President Bush called a "Cadillac production line for atomic-bomb parts."

Similar dangers are brewing elsewhere in the world, such as Iran, Syria, and Algeria, as nations operate clandestine atomic programs—often under the guise of generating electric power—in an effort to grasp the "nuclear brass ring." As we enter the post–Cold War era, "We face a new series of threats, and if we don't learn to deal with them quickly they could get worse than the Soviet nuclear threat," said Steven Dooley, research director of the private Nuclear Control Institute. "We have a world that's awash in bomb-grade materials."

It was in this context that Senator John McCain, a member of the United States Armed Services Committee, stated that Korea's nuclear ambitions may be "the defining crisis of the post–Cold War period," because if these ambitions are realized, the result may be the exponential growth of nuclear-armed regimes.

Energy Activists and Entrepreneurs

The nuclear industry meltdown, the attempted resurrection of nuclear power, the end of the arms race, and the emergence of nuclear terrorism as a global threat are all historical themes—a legacy of the first half century of the Atomic Age. Individually and collectively, these themes pose interesting questions for research and policy. However, from the perspective of social movements and public policy, the most intriguing question about nuclear power is how a grassroots antinuclear movement, comprising mainly laypeople and a handful of dissident experts, could have any lasting impact on an advanced energy technology that was perceived to be vital to the national interest and that was initially supported by major segments of the governmental, labor, scientific, and corporate elite.

The case studies presented throughout *Profiles in Power* support the viewpoint that the antinuclear movement has historically functioned as a political feedback mechanism that has articulated, at a broad cultural level, the unresolved public anxiety and expert skepticism regarding nuclear technology, safety, and economics. As a social movement, it has indeed fulfilled its early promise to challenge the nuclear industry. The pressing need for this challenge was examined in 1972 by Richard S. Lewis in his book *The Nuclear Power Rebellion: Citizens vs. the Atomic Industrial Establishment*. In a review of Lewis's book, Dean Abrahamson, a former reactor designer, made the following observation regarding the atomic industrial establishment (AIE) and its dual role of promoter and regulator of nuclear power:

> In no other instance has it been more clearly demonstrated that the promoter needs to be challenged. And in every case the challenge has been made by individuals who, often at great personal sacrifice and risk, have shown that the AIE has been technically incompetent, lacking in candor and honesty, and incapable of protecting the public health and welfare. . . . In no other instance has it been more evident that there can be no effective assessment of hazards without issues being raised and remedies provided by independent scientists working with an active and concerned public.[39]

Strategically, when *centralized* federal institutions (the Office of the President, the Supreme Court, and Congress, including the AEC and its successor, the NRC) did not respond to concerns raised by the antinuclear movement and its allies, the movement developed creative strategies for petitioning or pressuring *decentralized* local institutions (state courts and legislatures, public utility commissions, and county commissions) in order to effectively circumscribe the nuclear industry. These strategies gave nuclear industry opponents the legal ability to economically pressure utilities into canceling existing plants and abandoning long-range nuclear plans. In this way, despite an official pronuclear *national* energy policy, activists were able to influence *local* energy policies de facto by turning utilities away from nuclear power and, in many cases, toward renewable sources of energy.

Therefore, the central thesis of this study is that although the nuclear industry was stalemated during the 1970s primarily due to internal technical and external economic problems, the emergence of a sophisticated grassroots antinuclear movement increased the financial risk and liability of nuclear power to utilities and thereby played a significant role in foreclosing the nuclear option in the United States during the 1980s and early 1990s.

The antinuclear movement won major victories when it recast its strategy from that of a broad national critique of the moral, safety, and environmental problems of nuclear power into specific local debates on the economics of individual nuclear power plants. Paradoxically, this narrowing of the issue resulted in a significant expansion of the coalition opposing commercial nuclear power.

"The fate of nuclear power is far more than a function of reactor technology. Political, financial and even cultural trends exert tremendous influence over how the technology is perceived and deployed," notes Komanoff, an interdisciplinary energy expert.[40] If nuclear power had been commercialized around sound engineering and economic principles, then its critics would never have become more than marginal political gadflies. The endemic technical flaws and economic shortcomings that emerged over time gave critics the ammunition necessary to undermine the industry at its very foundation: the financial viability of nuclear power as a prudent investment for utilities. With increasing public support, the antinuclear movement applied "economic jujitsu" at the state and local levels to attack specific plants after the industry failed in its initial promise to deliver electricity at competitive prices.

In this context, *Profiles in Power* examines significant campaigns by antinuclear activists, utility executives, and energy entrepreneurs throughout the United States who developed successful strategies to stalemate nuclear power and promote renewable energy at major utilities and in the private sector. This study reviews from several perspectives the safety and technical questions raised by the reactor techies, the economic conflicts that sparked the ratepayers' revolt, and the new energy paradigm articulated by the conservation revolution and the energy entrepreneurs.

First, what factors led to the initial abandonment of nuclear power by the electric utilities? Second, what was the impact of the antinuclear movement on the nuclear industry? Third, what do these profiles teach us about citizen activism and nuclear politics?

Over the past two decades, antinuclear forces spearheaded a vigorous social movement that helped shatter the national consensus supporting nuclear power. Policy analysts have described in general terms the unique American political context—the institutional framework and decentralized state apparatus—that allowed dissident groups to gain access to the energy policy arena and to override the official policy favoring nuclear power. However, the actual strategies and mechanisms through which the antinuclear movement influenced policy makers have not previously been well documented or analyzed.

Certainly, there have been important case studies of local opposition to nuclear power, particularly of early citizen interventions in nuclear power plant citing and licensing,[41] of citizen mobilization around Three Mile Island,[42] of the regulatory process at Seabrook,[43] and even of antinuclear movements from a cross-national perspective.[44] However, there have been no comparative, nationwide, in-depth case studies of successful grassroots campaigns and entrepreneurial initiatives by safe-energy activists. This book is an original study of the strategies developed by key actors in the energy drama—scientists, activists, utility executives, entrepreneurs, and visionary thinkers, all of whom have made a significant contribution to our energy future.

Profiles in Power describes and compares pivotal points in the conflict between the antinuclear movement and the nuclear establishment through a series of case studies. The 10 profiles in power are organized by chapter into five case studies: "The Reactor Techies," "The Ratepayers' Revolt," "The Conservation Revolution," "The Energy Entrepreneurs," and "The Dawn of the Solar Age." Figure 1 outlines, in order of appearance by case study, the key participants—the dramatis personae, if you will—for each of the profiles in power and describes the main energy issues addressed by each profile.

Mobilizing Principles for Energy Activists

This study has explored the question: What do these profiles teach us about citizen activism and nuclear politics? Each case study (see chapters 2 to 6 in figure 1) illustrates a key "mobilizing principle" for en-

Figure 1.
Case Studies for Profiles in Power

Chapter 2: The Reactor Techies

Dr. John Gofman, radiation biologist, California. Dr. Gofman's research on the health effects of radiation and his crusade against the nuclear establishment illustrate how the near meltdown at TMI and the subsequent Chernobyl disaster revealed the catastrophic radiation and cancer-causing risks of nuclear power, forcing citizens, utilities, and governments around the world to reevaluate the safety and costs of nuclear energy.

Mark Oncavage, music teacher, Florida. As president of Floridians United for Safe Energy (FUSE), Mr. Oncavage spearheaded a legal citizen intervention that revealed how, at Florida Power and Light's Turkey Point and most other U.S. pressurized water reactors, corrosion of steam generators produced "the most expensive product failure in the history of American industry."

Chapter 3: The Ratepayers' Revolt

Nora Bredes, county commissioner, Long Island, New York. Ms. Bredes played a key role in the 15-year battle by county officials and citizen groups to stop Long Island Light Company's $5.7 billion nuclear plant from opening because of concerns over safety and inadequate evacuation planning.

Dan Leahy, public power activist, Washington. Mr. Leahy describes the struggle for public power in the Pacific Northwest and the consumer outrage at the electric "rate shock" that followed the financial fiasco of the Washington Public Power Supply System's $2.25 billion default on nuclear utility bonds, the largest default in utility history.

Chapter 4: The Conservation Revolution

John Bryson, chairman, Southern California Edison, California. Once he assumed the leadership of SoCal Edison, the nation's second largest utility, Mr. Bryson forged alliances with government officials, environmentalists, and independent power producers to transform this utility into the largest user of conservation and renewable resources in the world.

(continued)

Figure 1.
continued

David Freeman, general manager, Sacramento Municipal Utility District, California. After residents of the publicly owned SMUD voted to shut down the troubled Rancho Seco nuclear plant, Mr. Freeman, former director of the Tennessee Valley Authority, was hired to generate all of SMUD's future growth through the year 2010 by means of conservation and renewable energy sources, creating America's premier conservation power plant.

Chapter 5: The Energy Entrepreneurs

John Schaeffer, president, Real Goods Trading Corporation, California. Mr. Schaeffer built a small rural catalog company selling products for energy self-sufficiency to North California hippies into a successful $16 million public company that advises customers around the country about how to "get off the grid" and live independently.

John Perry, chairman, Energy Partners, Inc., Florida. After designing silent hydrogen-powered submarines for the military during the Cold War, Mr. Perry has applied his wealth and entrepreneurial skills to the design of the hydrogen-fueled, zero-emissions vehicle called the "Green Car," a major step toward the transition to a solar and hydrogen energy future.

Chapter 6: The Dawn of the Solar Age

Amory and Hunter Lovins, directors, Rocky Mountain Institute, Colorado. As founders of the Rocky Mountain Institute, Amory and Hunter Lovins have reframed the energy problem into a choice between "hard" and "soft" energy paths, breaching the nuclear establishment's perceived monopoly on technical credibility and providing the antinuclear movement with a viable vision of a nonnuclear world.

Christopher Flavin, vice president, Worldwatch Institute, Washington, D.C. As the coauthor of *Power Surge: The Coming Energy Revolution* and numerous articles on energy, Mr. Flavin has described a world economy that is poised for a sweeping shift away from imported oil and environmentally damaging coal during the next few decades owing to the deployment of new energy technologies by enterprising entrepreneurs and independent power producers around the world.

ergy activists in particular, and for citizen activists in general. These principles are outlined and summarized in figure 2.

The end of each chapter will examine how the subject of each case study impacts the energy issue and briefly highlight the mobilizing principle demonstrated by that case study. In conclusion, chapter 7, "Profiles in Courage," will revisit the case studies in the context of these mobilizing principles for energy activists to see what insights they provide into the impact of the antinuclear and safe-energy movement in particular and into the process of citizen activism and nuclear politics in general.

These case studies illuminate the debate on the impact of the antinuclear movement on the nuclear industry. They may also serve as examples of what is not debatable. Over the past two decades, antinuclear activists and energy entrepreneurs have confronted the nuclear establishment in the streets, in the marketplace, through the courts, before the public utilities commissions, at the NRC, and in Congress. At minimum, the profiles in power presented here demonstrate that even in this complex, technological era—the era of Chernobyl, Bhopal, Challenger, and Star Wars—private citizens can become effective players in the public-policy process.

Viewed from a broader historical perspective, the antinuclear movement in the United States is symptomatic of a general crisis of faith in science and government. This crisis erupted during the seven-

---

Figure 2.
Mobilizing Principles for Energy Activists

Chapter 2: The Reactor Techies
Establish truth force.
Chapter 3: The Ratepayers' Revolt
Define the issue so as to build broad coalition.
Chapter 4: The Conservation Revolution
Demonstrate viable alternative solutions.
Chapter 5: The Energy Entrepreneurs
Combine economics and environmentalism.
Chapter 6: The Dawn of the Solar Age
Create a new energy paradigm.

ties—the decade that saw the emergence of a national antinuclear movement—and produced widespread public protest against the arrogance of technology and the corruption of government.[45] Although the history of nuclear power may offer a classic example of how not to conduct public policy on the commercialization of advanced technology, it is not an isolated case. As science has developed the ability to restructure genes and change global climate, decisions that were once the exclusive domain of the scientific elite have become highly politicized. More and more, citizens will insist on "no technology without representation" and seek a voice in shaping the future of civilization.

In *Profiles in Courage,* President Kennedy lamented that we have forgotten the quality of courage in public life.[46] Fortunately, in the case of nuclear power, private citizens have exhibited that virtue with notable grace under pressure, often at great risk to their careers and reputations. Collectively, they have demonstrated the viability of a sustainable, nonnuclear energy future and successfully challenged the authority of the "nuclear priesthood" in an age of high technology. In the process, these individuals have emerged as profiles in power. For that, the nation owes them a debt of gratitude.

Chapter Two

The Reactor Techies

The problem of the nuclear power industry is that we have had too few accidents. . . . It's expensive, but that's how you gain experience.
—*Sigvard Eklund, general director, International Atomic Energy*
Agency, 1980

This is the statement of a madman.[1] There is a growing global consensus that the reactor route to "infinite power" is a chimera.

We are not sure if Mr. Eklund was speaking about Three Mile Island (TMI) or a possible Chernobyl. But it is clear that citizens worldwide do not think these are risks worth taking. This brings us to a fundamental question that even the next generation of so-called inherently safe reactors does not answer. Is there any acceptable risk scenario that involves a TMI-type accident or a Chernobyl-like catastrophe every five years?

The first people to raise these questions were the "reactor techies." Because the issues were complex and couched in the esoteric language of nuclear physics and radiobiology, most people did not feel comfortable challenging the experts. But the reactor techies did. Because they were willing to master the language of "nukespeak" and wade through reams of technical reports, often with the help of independent scientists and engineers, the reactor techies came up with shocking conclusions about reactor safety and the impact of radioactivity on human health.

25

No events have had greater public impact on the nuclear industry than the near meltdown at Three Mile Island in the United States on March 28, 1979, and the reactor explosion at Chernobyl in the former Soviet Union on April 26, 1986.

As the worst accident in the history of commercial nuclear power in the United States, TMI proved that "class nine accidents," which the NRC had dismissed as possible but "incredible" accidents that could supposedly never happen, could and do occur. The near meltdown of Unit 2 at TMI and the release of radioactivity forced Pennsylvania governor Thornburgh to call for the "precautionary evacuation" of people living within a five-mile radius of the plant.

More broadly, the accident definitively undermined the credibility of the nuclear industry by confirming the earliest suspicions of the reactor techies. These were dissident scientists and gadfly citizens who penetrated the labyrinth of secrecy surrounding the industry. Armed with insider technical information, the reactor techies had for years been sounding arcane warnings about the possible disastrous effects of "common mode failures" and "emergency core cooling system malfunctions," which could lead to accidents, meltdowns, and possible exposure of the public to cancer-producing radioactive isotopes.

The multiple explosions that rocked the Chernobyl nuclear plant created the worst peacetime catastrophe in the history of humanity. As recently as November 1996, it appears that new spontaneous fission occurring in the wreckage could lead to another meltdown within the battered hulk of the reactor.

The Chernobyl detonations blew the top off the upper section of the reactor, discharging into the atmosphere over the Ukraine and Byelorussia 300 to 400 times the amount of the long-lived radionuclides released at the atomic bombing of Hiroshima. Within days, much of Europe was experiencing the highest levels of radioactivity ever recorded. According to information made public between 1986 and 1991, the short-term direct costs of the accident included at least 1,000 immediate injuries, 31 deaths, 135,000 people evacuated from their homes in the Ukraine, hundreds of thousands of people exposed to radiation, and at least $3 billion in financial costs at the reactor site alone.[2]

The staggering economic impact of the disaster was outlined in a 1990 report by Yuri Koryakin, chief economist of the Research and Development Institute of Power Engineering, the Soviet government institute that designed the Chernobyl reactor. Assessing the comprehensive total economic impact up until the year 2000, Koryakin projected figures between \$283 billion and \$358 billion. The economic conclusion suggests that the former Soviet Union (now Russia) would have been financially better off never to have developed nuclear energy.[3]

Unfortunately, the true, less easily quantifiable long-term losses are more far-reaching: almost half a million mothers and children were evacuated from the region in 1986; nearly another 300,000 were slated for resettlement in the early nineties; an additional four million people live under contamination conditions; and the health of people in the Ukraine and Byelorussia, and throughout Europe, will be affected for decades and possibly centuries. Taking the effects of low-level radiation into account, independent experts estimate that the resulting "all-time" cancer fatalities (excluding nearly half a million nonfatal cancer illnesses) from Chernobyl will range upward to 475,500 over the next century. These grim figures could surpass even the immediate deaths resulting from the combined atomic bombing of Hiroshima and Nagasaki at the end of World War II.[4]

Although the full health impact of the radioactive fallout from Chernobyl will occur over a century, the political fallout of Chernobyl has already taken its toll on the worldwide reactor industry. In the former Soviet Union and Europe, government credibility eroded even further with charges that officials failed to warn citizens about the health threat of Chernobyl. In the United States, public support for further nuclear development plummeted from 64 percent in 1975 to 19 percent in 1986.[5] After Chernobyl, many nations abandoned their nuclear plants and plans. Antinuclear scientists and advocates were no longer shunned as eco-extremists and naysayers. They were joined by prime ministers and presidents, who now endorsed the view that the long-term costs of nuclear power—in capital, waste disposal, accidents, public health, and even terrorism—exceeded *any* conceivable benefit.

With the notable exception of *Time* magazine's "Man of the Century," former Soviet prime minister Mikhail Gorbachev, most political leaders in the industrialized nations have failed to respond to the terrible tragedies that pronuclear governmental policies have created. As a direct response to his having been in charge of the Soviet Union at the time of the Chernobyl incident, Gorbachev has continued to dedicate his ceaseless efforts and personal funds to aid the Children of Chernobyl organization in its attempts to provide desperately needed medical services to the young victims of the disaster. By his actions, Gorbachev has sought to focus attention on the grave responsibility assumed by all political leaders who continue to operate highly dangerous nuclear facilities.

The nadir to which nuclear power has fallen in the aftermath of TMI and Chernobyl would have been unimaginable in the early halcyon days of atomic energy. In that heyday of technological optimism and the Apollo Project, science was lauded as the United States' savior in the Cold War, producing thermonuclear weapons to ensure victory on the battlefield and atomic power plants to fuel the economy.

Physicist Glenn Seaborg, who shared the 1951 Nobel Prize in Chemistry for the discovery of plutonium, believed he had discovered a new element that would be "the salvation of mankind." As a hero in the world of science, Seaborg believed the future of civilization itself was in the hands of the elite nuclear scientists, who would "build a new world through nuclear technology." Science was the new religion; plutonium its sacrament.[6]

A generation of scientists and politicians was inspired by Seaborg's "visionary dream of atomic-powered plenty." Nuclear energy was the alchemist's elixir that would free humanity from all possible limitations. Homes would be heated, factories powered, deserts made to bloom, sea water made drinkable, and mountains removed—all as a result of the giant nuclear power stations, each surrounded by its "own little Eden" in the form of agro-industrial manufacturing centers. These predictions of a technological utopia gave nuclear power great prominence and prestige in the postwar decades as scientists and legislators, industrialists and bankers, joined the "great nuclear bandwagon" in a massive campaign to commercialize atomic power. Most leaders of this postwar generation were swept up in the technological euphoria of engineering a "new civilization" to be fueled by an "unlimited source of energy"—by nuclear power "too cheap to meter."

This enthusiasm continued well into the 1970s. Alvin Weinberg, the theoretical physicist who patented the first design for a water-cooled reactor, shared Seaborg's optimism. Weinberg predicted that there would be 1,000 nuclear plants, generating nearly one-half of the United States' energy, by the end of the century. The only cautionary note he sounded was that the price we would have to pay for this limitless supply of nuclear energy would be the need to install a permanent "nuclear priesthood" to maintain eternal vigilance over this potent technology.

In this atmosphere, it would take a man of great courage and momentous conviction—willing to risk his entire career, the ridicule of his peers, and the opprobrium of his country—to question the safety of atomic energy and the wisdom of proceeding with nuclear power.

Dr. John Gofman was such a man.

From Three Mile Island to Chernobyl: Dr. John Gofman, Radiation Biologist

There can be no doubt that the promoters of nuclear power . . . are indeed committing these crimes against humanity. Americans would be justified in demanding that Nuremberg-type trials be held for these individuals.
—*Drs. John W. Gofman and Arthur Tamplin,* Poisoned Power, *1979*

"I've already gotten the data from the World Health Organization, the EPA, and my numbers add up to something over 300,000 fatal cancers and 300,000 nonfatal, plus about 12,000 to 15,000 leukemias. And that with only fragmentary data in. East Germany has provided nothing. The Soviet Union has provided only a wee little bit of data for the Ukraine, and the data they have provided don't even address the biggest source of future deaths, namely, cesium. Chernobyl could produce a million total cancers, but I don't know that now."[7]

Dr. John W. Gofman continued his calculations as he gave his third interview of the day. It was June 5, 1986, a little more than one month after the Chernobyl disaster had shocked the world. He swiveled frenetically in his chair, reaching for computer printouts and reports piled haphazardly around his crowded basement office in San Francisco. Not far across the bay was the spacious office Dr. Gofman once occupied as associate director of the U.S. government's prestigious Lawrence Livermore Laboratory, one of the world's foremost research institutions in applied physics. Yet that had been two decades earlier, before he had been branded a renegade, "incompetent" scientist by the U.S. government and the nuclear establishment. But today, in the aftermath of Chernobyl, reporters and officials from around the world were not calling Livermore. They were calling Dr. Gofman, because he was one of the few scientists who had dared to denounce the "cult of the atom" and who had consistently been proven right about the effects of radioactivity on human health.

"These are the numbers for full-body radiation," he continued. "They're minimums, remember, because I don't have the cesium 134 data that I need. Sweden, 788 millirads average; Austria, 51; Poland, 31.2; Czechoslovakia, 12.4; Denmark, 14.8; West Germany, 132; Italy, 44.8; Ukraine, 86. I'm sure that's a minimum ... It could go to 850 or more."

As a scientist, Dr. Gofman loved the numbers. In terms of radiation biology, the field he had helped pioneer, the numbers allowed him to predict the number of cancers that would be caused by the fallout from the Chernobyl accident.

As a physician who considered every cancer a tragedy, Dr. Gofman hated the numbers. They were harbingers of death for thousands of Soviet and European citizens.

"Now, when I had one measurement, what I did is I assumed that— we'll divide it in half. I'll assume that one half of the country got that measurement and the rest of the country got zero. I don't know that zero is right. But I wanted to be conservative. Now take down these numbers. They represent population, dose, and fatal cancers:

"Sweden: 8,330,000 population, 788 millirads, 24,400 fatal cancers. I won't give you the nonfatal cancers because they're exactly the same. And leukemia is 1,000. West Germany: 62,400,000 people, gets 132 millirads, about 30,200 fatal cancers. United Kingdom: 54,000,000, 180 millirads, 36,300 fatal cancers. Ukraine: 50,667,000, 85 millirads, 16,800 fatal cancers. But I regard that number for the Soviet Union as ludicrously low. If I get some real data from the Soviet Union, I think that 300,000 deaths is going to look very low."

Dr. Gofman concluded the interview and slumped back in his chair. He rubbed his tired eyes and pondered what the numbers scattered about his office meant in future illness and suffering. The phone rang again. It was a German newspaper correspondent.

The professor told the German correspondent, "Back in the 1950s, people estimated about 200,000 total fatalities from the Hiroshima-Nagasaki bombings."

There was a long pause as the German reporter listened in disbelief. "So, Dr. Gofman, you are saying that the Chernobyl accident will cause more fatalities than—more than Hiroshima and Nagasaki?"

"Yes," Dr. Gofman replied. "I'm saying that although the Chernobyl fatalities will be later, aside from the acute radiation sickness fatalities which will come quickly, long range, it would be worse than the combination of Hiroshima and Nagasaki. Unfortunately, since radiation has the worst impact on children, say young children up to nine years old, they will bear the brunt of this."

It was a little more than a month after the explosion at Chernobyl, and the real impacts of the disaster had just begun to be understood.

"What Will Become of Us?" Ironically, the events that led up to the accident at the Chernobyl nuclear power plant began with a safety test. As with most accidents, this one resulted from a combination of human error and reactor design weakness—and could have been stopped at many points. Chernobyl is a small town of about 12,500 people in the Ukrainian Republic of the former Soviet Union. It is located about 105 kilometers north of Kiev, capital of the Ukraine. Twenty-five miles northeast of Chernobyl stood the nuclear power stations, which by 1986 had four of the most modern Soviet RBMK-type reactors in full operation, with two more under construction. Five miles away from the reactors was the city of Pripyat, with 45,000 people.

RBMK is a Russian acronym that stands for a water-cooled, graphite-moderated reactor. The RBMK is one of the two types of reactors the Soviets have built to generate electric power; the other, the VVER type, is similar to the United States' pressurized-water reactor. By 1986 the Soviets had developed a strong nuclear power program, generating about 10 percent of the world's nuclear energy from 43 operating reactors, with 36 under construction and another 34 in the planning stages. Even before the accident, the Soviets had planned to shift away from the graphite to the pressure-vessel reactors, a decision that implied Soviet recognition that the graphite reactor's design was unsafe and obsolete.

In terms of Soviet reactor design, Chernobyl represented a compromise. It had only a partial containment vessel—to prevent the leakage of radioactive gases due to an accident. Earlier versions of the RBMK reactor did not have even a partial containment building. However, the United States TMI accident in 1979 caused a full-scale review of reactor safety and containments in all countries, including the Soviet Union. The RBMK is a huge reactor. It is topped with a tall building, housing a fuel machine at the top that replaces the uranium as it is used up. Although the pipes below the reactor core were enclosed in a containment vessel, all the steam pipes above the core were inside ordinary industrial buildings. When these pipes broke during the accident, huge amounts of radioactive gases were released into the atmosphere.

At 1:00 A.M. on April 26, the Chernobyl reactor operators were one full day into a unique safety test.[8] The test goal was to determine if the residual energy of a spinning turbine could provide sufficient power to the reactor in case of an emergency shutdown with loss of off-site power. During the test, operators purposely disconnected key safety systems and consciously violated normal operating procedures in order to maximize the test results. As the operators departed from normal operations, the plant became more and more unstable. Soon the operators were running the plant "blind." The emergency core cooling system had been shut down; safety mechanisms had been disconnected; and all the control rods that moderated fission in the reactor's core had been at least partially pulled out—a fundamental violation of procedure that could not have been legally authorized even by then–general secretary Gorbachev. When it became clear that the reactor was becoming dangerously unstable, the operators slammed the emergency AZ-5 button to drop the control rods back into the core. But it was too late. The rods could not enter the deformed core.

A few seconds later, shocks were felt in the control room, followed by two large explosions. As the reactor's power level soared to 120 times its rated capacity, a surge equivalent to a "slow nuclear explosion" ripped open the 2,000 fuel rods in the reactor's core. As the superheated cooling water flashed to steam, a huge explosion blasted through the 1,000-ton concrete slab above the reactor, spitting hot, highly radioactive nuclear fuel into the Soviet night. For the first time in history, the lethal radioactive isotopes of a large reactor were scattered into the atmosphere, blasted high enough to be carried over Europe by wind currents. Initial efforts to seal the reactor were only partially successful. The graphite-encased core continued to smolder for several days, allowing more and more radioactivity to be released.

It is estimated that between 3 and 4 percent of the radioactive isotopes in the core were released into the environment—about 7,000 kilograms (representing 50 million to 100 million curies) of radioactive materials, more than 1,000 times the amount released at Three Mile Island. These included up to 50 radioactive isotopes with half-lives ranging from two hours to 24,000 years.

Chernobyl: The Human Cost   Human injury from radioactivity can occur in three ways: being exposed to gamma rays in radioactive materials outside the body (in the sky, on the ground), inhaling radioactive gases and dust, and digesting contaminated food or water.

Although all three types of injury occurred, the largest concern in the surrounding nations of the Ukraine and Byelorussia continues to be ingestion, because radioactive materials fell on soil and on vegetation that was consumed by people or by grazing animals. The largest number of deaths will be due to cancers caused by exposing living tissues to ionizing radiation, which damages cells' genetic materials. The greatest danger is from cesium 137, which, like potassium, goes to all cells. Scientists estimate that one-tenth to one-sixth as much cesium 137 was emitted at Chernobyl as has entered the environment from all nuclear weapons tests to date. Today nearly 70 percent of Byelorussian territory is still contaminated at more than 5 curies per square kilometer for cesium. Uncontaminated food for babies must be imported from outside. The Kurchatov Institute of Moscow has reported that 250,000 people are still living in locations where levels of contamination are more than 15 curies per square kilometer. In Western radiation laboratories, work is stopped and decontamination procedures are started at less than 1 curie per square kilometer.[9]

In the days following the disaster, Olga Korbut, the former gymnast and Soviet Olympic gold medalist, went about her life as usual in Minsk.[10] She planted her garden, celebrated the coming of spring, and with her husband and son walked in the May Day parade, just days after the accident. Like most Soviet citizens, she was kept in the dark by her government and did not realize the cataclysmic nature of the event. Two days passed before a brief announcement was made on Radio Moscow. Officials tried to assure the world that the reactor was "under control." On the 11th day after the disaster, *Pravda* released an extensive description of the accident. One week later, Gorbachev made a televised statement to the nation.

For Ms. Korbut, the news came too late to prevent her family's exposure. "When we were finally told about the catastrophe, it was too late. A dreadful fate has been sealed for my beautiful Byelorussia and its children," she later wrote as an international emissary for the Children of Chernobyl. "We heard the rumors and guessed at the truth. Over the years we watched friends and neighbors get mysteriously sick, but there was never an explanation."

Soviet credibility at home and abroad was severely damaged in the aftermath of the accident. The lack of information following the accident brought denunciations from Western governments. Beyond its economic and biological effects, Chernobyl has played an enormous role in shaping a new Soviet political consciousness. "It exposed the

Communist Party, all the secrecy, the callousness, the self-interest. On May Day, they ordered the children into the street. People don't forgive when it affects their children. They never forgave; they began to curse the party," said Dr. Yuri Sherbak, a physician and founder of the environmental movement in the Ukraine.[11] The accident also furthered the alienation of the Republics of the Ukraine and Byelorussia and was a key element in their independent movements, which contributed to the breakup of the Soviet Union.

Today, beyond the power plant, an 18-mile "forbidden zone" surrounds the burned-out sarcophagus of the entombed reactor. Visitors to the zone begin to notice that something is wrong with the towns that surround the area. There are no children. In fact, there are few people at all. The only evidence that the area is a radiological hell is the occasional evacuated town, its entrance blocked by a sign reading: "Entry Forbidden, Radiological Danger." Hidden from view are the thousands of radiation-related illnesses yet to appear, the hospital wards full of victims, and the thousands of uprooted families. None of the grim statistics convey the psychological stress felt daily by families dealing with the uncertainties of nonfatal cancers, potential genetic defects, and other diseases such as the widely reported Chernobyl AIDS syndrome.

For the citizens of the Ukraine and Byelorussia, the long shadow of Chernobyl has cast a curse on their lives and land and destroyed the myth of heroic Mother Russia rising up, as she did in World War II, to overcome all obstacles. As one elderly Ukrainian woman put it: "During the Second War, the Germans conquered Ukrainian territory and openly killed millions of inhabitants of this land. The catastrophe of Chernobyl, however, is destroying our soul, our land and our air, and even our future." The cries from the poisoned Ukraine are now heard around the world. Echoing the silent question that "can be seen in the eyes of hundreds of thousands of children," Volodymyr Yavorivsky, a novelist, asks, "What will become of us"?[12]

The Rites of Power   Dr. Gofman knew only too well what would become of them.

As professor emeritus of molecular and cell biology at the University of California–Berkeley, as a physician with a doctorate in nuclear and physical chemistry, and as one of the world's foremost radiation researchers, he had devoted decades of his life to the study of radiation. In the early 1940s, Dr. Gofman had codiscovered uranium 232 and uranium 233 while still a graduate student a Berkeley. There, he continued research related to the atomic bomb and isolated the world's first workable amount of plutonium for the Manhattan Project.

In those heady early years, Dr. Gofman displayed many of the qualities author Tom Wolfe called "the right stuff" in describing the astronauts of NASA. Dr. Gofman had rapidly climbed to the pinnacle of the scientific ziggurat, where he enjoyed a life of prestige and comfort. His early career had rapidly progressed from radiation chemistry (the Manhattan Project), to biomedical pioneering in heart disease research ("bad" and "good" cholesterol), and then back to radiation (now in health effects, not chemistry) in 1963 when he set up the Biomedical Research Division at the U.S. government's Lawrence Livermore National Laboratory. Here, he was on the cutting edge in the exciting new field of molecular genetics, the field now producing major discoveries about the relationship of chromosomal abnormalities to cancer and inherited diseases. And radiation was proving to be a champion chromosome wrecker.

However, Gofman's ascent to the upper echelons of the radiation establishment ended abruptly when he voluntarily jumped off the ladder to success. Faced with a clear choice between extolling scientific truth and perpetuating official lies about "safe" radiation, he declared that the atomic emperor wore no clothes. Unable to compromise his findings, which he documented in the 900-page *Radiation and Human Health* (1981), and more recently in *Radiation-Induced Cancer from Low-Dose Exposure* (1990), Dr. Gofman left the Livermore Laboratory to help lead the revolt of the guinea pigs.[13]

In 1963 the Atomic Energy Commission hired Dr. Gofman to establish the Biomedical Research Division at the Livermore Laboratory and to investigate the impact of radiation on humans. By 1969 Dr. Gofman and his colleague Dr. Arthur Tamplin had concluded that *all* forms of human cancers can be induced by radiation, that an increase of radiation dose produces *a linear increase* in cancer incidence, and that children are far more susceptible to radiation-induced cancers than are adults.

Their work argued that if everyone in the United States received the official "permissible" average dose of radiation from nuclear power plants, at that time 170 millirems per year, an additional 16,000 to 32,000 cancer deaths would be caused annually. From the point of view of the nuclear industry and the government, the most damaging findings were that all and any radiation causes cancer and that there was probably no safe, "permissible" exposure to low-level radiation for humans. Gofman did not conclusively prove this latter finding until the late eighties.

The AEC was appalled by the findings and forced Gofman and Tamplin out of their positions at the laboratory. In fact, the nuclear industry had already launched a witch-hunt to undermine the careers of other researchers—such as Dr. Edward Sternglass in the United States and Alice Stewart in England —who had the temerity to report that radiation could kill at higher rates than expected. These findings meant that nuclear power plant workers, nuclear shipyard workers, soldiers and citizens who had been exposed to radiation during the above-ground nuclear weapons testing era of the forties and fifties, and even patients exposed to medical X rays faced a long-term danger of contracting cancer.

By 1986 Dr. Gofman had become sanguine about the government's attempts to discredit him.

> Well, the Atomic Energy Commission gave me $3.5 million a year for six and one-half years to study this question. Then, two weeks after I concluded that radiation was more harmful than they thought, they were very displeased and suddenly I was officially "incompetent." ... Now, when we arrive at 1985, the National Institutes of Health are only three-fold away from me on breast cancer. So the AEC, which is probably one of the worst agencies in the history of the U.S. government, had taken upon itself the dual role of regulating and promoting nuclear power. If I had never said anything, I would be their fair-haired boy, but I've taken care of too many patients with cancer and leukemia to lie for the Atomic Energy Commission. I consider every cancer case a disaster.

Crimes against Humanity   In their book *Poisoned Power,* first published in 1971, Gofman and Tamplin described their findings and openly declared war on the nuclear industry: "About a year ago, we began to perceive the dimensions of the massive hoax being perpetrated on the public. It was very difficult for us to believe that what we observed to be occurring could truly be real. Indeed, up to that time we, deeply immersed in atomic energy research, had been lulled into the belief that nuclear electricity was the one atomic energy program which posed little threat to society. How wrong we were. There is a real potential disaster ahead."[14]

They concluded that the public has been, and *is being,* deceived by a clever, well-financed propaganda campaign of delusions concerning "cheap, clean, safe nuclear power" and that concealing the truth from the public was regarded as essential. They further stated:

> Radioactivity represents one of the worst, maybe the worst of all poisons. And it is manufactured as an inevitable by product of nuclear electricity generation. One year of operation of a single, large nuclear reactor plant generates as much long-persisting radioactive poisons as one thousand Hiroshima-type atomic bombs. There is no way the electric power can be generated in nuclear plants without generating the radioactive poisons. Once any of these radioactive poisons are released to the environment, and this we believe is likely to occur, the pollution of our environment is irreversible. . . . It is important that people learn *how* they are likely to be exposed to such poisons and *how* death dealing injury is thereby produced in the individual and in all future generations.[15]

In the aftermath of TMI, Dr. Gofman redoubled his efforts to educate the public on the dangers of radiation. He pointed out that

> it is a simple calculation indeed to estimate the number of fatal cancers and leukemia which are produced by any nuclear accident, provided we know the dose received. The . . . process can be summarized . . . by a single equation:

$$\frac{(no.\ of\ rems)}{hour} \times (no.\ of\ hours) \times \frac{(no.\ of\ persons\ exposed)}{300\ person\text{-}rems} \times (1\ death) = \begin{array}{c} no.\ of\ deaths \\ which\ will \\ occur\ later^{16} \end{array}$$

The first term of the equation is read "number of rems per hour" and the fourth term is read "one death per 300 person-rems." Because the persons, rems, and hours in the equation all cancel each other out, the solution is the total number of deaths.

Dr. Gofman was enraged by the deceptiveness of the NRC in the wake of the TMI accident. He noted that a few days after the accident began, the NRC began reporting radiation doses to the public as "a few millirems per hour"—inevitably pointing out that the doses were "low" while neglecting to mention that "it is not just the millirems per hour which matters, but rather the *total* numbers of millirems received by the people."

Although the industry claimed, and continues to do so today, that "no one died at TMI," Dr. Gofman had a different view. "In the first printing of *Poisoned Power,* we used figures that were called overestimates of the hazard by atomic energy 'experts.' Those 'experts' were wrong then, and they are even more wrong now, for new evidence in the last eight years shows that we had *underestimated* the hazard." Plugging the data in to his equation, Gofman projected that there would be "333 fatal cancers or leukemias" caused by the accident at Three Mile Island.

"Believe it or not," he continues, "the Nuclear Regulatory Commission permits giant nuclear plants to operate without having [radiation] monitors installed and operating at all times in every populated area within 50 miles of the plants. . . . the no-monitor policy is no accident, for it helps to protect the utilities from lawsuits for personal injury." Therefore, Gofman concludes, "The true doses at TMI itself and the true numbers of cancers will never be known."

After TMI, Gofman, appalled by the arrogance of the industry, launched an all-out attack on the industry and the government—one that got him branded as an "extremist." Initially he and Tamplin had criticized the "top leadership" of the "nuclear juggernaut" for displaying a "total lack of comprehension of radioactive poison and its effect. . . . Worst of all, this same top leadership has demonstrated a lack of responsibility in meeting the moral obligation to provide the public with honest information concerning the real hazards which must be faced.

"We are not speaking of unusual 'individual accidents.' Rather, we are concerned over the hazards of major calamities to human health and life, unparalleled in human history."

But in the introduction to *Poisoned Power,* reissued after the TMI accident, Gofman went much further: "This book . . . is about the lies, the cover-up, and the callousness of those who are willing to trick you into accepting nuclear power so that they . . . can make money or expand a bureaucratic empire, even though their activity kills people." Gofman argued that if the promoters of nuclear power are really ignorant about the effects of "low" doses of radiation, then they are conducting a mass experiment on humans without their consent, under a philosophy of "expose people first; learn the effects later."

Alternatively, if they do know the effects, then the charge against them is not simply "experimentation on humans, but rather it is planned, random murder." He concluded that "Americans would be justified in demanding that Nuremberg-type trials be held for these individuals."[17]

Reflecting on the legacy of Chernobyl, Dr. Gofman believes the world has created a highly toxic nuclear mausoleum that must be "sealed off for a couple of hundred thousand years" because of plutonium. Plutonium is a long-lived transuranic isotope, dangerous for 10 times its half-life of 24,000 years, or for 240,000 years. Consider this folly in light of the fact that our species, Homo sapiens, has been on earth for only about 35,000 years. "Also the NRC does not even like the idea of sealing it off. They say that the radioactivity will outlast the concrete. But you could have people go in every 300 to 400 years, put a new concrete structure on it, and replace the bronze plaque that says, 'A Monument to the Idiocy of the Twentieth Century.' "

Upon showing that all radiation is dangerous, Dr. Gofman spent his "retirement" crusading against nuclear power, nuclear pollution, and careless radiation overdosing in medicine. After being defrocked by the nuclear priesthood for violating the unwritten code to "speak no evil" about radiation, he has launched a personal crusade to warn people about the retroactive alteration of radiation health databases by the governments that control them. He calls it "Orwellian science" and adds, "if the scientific databases on health effects are false, then even an Einstein will get the wrong answers from them."

As the veil of secrecy that has shrouded the nuclear industry worldwide has been lifted, Gofman's study of radiation has given experts and the public a deeper awareness of the health dangers of major nuclear accidents and radiation experiments. Prominent among these accidents are the nuclear explosion of buried atomic wastes near Kyshtym (U.S.S.R) in the Urals in 1957, the Windscale reactor fire that littered the British landscape with radioactivity in 1957, the fire at the Fermi plant in Detroit that led to a partial meltdown in 1966, and the misinformation regarding the ongoing impact of the TMI and Chernobyl accidents. Significant among the experiments are the Department of Energy's revelation of illegal government radiation experiments conducted on Americans during the Cold War, and, in 1995, Gofman's own research, which shows that past exposure to ionizing radiation—primarily through flagrant use of medical X rays—is *responsible* for up to 75 percent of current U.S. breast cancer cases.

Reflecting the primacy of conscience and truth above career, Dr. Gofman's pioneering work parallels that of Rachel Carson, the marine biologist who in *Silent Spring* first alerted the world to the ways in which pollution threatens human health and animal life.[18] Having descended into the abyss of human death and destruction generated by the radiation spewed out by Chernobyl, Gofman rises above the nuclear fire like a phoenix to become a messenger for the Children of

Chernobyl and a respected antinuclear advocate of a safer and saner world.

Strangely, it was not radiation but plumbing problems that helped stalemate nuclear power in the United States.

The Green Grunge at Turkey Point: Mark Oncavage, Music Teacher

Steam generator failures are the largest product failure in the history of American industry.
> —*Ralph Nader, consumer advocate and founder,*
> *Critical Mass Energy Project*

Mark Oncavage and John Gofman had little in common. Mr. Oncavage was a music teacher at Hialeah Elementary School. Dr. Gofman was an eminent health physicist. Their lives intersected when Oncavage became a reactor techie and petitioned the NRC to challenge the $500 million repair of the corroded steam generators at Florida Power and Light Corporation's (FPL) Turkey Point nuclear power plant.

Dr. Gofman counseled Oncavage that "the NRC is a kangaroo court and you are wasting your time if you think you are going to get a fair hearing there. Still, it's the only forum you have to bring these issues before the public."[19] Oncavage decided to go ahead. His petition to intervene started "the battle of Turkey Point," which would bring the safety problems of steam generator corrosion and embrittlement at aging U.S. reactors to national attention and raise the issue of who should pay for expensive reactor repairs needed to maintain reactor safety.

Oncavage never intended to join the antinuclear movement. As a graduate student in environmental studies at Florida International University (FIU) in Miami, he was simply looking for a topic for a research paper when he visited the public-documents room at the library to research Turkey Point.

Reading arcane announcements in the *Federal Register* and leafing through three volumes of FPL's *Steam Generator Repair Proposal* to the NRC, Oncavage realized that his local utility had plans to repair, replace, and store the radioactive steam generators at the Turkey Point nuclear plant, located only 12 miles from his home in Dade County, Florida.

Oncavage became fascinated by the scope of the proposed repairs. As he leafed through the pages, he soon realized that FPL's "simple maintenance" was no backyard repair job. The grinding, cutting, and sandblasting would expose thousands of workers to radiation. The original repair plan called for storing the six corroded, 200-ton radioactive steam generators in an earthen-floor building next to Biscayne Bay, a national aquatic monument. One hundred thousand gallons of radioactive primary reactor coolant would be dumped into the porous limestone cooling canals surrounding the plant. There was no scientific evidence that the repair would work. Westinghouse Corporation, which had manufactured the original faulty steam generators and would now provide the replacements, was offering only a 12-month guarantee. And, to top it off, FPL wanted to pass the $500 million in repair costs on to the Oncavage family and the rest of FPL's customers.

Oncavage began to write letters to the NRC. Was this repair safe? Would it work? Had any other steam generator repairs been successful? Should radioactive materials be stuck in a building with only an earthen floor? Could a hurricane send a storm surge through the building, releasing radioactive wastes into the environment? Oncavage asked this last question more than a decade before Hurricane Andrew, the worst natural disaster in U.S. history, sent a wall of water surging through Turkey Point.

His letters went unanswered. Oncavage began to lose interest. He started spring break wondering if he would get enough information to complete his report. On March 29, 1979, just before classes were about to begin again, Oncavage picked up the morning paper in front of his house. The headlines screamed: "Nuclear Accident at Three Mile Island." Over the next week, Oncavage followed the details of the TMI accident with a keen interest. He decided that he must get his questions answered. He had to do everything possible to prevent what had happened at TMI from happening at Turkey Point.

The "Green Grunge" Turkey Point was a product of the early 1970s, a time when utilities were counting on safe, cheap, and reliable nuclear power to generate electricity. At a cost of only $212 million, Turkey Point's Unit 3 and Unit 4 were a bargain for FPL and a loss leader for Westinghouse, which was then trying to establish the utility market for pressurized water reactors (PWRs).

Behind the scenes, however, all did not go well at Turkey Point. As early as 1974, FPL first detected deterioration in the steam generator tubes—and the deterioration seemed to increase over time. The steam generator in a PWR such as the ones at Turkey Point is a tall, radiator-type device that transfers the heat generated by the nuclear fission process in the primary system to the secondary system, where water is turned into steam. The steam turns a turbine, which in turn generates electricity.

At Turkey Point there are two nuclear units, each with three steam generators. In each steam generator, hot water from the primary system circulates under enormous pressure (about 2,200 pounds per square inch) through 3,500 tubes, which are typically 0.05 inch thick and have a diameter of approximately .75 inch. Feed water in the secondary system flows around these tubes, taking up some of the heat and turning to steam. It is important that both the tubes and the steam generators maintain their integrity because they perform two very important safety functions. They remove the intense heat of the fission process (which reaches 500 degrees Fahrenheit) and act as a barrier so that radioactivity from the primary system does not contaminate the secondary system and leak into the environment.

But by the early 1980s, according to the NRC, steam generators were breaking down at 25 nuclear power plants across the United States—representing about three-fourths of all PWRs then in operation.[20] Denting and corrosion had caused degradation of both the steam generator tubes and the support plates that hold the tubes. The villain of support plate degradation is a hardened corrosion product that settles between the tube and the support plate. This substance expands under the intense reactor heat with sufficient force to dent the tube and crack the support plate.

This corrosion, nicknamed the "green grunge" by the press, can eventually weaken the tubes and cause leaks of radioactive primary coolant into the air. According to the NRC, a worst-case scenario involving tube burst and loss of feed water could result in the feared loss-of-coolant accident (LOCA), in which the core is uncovered and the fuel melts.

When FPL first contacted Westinghouse about the problem in 1974, Westinghouse suggested changes in the water chemistry treatment. But the change to a new phosphate treatment only succeeded in speeding up the corrosion. In 1975 another temporary solution was devised. Then an inspection program was instituted that enabled FPL to target potentially leaking tubes and decommission them.

This work of plugging the steam generator tubes was carried out by temporary workers called "jumpers" or "sponges," who jumped into the steam generator for 30 to 90 seconds and plugged tubes with an explosive plug device. After these sponges had absorbed 3 rems of radiation, the maximum allowable for a year, their employment was terminated. At severely affected plants such as Turkey Point, the NRC required that each unit be shut down every six months for a 30-day period. In order to keep Turkey Point running until a permanent solution was found, thousands of workers were "burned out," and FPL underwent expensive downtimes.

Although the public remained unaware of the problem at Turkey Point, the NRC was extremely concerned. They knew that 20 percent of the steam generator tubes had been plugged in each of the nuclear units at Turkey Point. The NRC had already ruled that when this figure reached 25 percent, the commission would require FPL and other affected utilities to derate the nuclear units because the loss of heat transfer could affect the safety systems of the plant. Derating required running the plant at lower power and losing large sums of money.

To continue operating with this loss of generating capacity would affect FPL's profits. At this point, FPL management made a corporate decision to repair Turkey Point by replacing the massive Westinghouse steam generators at a cost of $138 million for all repair-related capital costs. This $138 million repair cost, plus the $360 million in replacement power costs that FPL would need in order to purchase oil during the 18 months the plant would be shut down for the repairs, brought the total steam generator replacement costs to nearly $500 million. Ultimately, FPL planned to pass all of the repair costs on to its Florida consumers.

FPL's management was pleased. They had found a permanent solution to steam generator corrosion and could keep running Turkey Point at full power. FPL shareholders were pleased; the consumer would pay for the repairs. The NRC was relieved; steam generator replacement could provide a solution for all the PWRs around the country suffering from the "green grunge."

However, none of them had counted on the tenacity of Mark Oncavage.

The Battle of Turkey Point Oncavage returned to class from spring break with more questions than answers for his environmental studies teacher, Dr. Jerry Brown.[21] "How can I complete my report if the NRC won't answer my questions? I see 14 problems with the FPL's repair proposal, but who will believe me—I'm a layperson? How can I get copies of FPL's repair documents? How can I ensure the safety of the repair process? How can I stop them from putting the nuclear waste next to Biscayne Bay, where I like to sail on weekends and my kids love to swim?"

Fortunately, Dr. Brown had some of the answers to Oncavage's questions. As a former national grape boycott coordinator for Cesar Chavez's farmworkers' movement, Dr. Brown had broad experience with the process of raising funds, working with the press, and educating the public on controversial issues. He explained to Oncavage that if he wanted to have his questions answered, he would have to become a citizen "legal intervenor" in FPL's repair petition to the NRC. That the intervention could take years to prepare and would cost hundreds of thousands of dollars, mainly in expert witness fees. That Oncavage would have to become a technical expert on Turkey Point in particular and on steam generator problems in general. And, last, that although Oncavage had little chance of winning, if he were granted legal status as an intervenor, he could bring greater public scrutiny and safety to the repair and waste disposal process.

"Are you sure you are right about this?" Dr. Brown asked Oncavage.

Oncavage stared back at Dr. Brown with an honest innocence backed by a steel determination that would serve him well over the next years and replied, "I have never been so certain about anything in my life."

Dr. Brown introduced Oncavage to Bruce Rogow, a law professor at Nova University and an expert in First Amendment issues. Working closely with Oncavage, Rogow transformed the 14 problems Oncavage saw with Turkey Point into 14 "contentions" formulated into a legal "Petition for Leave to Intervene." Oncavage sent his petition to the NRC and turned it in as his final report to Dr. Brown's class. He got an A in the class. He waited anxiously for the NRC's response.

In the summer of 1979, the NRC convened a special hearing of the Atomic Safety and Licensing Board (ASLB) at the Howard Johnson hotel in downtown Miami to gather information about Oncavage's petition. Representing the NRC were a nuclear engineer, an NRC attorney, and an environmental engineer—all of whom sat on the dais behind the seal of the U.S. Nuclear Regulatory Commission. Five NRC staff members argued against Oncavage's petition, along with 11 attorneys from Steel Hector and Davis, the prominent Florida law firm that represented FPL.

Seated alone was Mark Oncavage, dressed in his yellow polyester sports jacket and peering back at the hostile crowd through his horn-rimmed glasses.

"Mr. Oncavage, what are your credentials to comment on the process whereby radioactive flux fields corrode steam generators in nuclear plants? Have you done original research in this area?" the head of the ASLB queried.

"I am a music teacher at Hialeah Elementary School. I plan to hire experts in nuclear chemistry to comment on this process," he replied.

"Mr. Oncavage, do you have legal counsel to assist you in building a sound and responsible record in this legal proceeding, should you be granted standing as an intervenor?"

"I will have to rely on volunteer attorneys," Oncavage replied.

"Mr. Oncavage, do you have the resources to sustain this intervention? It has been our experience that it can cost upward of $10,000 for intervenors to litigate each contention—that is, question—that you have raised. And you have 14 contentions."

Oncavage fumed. It seemed to him that his chances were dimming and that the price of democracy in the nuclear age was getting very expensive.

FPL argued vigorously that Oncavage's petition, more than a year late, was "untimely" and "irresponsible" and that as a music teacher, Oncavage could obviously contribute nothing of merit to a process that FPL, the utility, Westinghouse, the manufacturer, and the NRC, the final arbiter of safety at all U.S. nuclear plants, had analyzed and evaluated for years. Approving the intervention would result only in a waste of time and costly delays for Florida consumers.

But Three Mile Island weighed more heavily on the minds of the NRC commissioners than did FPL's protests. The accident had placed the NRC under greater public and congressional scrutiny than at any time in its history. A presidential commission had been convened to look into the causes of the accident. The NRC staff was on a hair-trigger alert to address all possible reactor safety issues in depth. On August 3, 1979, the ASLB granted Oncavage's request for a full public hearing on the health and safety issues of the proposed repairs to FPL's Turkey Point nuclear reactors, to be litigated at a hearing scheduled for January 1980 in Miami.

The NRC began requesting information from Oncavage and FPL. FPL began complaining about expensive and unnecessary delays. Oncavage began gathering public support. Oncavage and Dr. Brown organized a community group under the banner of Floridians United for Safe Energy (FUSE). FUSE's purpose was not to stop nuclear power but to "make the Turkey Point repair safe." FUSE enlisted a broad base of support in the form of energy experts, public-interest attorneys, and businesses and citizens who contributed funds to legally oppose a repair and waste disposal plan that now appeared to be inherently dangerous and of questionable value.

Early in 1980, Oncavage learned that he was involved in not only a nuclear safety issue but a major product failure. FUSE's lead attorney, Neil Chonin, a seasoned litigator and product liability expert, discovered that FPL had filed suit in federal court in 1978 against Westinghouse, the manufacturer of the steam generators at Turkey Point and of those at most PWRs around the country. The suit charged that Westinghouse had supplied the utility with faulty steam generators. FPL was suing for damages resulting from what they alleged to be negligence and breach of warranty.

Immediately, Oncavage and his attorneys filed suit also to intervene in the case on behalf of all FPL consumers, who had already paid huge fuel costs because of the faulty product. A battery of FPL and Westinghouse attorneys now joined forces to keep Oncavage out of *their* lawsuit. When Chonin went to examine the legal brief, he found that the case had been sealed. But the lawsuit would eventually prove to be Oncavage's trump card.

Suddenly, on May 28, 1981, a curt mailgram arrived at Neil Chonin's office. The ASLB had decided to "grant a summary disposition of all intervenors' contentions." The mailgram notified Oncavage that after two years of preparation and expenses for expert witnesses, the hearing scheduled for June 2 was now summarily canceled, and an official order would follow. FPL had won and could proceed with the repairs.

"Darn it," Oncavage exclaimed when Chonin read him the notice. "Dr. Gofman was right. The NRC is a kangaroo court. The case is over."

Nuclear News   During his darkest moment, Oncavage received a boost from a major publicity coup that would ultimately propel him and FUSE to victory in their battle with FPL. For two years, Oncavage had been bombarding the *Miami Herald* with press releases about Turkey Point. "Are you picketing the plant?" "Are you chaining yourself to the fence at Turkey Point?" reporters would ask, looking for a public confrontation. "No," Oncavage replied, "we are not *that* kind of antinuclear group; we are a legal and research group." But to no avail. Not one word appeared in the *Herald*.

But for months, freelance writer John Rothschild had been quietly gathering information about Turkey Point. His article finally appeared as the April 12, 1981, cover story of the *Herald*'s *Tropic Magazine,* a widely read Sunday supplement. The cover carried a full-page color picture of Turkey Point and an open letter to readers stating that "this is one of the most important articles ever published by this magazine. It outlines FPL's controversial plan to cut open the plant, fix the problem, and perhaps make the same mistake over again." Inside the article was a ballot that asked readers if "Turkey Point should be fixed or shut down forever." Rothschild questioned the economic feasibility of repairing the plant and questioned whether Turkey Point could be phased out and replaced with a stringent conservation program.

The article created a public furor that neither FPL, FUSE, nor the *Herald* anticipated. Ballots poured in to the *Herald* for weeks as the public conducted its own nuclear referendum. In a follow-up article on May 31, 1981, the *Herald* reported the results. Almost 7,000 ballots had been received, but of the 5,500 actually counted, Miamians voted *for* nuclear power but against the Turkey Point repair, against the NRC's making the repair decisions, and overwhelmingly against paying for the repair. Out of 5,527 readers who responded, 4,053—or nearly 75 percent—answered no to the question "Do you think you, as a consumer, should pay for the repair?"

Now all the major newspapers and TV stations began to besiege FPL and FUSE for interviews. "What do you think about the 'news' in the *Herald*?" reporters asked Oncavage. Oncavage would smile to himself at this question, wondering why this hadn't been "news" two years ago when he started the intervention. Still, he was pleased to finally have a public forum. On local TV, he expressed his concerns that a hurricane could breach the planned storage site at Turkey Point, spilling radioactive waste into the environment. As soon as the stories about FPL's plans to store radioactive waste next to Biscayne Bay hit the press, the utility announced that it was revising its plans. Eventually FPL announced that the old steam generators would be barged to the Barnwell nuclear waste site in South Carolina.

FUSE convened an emergency meeting at Neil Chonin's offices to consider its options. With its funds dwindling and its energy sapped by the NRC intervention, but with public support rising, what could the organization do? Disbanding would be irresponsible. Appealing the NRC ruling would be too time-consuming and had little chance of success. Calling for a statewide referendum on Turkey Point was too big an undertaking for a small group. Finally, Oncavage read the *Herald* survey aloud. Obviously, the public did not want to pay for the repairs. He suggested that FUSE change its focus from Washington, D.C., to Tallahassee, Florida, and intervene to stop the Florida Public Service Commission (PSC), the public body that sets utility rates, from allowing FPL to pass the repair costs on to the consumers.

"OK," said Chonin, "the PSC is made up of five people appointed by the governor of Florida. Many of them have political ambitions, so they are sensitive to public concerns. But now you've got another intervention, a new forum, a different set of witnesses—utility rate experts, economic experts. After what we just went through with the NRC over the past two years, how are you ever going to pay for all of this?"

Oncavage's eyes lit up. "We've got a massive product failure on our hands. We are now making this a consumer issue, not a nuclear issue. Let's call America's preeminent consumer advocate. Let's ask Ralph Nader to help us make our case!"

Ralph Nader to the Rescue   Nader arrived at the FUSE fundraiser two hours late. He had a bandage over his left eyebrow and, hobbled by a badly sprained ankle, walked with a cane and had to speak sitting down. Nader apologized for arriving late, explaining that he had slipped at home and injured himself. But he received a standing ovation from the 400 guests assembled at a private home when he urged them to oppose FPL's request for a $281 million rate increase.

He spoke about the potential dangers of an accident, a meltdown, or an explosion at a nuclear power plant. He cited a just-released NRC study of the consequences of accidents at all 91 U.S. reactor locations. The study estimated the results of a "one-in-a-billion" combination of mechanical failures at the Turkey Point nuclear power plant and weather conditions favoring the spread of radioactivity. The worst-case accident at the South Dade County reactor could cause 29,000 deaths in the Miami area, 45,000 injuries in Dade and Broward County, and more than $43 billion in property damage, according to the government's Sandia National Laboratories.

This was significant because the Turkey Point plant had not only all the customary problems of nuclear plants, such as corrosion and lack of a final waste disposal site, but also an "embrittlement problem." Nader explained that embrittlement occurs when the protective steel containment vessel around the radioactive gases and fuel rods becomes brittle because of neutron bombardment. In the case of an accident, the embrittled shell could shatter, much as a cold glass would if taken from the refrigerator and thrown into a container of hot water. The Turkey Point reactors were numbers three and four, respectively, on a list of the worst-embrittled nuclear power plants in the United States, and they could suffer a breach of containment in an accident that required flooding the reactor with emergency core cooling water.

"You are a community, without any exaggeration, that is sitting under a cloud of jeopardy, economically and from a radioactive explosion," Nader said. "The radioactive material in a nuclear plant the size of Turkey Point utterly dwarfs the radioactive fallout from a nuclear bomb."

"Turkey Point," he continued, "you have the best named nuclear generating plant in the United States."[22] The FPL plants should be shut down, argued Nader, who advocated closing down all nuclear power plants around the country.

Nader railed against FPL's current request for a $281 million rate increase, part of which was earmarked to cover a portion of the repair costs for the Westinghouse-supplied steam generators at Turkey Point. The equipment was supposed to last for 40 years but broke down in less than 10. Now FPL was suing Westinghouse but was buying the replacement equipment from the same company.

"Florida Power and Light got a 12-month warranty," said Nader, who first achieved national attention for his exposure of General Motors's poorly designed Corvair. "Even General Motors does better than that."

Nader endorsed FUSE's efforts to stop FPL from charging customers a half billion dollars for repairs to the broken steam generators. "It is understandable that you do not want to pay for what the utility messed up," Nader continued. "FPL is requiring you as consumers to be unwilling investors without a vote and no hope for dividends. You pay for the losses and blunders, shenanigans, expense accounts and propaganda that floods out to persuade people that the two plants are nothing more than pale colored tulips in disguise."

Nader went on to outline the global scope of the steam generator problems. Earlier that year, the Ginna nuclear plant near Rochester, New York, had been brought to a cold shutdown because of a steam generator tube rupture that leaked radioactive gas into the air and flooded the containment building with 11,000 gallons of radioactive water. At Arkansas II and Sequoyah I (Tennessee), tube leaks occurred within two years after start-up. Steam generator tube degradation had already been recorded at the Almarez II (Spain) and Ringhals III (Sweden) reactors, both of which came on-line in 1981. Twenty of the 38 foreign reactors suffering from internal corrosion were designed by Westinghouse Electric Corporation. "If it's Westinghouse, you better be insured," Nader joked.

"In California, Virginia and now here in Florida, nuclear plants have already been shut down for steam generator repairs that will take at least nine months. Given the scope and cost of the repairs—$3.8 billion for at least 15 seriously corroded plants—steam generator failures are the largest product failure in the history of American industry," he observed.[23]

"The ultimate goal of this struggle," Nader concluded, "is not just to reduce the risk of catastrophe but to reduce the burden on utility bills and establish a proper direction for a more benign, adequate and self-controlled energy system."

When Nader finished his remarks, the guests gave him another standing ovation. As Oncavage rose to speak, he looked out over the crowd, which included county commissioners, state senators, business leaders, community activists, and media representatives. It was not that Nader had told those gathered at the home of Lucille and Belvin Friedson, founders of Windmere Corporation, anything they hadn't heard or read before. But Nader's presentation and reputation made a tremendous impression. Oncavage felt vindicated. It was as if the pope of public advocacy himself had blessed his cause. Oncavage knew he was finally getting the public hearing on Turkey Point that he had fought so hard and long for.

FPL Investors Must Share Costs   On September 14, 1982, nearly a month before Nader's visit, FUSE had presented its case against the FPL rate increase to the Florida Public Service Commission. FPL's 2.3 million customers were paying too much for investment risks that should be borne by shareholders, argued John Stutz, a Boston utility economist hired by FUSE to testify against the FPL request for a $281 million rate hike.

"The interests of investors are served, at the expense of ratepayers, to an unreasonable extent," Stutz argued. His testimony centered on who—stockholders or customers—should pay for $190 million in repairs. Building the Turkey Point plant was a typical business investment risk, Stutz argued. When the plant worked, it produced power significantly less expensive than power produced by oil-fired plants. But when the plant was out of service, FPL was paying for the debt on the plant, the repairs, and the cost of oil to replace the lost power—at about $700,000 a day. FPL executives testified that the failures at Turkey Point were costing the company a total of more than $470 million in such added expenses.

Articulating FUSE's "risk-sharing plan," Stutz suggested to the commissioners that the answer was to allow FPL to recover from customers its actual repair costs, spread out over a decade, but not earn a profit on those repairs by placing them in the rate base. FPL's plan would have allowed common stockholders to earn a 19 percent annual profit on the Turkey Point "mistake" if FPL's current rate increase were granted. Under FUSE's plan, Stutz concluded, both customers and stockholders would share the costs.

Testifying before the commission, FPL officials rejected Oncavage's call for risk sharing and equity for consumers. Professor Charles J. Cicchetti, a utility witness, stated under oath that "equity must be left to rabbis, priests and ministers."[24]

But the case was now also being tried in the press. Oncavage had tapped a groundswell of citizen outrage at FPL's "damn-the-public attitude." He countered FPL by arguing that "consumers are already paying for Turkey Point. They should not have to pay twice for nuclear lemons."

Without shifting the risk to FPL management and shareholders, FPL would have no incentive to correct its mistakes, and a dangerous precedent would be set whereby Florida consumers would face a future of multimillion dollar increases in electric power costs caused by breakdowns in nuclear technology. Further, Oncavage pointed out, steam generator corrosion had already appeared at FPL's St. Lucie 1 and at Florida Power Corp.'s Crystal River 3 reactors, both of which began operation in the mid-1970s.

FUSE's attorney then painted the commission into a corner by pointing out that FPL was already suing Westinghouse for negligence involving the original generators and that FPL and its customers had no guarantee (other than a 12-month warranty) that future steam generator failures would not occur even after the massive repairs were made.

If FPL won the case against Westinghouse, then FPL would recover its costs from the manufacturer—so why should the consumer pay? If FPL lost, then Westinghouse would have proven that FPL did not operate and maintain the steam generators correctly, so why should the consumer pay? Apparently, the commission was impressed by both FUSE's arguments and the firestorm of public protest against "unfair" rate increases. It ruled against FPL and, in a subsequent intervention brought by Oncavage, refused to let the utility recover replacement power costs. FPL and its shareholders were not going to make customers pay for the billion-dollar boondoggle caused by the "green grunge."

During the intervention, Oncavage had made a habit of dropping in to the public-documents room at FIU to keep a lookout for new developments at FPL and Turkey Point. Curious, he picked up FPL's Ten Year Site Plan, completed in 1982. Buried in the text was a small announcement that FPL was abandoning its plans to expand Turkey Point into a nuclear industry park that would house six additional power reactors. The utility cited "regulatory rachetting" in Washington in the wake of the TMI accident and increasing nuclear power plant costs as the main reasons for its decision to forsake the nuclear path for the foreseeable future.

Oncavage breathed a sigh of relief. Now maybe he could get back to spending weekends sailing with his son on Biscayne Bay, instead of worrying about Turkey Point.

Impact of the Reactor Techies   Already reeling from TMI-related expensive reactor safety retrofits and the shock of record new plant cancellations in the early 1980s, the nuclear industry now faced a serious economic challenge that would dog it throughout the decade. Most reactors were showing declining performance as they aged. Specifically, many PWRs were experiencing enormous and expensive problems with steam generator leaks and reactor pressure vessel embrittlement. As the first generation of nuclear plants deteriorated and repair and replacement power costs mounted into the billion dollar range, consumers began staging increased resistance to footing the bill. In many cases, as the focus of the antinuclear battle shifted from safety issues decided in Washington, D.C., to economic issues litigated in state capitals, consumers were winning.

By winning the first citizen-contested steam generator rate case, Oncavage had unknowingly forged an important strategic alliance between antinuclear activists and consumers, and this alliance held the potential to significantly increase support for the movement. With nearly three-quarters of all PWRs facing steam generator problems, the Florida decision portended increasing economic troubles for the nuclear utilities. The Florida PSC was rated by Wall Street as one of the most sympathetic to utilities in the country. Regulators in other states were expected to take an equally hard line against passing on major repair costs to consumers. According to rough estimates made by FUSE, replacing steam generators in all plants facing problems could cost nearly $4 billion in direct costs and another $4.5 billion in replacement power costs.

In the wake of the Turkey Point decision, other state commissions went even further and began to deny utilities the right to pass along *any* replacement power costs involving nuclear plants that had been forced out of service. For example, the Pennsylvania commission ordered Duquesne Light to refund $12.5 million for replacement power purchased when the NRC ordered it shut down in 1979 for strengthening to resist potential earthquakes. Baltimore Gas and Electric Company was made to pay for 75 percent of the costs for replacement power for Calvert Cliffs when it was shut down because of a technical error that accidentally allowed 6,000 gallons of salt water to leak into the plant. Activists claimed a major victory when the North Carolina Utilities Commission penalized Carolina Power and Light for the "poor performance" of its Brunswick nuclear units.

The utilities were now caught between the proverbial rock and a hard place. On the one hand stood the NRC, which was now demanding expensive measures to increase safety, retard corrosion, and slow embrittlement. On the other stood state public service commissioners, who were becoming more and more reluctant to pass these costs on to ratepayers.

In 1995, nearly 15 years after Oncavage raised the issue of steam generator repair costs, the issues of steam generator corrosion and embrittlement remained unresolved. On December 4, 1995, the Union of Concerned Scientists publicly released documentation from a whistle-blower charging the "management of the Maine Yankee nuclear power plant with deliberately falsifying computer calculations to avoid disclosing that the plant's cooling systems are inadequate to mitigate a loss-of-coolant accident, increasing the probability of a core meltdown."[25] The documents were sent by a longtime Yankee Atomic Electric Company employee who claims that management deliberately falsified reports to the NRC in order to receive approval to increase the reactor's power level to full power after recent steam generator repairs. On December 20, 1995, as a result of a review of these documents, the NRC stopped the restart of the Maine Yankee reactor.

Robert Pollard, a senior nuclear safety engineer with the Union of Concerned Scientists and a former NRC project manager, noted that "Unfortunately, sleeving 17,000 tubes further degrades the ability of the emergency core cooling system to prevent a meltdown. . . . It is necessary to determine, using a computer model that has not been falsified, that the cooling systems are adequate to protect the public."[26]

Pollard further noted that "The 1979 Three Mile Island accident at Harrisburg, Pennsylvania was a loss-of-coolant accident that showed existing computer models were inadequate to prevent core melting. Thereafter, the NRC required all plants to review and, if necessary, revise the computer models used to calculate the effectiveness of emergency core cooling systems."[27]

A major factor influencing the jump in reactor operating costs has been the need to retrofit existing reactors to meet safety standards. Major accidents at U.S. nuclear reactors—including the partial meltdowns at Fermi Unit 1 (Michigan) in 1966 and Three Mile Island Unit 2 (Pennsylvania) in 1979; the fire at Browns Ferry Unit 2 (Alabama) in 1975; and steam generator tube ruptures at Ginna Unit 1 (New York) in 1982, North Anna Unit 1 (Virginia) in 1988, and McGuire Unit 1 (North Carolina) in 1989—increased public, utility, and regulatory awareness of nuclear power plant safety risks.

Public and congressional pressure, brought about by the work of reactor techies around the nation, caused the NRC to order utilities to correct hundreds of unresolved and newly identified safety issues discovered after reactors were already licensed to operate. In some cases, major chronic safety repairs may eventually cost so much that utility management and stockholders will decide to close reactors rather than sink more money into maintaining operations. Since 1988 six reactors, including Rancho Seco in California and Shoreham in New York (both of which are chronicled in this book), have been permanently shut down for economic reasons, safety concerns, or related problems, long before the end of their 40-year life expectancy. This trend of premature closings will likely continue. A January 1993 report by Shearson Lehman Brothers predicted that "of the 110 commercial nuclear plants [then] operating in the U.S., as many as 25 of them could face premature shutdown in the next several to 10 years."[28]

Ironically, both Westinghouse and General Electric—the primary U.S. manufacturers of nuclear power systems—stated that they expected most of their future nuclear profits to lie in reactor repairs and foreign sales. At the same time, antinuclear activists and consumer advocates were reframing the national nuclear debate into a series of local economic contests that focused on preventing the industry from profiting on problems it had created.

The battle of Turkey Point was the harbinger of a ratepayers' revolt against the $100 billion bailout of failed nuclear power plants that would soon sweep the nation.

Mobilizing Principle 1:
Establish Truth Force

Because the antinuclear movement based its claims on fundamental truths about the economic costs, public health dangers, and technical flaws of nuclear power, the movement gained credibility, and the nuclear industry lost credibility, as more often than not the central claims of the antinuclear movement were independently verified. The tragic zeniths of this process of de-legitimization were the accidents at Three Mile Island and the disaster at Chernobyl. The industry's arrogant rejection of the issues raised by the antinuclear movement seriously backfired and contributed over time to the erosion of public confidence in nuclear power. Eventually, the public came to view nuclear power itself as problematic and blamed the government, the nuclear industry, and the utilities for prematurely promoting the commercialization of nuclear power technology.

Chapter Three

The Ratepayers' Revolt

*Only in Asia are governments continuing to invest enthusiastically in
nuclear power. They are making an expensive mistake.*
—Editorial, the Economist, *1995*

It was on the bitter fields of economic reality that nuclear power met
its Waterloo, both domestically and internationally. In a 1995 editorial,
"Asia's Energy Temptation," the *Economist* warned China, Taiwan, In-
donesia, South Korea, Pakistan, and India that they were "making a
mistake" in looking to nuclear power as a solution to their 8 percent
per year growth in electricity demand. "The economic arguments for
building new nuclear plants are flawed," stated the *Economist* in a
stern warning to "those still charmed by nuclear power (as the *Economist* was, a decade ago)."[1]

Today nuclear power supplies 5 percent of the world's energy from
more than 400 plants. However, with the important exceptions of
Japan and France, the First World—the rich world—has stopped or-
dering new reactors. Today worldwide reactor construction starts
have dropped to their lowest level since the early sixties. In every year
since 1986, the cumulative nuclear capacity of plants that have been
decommissioned exceeds the capacity of new plants under construction. From 1990 to 1994, total installed nuclear generating capacity has
inched up from 329 to 339 gigawatts. Given the paucity of new orders,

it is likely that worldwide nuclear capacity will peak before the turn of the century.

Thus, this worldwide slowdown parallels the collapse of the U.S. nuclear industry that began in the 1970s, driven by the growing realization that nuclear power has failed in its early promise of cheap electricity and emerged as the most expensive conventional source of energy (including oil, gas, and coal). The claims and counterclaims surrounding domestic nuclear power economics highlight the struggle of antinuclear activists to prove that nuclear power is the most expensive conventional energy option and, therefore, not an economically viable solution to the energy dilemma.

Nuclear industry proponents argue that nuclear power is an economical method of generating electricity, that nuclear power is one of the few reliable domestic sources of energy that has a promising future, and that continuing federal subsidies are essential.

In rebuttal, the Safe Energy Communication Council, an antinuclear research and communications group, argues that "construction, operating, decommission and radioactive waste storage costs have combined to drive the average cost of nuclear power higher than all other conventional technologies."[2] Although the marginal cost of producing power from nuclear fuel is cheaper than from any other conventional source, the full *life cycle costs* of the nuclear power supply system have generated the following higher costs:

Construction cost overruns. In 1986, the U.S. Department of Energy analyzed the original construction cost estimates and the actual final cost of 75 nuclear plants that had construction starts between 1966 and 1977. Whereas the original total cost estimate for these reactors was $45 billion, the actual cost, not including interest or finance charges, was $145 billion—a $100 billion cost overrun.[3]

High operating costs. The original justification for nuclear power was that low and predictable operating costs would offset the higher construction costs. Between 1974 and 1993, as nonfuel operating costs escalated from an average of $37 million to $126 million per reactor per year, this justification collapsed under the weight of the empirical evidence to the contrary. According to research by the Nuclear Power Advisory Committee of the Edison Electric Institute, the utilities' trade association, only 25 percent of U.S. nuclear power plants produced power more cheaply than available replacement power as of January 1993.[4]

Reactor decommissioning costs. The ultimate costs of decommissioning reactors retired after their 40-year life cycle are uncertain. But the escalating projections are contributing to questions about the competitiveness of existing plants. In 1985 the Yankee Atomic Electric Company raised its decommissioning-cost estimate for the Yankee Rowe nuclear plant in Massachusetts from $30 million to $68 million. However, after the plant was closed in 1992, the estimated cost of dismantling the plant had increased again to $370 million—almost 10 times its construction costs. In 1994 Commonwealth Edison announced that it was doubling the estimated decommissioning costs for its 13 Midwestern reactors to $4.1 billion. Although regulators require that utilities collect sufficient funds from ratepayers during a reactor's operating life to cover the expense of decommissioning, as of 1993, only 13.8 percent of the projected decommissioning costs for the United States' aging reactors had been collected—even though these plants had already completed one-third of their projected 40-year life cycle.[5]

Waste storage costs. Certainly, as physical superstructures, Hoover, Shasta, Bonneville, and Grand Coulee, the giant concrete dams built during the 1930s, will outlast the carbon steel–reinforced containment buildings of contemporary nuclear power plants. But even these megaliths will not outlive the environmental problem posed by the radioactive waste generated by nuclear power. Some radioactive isotopes remain extremely lethal for hundreds of thousands of years, posing unique economic and environmental problems. The federal Nuclear Waste Policy Act of 1982 requires all nuclear utilities to contribute 0.1¢ for every nuclear-generated kilowatt-hour to a national trust fund to pay for the disposal of the high-level nuclear waste produced primarily by spent fuel rods. A draft report by the DOE projects that the total life cycle cost of commercial waste disposal will be at least $34.6 billion.

Based on life cycle costs (including direct reactor costs, plus decommissioning, waste disposal, and federal support), the average cost of nuclear-generated electricity between 1968 and 1990 was 8.8¢ per kilowatt-hour, or nearly twice the cost of electricity from coal, oil, or gas during that same period.[6] Projected ongoing escalations in operating, decommissioning, and waste disposal costs—all of which utilities will attempt to pass on to ratepayers—suggest that nuclear power will continue to be the United States' most expensive energy option for the foreseeable future.

For nearly 50 years, extensive federal subsidies have been allocated to the research and development (R&D) of nuclear power, often at the expense of cheaper, safer, and more environmentally benign energy options. According to the Congressional Research Service, between 1948 and 1994, nuclear power received 60 percent of all federal R&D energy spending (in constant 1994 dollars). In the same period, fossil fuel received 24 percent, renewable energy 10 percent, and conservation only 6 percent. However, R&D support represents only one aspect of the overall federal support for nuclear power, which also includes subsidies for nuclear regulation and uranium enrichment and tax breaks for nuclear utilities. A study by Komanoff Energy Associates found that since 1950 the federal government has spent approximately $97 billion on developing, commercializing, and supporting nuclear power. How such subsidies will fare under congressional efforts in the 1990s to balance the federal budget will be a litmus test of the continuing power of the nuclear industry and the prospects for a revival of nuclear power in the United States.

In 1954, at the beginning of official boosterism for nuclear power, Lewis L. Strauss, chairman of the U.S. Atomic Energy Commission, issued the now famous prediction that nuclear power would provide "electrical energy too cheap to meter."[7] More than 40 years later, the economic realities of commercial nuclear power have, in general, produced a dismal reality.

As nuclear power costs escalated and the crisis and cancellations surrounding nuclear construction spiraled out of control into a $100 billion to $200 billion damage bill, a seismic wave of "rate shocks" spread out from nuclear utilities to their consumers—who were being asked to bail out the failed plants and foot the growing cost of having expensive nuclear units in the rate base.

It was here that the lone voices of the reactor techies were joined by the multitude of voices of utility consumers. It was here that the antinuclear movement grew from an esoteric exercise in elite environmental organizing into a mass popular movement. This was the fuel for the firestorm of the ratepayers' revolt. This was the conflagration that blackened the credit rating of the nuclear utilities and burned out the money machine of Wall Street financing for nuclear power plant construction.

In the nuclear age, not all utilities are created equal. As far as economic disaster is concerned, two stand out. The Washington Public Power Supply System (WPPSS) is remarkable not just for a 500 percent cost overrun on a five-plant nuclear project, which led to the mothballing and abandonment of most of the project and to a $2.25 billion bond default. Most noteworthy is that this default of AAA-rated utility bonds was the first in U.S. history since regulatory safeguards were instituted to protect bond investors after the Great Depression of 1929. But according to Karl Grossman, the author of *Power Crazy,* "leading the U.S. utility industry in all categories of mismanagement, ineptitude and worse is the Long Island Lighting Company (LILCO).... [which] *has built per proposed kilowatt the most expensive nuclear plant in the world.*" By 1986 the total projected cost of the Shoreham plant had grown to $5.7 billion.[8]

The "siege of Shoreham" and the "financial fiasco in the Northwest" were the battering rams with which the antinuclear movement breached the castle walls of reactor financing and publicly shattered the nuclear industry's myth of economic viability. Like military strategists in a medieval army, Suffolk County legislator Nora Bredes in New York and energy activist Dan Leahy in Washington were prepared for a long assault on the bulwarks of the nuclear industry.

The Siege of Shoreham:
Nora Bredes, Suffolk County Commissioner

The Shoreham Plant must open! If it doesn't, the signals will be the low point in this industry's history. If it does, we are going to begin a brand new era.

—U.S. Energy Secretary John S. Herrington,
Nuclear Power Assembly, 1985

Long Island, New York, has played a pivotal role in the history of the nuclear age. It was in Piquonick, on the eastern end of Long Island, where Albert Einstein and Leo Szilard inspired the Manhattan Project by composing a letter in 1938 to President Franklin D. Roosevelt urging the United States to build the atomic bomb before the Nazis did. It was there in 1947 that the federal government established the Brookhaven National Laboratory to draw on talent from the government, military, academia, and corporations to research "the peaceful aspects of nuclear science." It was there on April 13, 1966, that the Long Island Light Company (LILCO) announced its plans to "rezone a portion of a site on the north shore of Suffolk County for the Company's first nuclear electric generating plant"—the Shoreham plant—as the first step in establishing a nuclear park that would eventually provide power for most of the northeastern United States.

It was also here in the rolling hills of Long Island that the siege of Shoreham raged for nearly two decades until the plant was prevented from opening. This siege started as a local antinuclear movement and eventually grew to pit the Republican-controlled Suffolk County Legislature and Democratic New York State governor Mario Cuomo against LILCO and the federal government. Eventually the siege of Shoreham became the most intense government-versus-government conflict over nuclear power in U.S. history. The issues over which the siege was waged—home rule, rate shock, public versus private power, and the feasibility of evacuation in the case of a serious nuclear accident—have become central issues in the economic debate about nuclear power across the nation.

Huntington, Long Island, is also Walt Whitman's birthplace. In *Leaves of Grass,* his immortal song to a young America, Whitman wrote, "The proof of a poet is that his country absorbs him as affectionately as he has absorbed it."

Nora Bredes, the woman who laid the political groundwork for the siege of Shoreham, grew up in Huntington. When she founded the Shoreham Opponents Coalition and ran for local office on a "Stop Shoreham" platform, the citizens of Suffolk County, Long Island, "absorbed her" and elected her as a Suffolk County legislator.

The Most Expensive Nuclear Plant in the World

According to antinuclear activist Karl Grossman, a journalist who documented the early stages of the LILCO battle in *Power Crazy,* LILCO had become the most mismanaged, inept, arrogant, and powerful utility in the United States. To support his case, Grossman argued the following points in his 1986 book:[9]

- Although other U.S. utilities have built expensive nuclear power plants, LILCO has built per proposed kilowatt the most expensive nuclear plant in the world.
- Although in nuclear power plant construction there have been cost overruns of 30 to 100 percent, indeed even WPPSS's 500 percent, LILCO's cost overrun on its Shoreham plant is 7,600 percent and still rising.

- Although other utilities have high rates, LILCO's are the second highest in the nation (after Hawaii) and could jump 81 percent if Shoreham goes into operation—making LILCO the most expensive in the United States by far.
- Shoddy, slipshod construction is far from unknown in nuclear plant construction. In fact, although 97 percent complete, the license for the Zimmer plant in Cincinnati was eventually pulled by the NRC because of poor construction. However, LILCO at Shoreham has set a new low, according to former Shoreham inspectors and workers on the project.
- Although many utilities have ties to the U.S. government's energy establishment of national laboratory and federal energy agency bureaucrats, none has more intimate links than LILCO. The utility's chief (in 1986) is the former assistant director of Brookhaven National Laboratory, whose scientists had a role in inspiring, and have been leading the promotion of, LILCO's nuclear program.
- Other utilities in precarious financial shape have been aided by banks, but LILCO has been kept from bankruptcy only with massive assistance from the United States' top banks; indeed, from some of the world's top banks, led by Citibank of New York.
- Although many utilities have influence on the media that covers them, LILCO wields enormous influence over two of the most prestigious papers in the United States, *The New York Times* and *Newsday.*
- Other utilities have engaged in heavy political action. In fact, utilities are often among the most effective lobbies in their home states. Yet few have lobbied as intensively as LILCO, who in its home territory has become so powerful that people fear "government by LILCO" on Long Island.
- In Washington, D.C., LILCO's political operations have included the use of former federal officials such as Lyn Nofzinger, who was President Reagan's chief political aide, and William Casey, who left his seat on the LILCO board of directors to run the Central Intelligence Agency under President Reagan.
- Although all operating U.S. plants were important to the industry, the federal government picked the Shoreham plant as a symbol of the nuclear industry's future. "The Shoreham

plant must open!" declared U.S. Energy Secretary John S. Herrington at a Nuclear Power Assembly in 1985 in Washington, D.C. "If it doesn't, the signals will be the low point in this industry's history. If it does, we are going to begin a brand new era."

- Last, if Shoreham were to open and a major Chernobyl-like accident occurred, the consequences would be far more serious than for a similar accident at almost any other U.S. plant because Shoreham is located 50 miles east of New York, the largest city in the United States, and midway out on densely populated Long Island.

Thus the siege of Shoreham was as much a battle against LILCO as it was a crusade against the Shoreham nuclear power plant. For, as Grossman concluded:

LILCO has, with its Shoreham project, managed to combine the negative aspects of many electric utilities—and outdone all the competition *in extremis.* Thus the story of how LILCO became the way it is today and where it is heading provides a clear picture of the forces at work throughout the U.S. utility industry. It is a story not just involving electric power. It is about political power—and of profound threats to both democracy and human life.[10]

The Shoreham Opponents Coalition   It was Nora Bredes's almost mystical attachment to the waters of Huntington Bay, Long Island, that moved her to lay siege to Shoreham.

I grew up in Huntington by the Huntington Bay and started swimming a lot. It's very hard to describe, but I developed a kind of significant attachment to the water, to the bay and to the area. When I heard about Three Mile Island, as we all did, it was frightening and shocking. I knew that Shoreham was somewhere east of me and on the Long Island Sound. It was unsettling to think that the same thing could happen to the place where I grew up and where I had so many strong attachments. It led me to read more about it, it led me to decide that this was something to pay close attention to and study, and I did.[11]

In 1978 Bredes started to hear of protests at the Shoreham nuclear power plant. At that time, an organization called the Shad Alliance was very active and influential. It was one of the nonviolent, direct-action antinuclear groups that grew out of the "alliance movement" started in New Hampshire by the Clam Shell Alliance, which was mobilizing against the Seabrook plant. The Shad Alliance organized a "pro–Sound Hudson" campaign against atomic development, linking antinuclear activists on Long Island, in New York City, and throughout the Hudson River area against both the Indian Point and Shoreham plants.

The Three Mile Island accident of 1979 moved Bredes to take action on the energy issue. On June 3, 1979, she attended at large demonstration at Shoreham organized by the Shad Alliance. About 18,000 people marched on Shoreham, and 500 climbed the fence to occupy the plant in an act of civil disobedience. For Bredes, it was a watershed demonstration. She looked at the demonstrators, representing a broad spectrum of people who had come from all over—from New York City, from Nassau and Suffolk county, from the farms and tourist resorts of eastern Long Island.

Bredes knew these people well. They were not prone to demonstrations and public protests. Politically, she sensed that for many people, the Shad Alliance demonstration represented just one possible "expression of the people" against Three Mile Island and Shoreham. She knew that her neighbors' fundamental objections to Shoreham and LILCO "hadn't yet reached the political arena, hadn't really affected county policy, hadn't affected state policy, and would not affect the anarchy in the courts, if that's where the battle ended up."

At that demonstration, Bredes realized that Shoreham could become a *political issue,* and she decided to take political action. She spent the summer determining what she could do to organize a "legislative strategy to push the Suffolk County legislature to become a stronger intervenor against the Shoreham plant." At that time the county was a "neutral intervenor," which meant that it took no position on Shoreham. Bredes began to mobilize people to become involved in the political process, to visit the Suffolk County legislature, and to urge legislators to have the county actively oppose Shoreham.

Her political forays caused a good deal of dissension in the local antinuclear movement. Most of the alliance groups were philosophically committed to civil disobedience and direct action. Jack Cutler, who was very active in the Shad Alliance and had organized the Shoreham demonstration, argued that "if you became too involved in the system, too attached to the system, you'd be co-opted, even sort of tainted by the same political abuses that started nuclear power." Therefore, you had to stand "outside the system and demand action."

Bredes argued vehemently with Cutler throughout the Shoreham campaign. She also married him, building an intimate alliance between the political activists and direct-action advocates against Shoreham. Bredes then set out to prove her theory that it would take sustained political action on Long Island to ultimately stop Shoreham. After a series of strategy meetings, Bredes formed a core political group that mobilized hundreds of people to visit the county legislature during the summer of 1979. They raised several issues in an effort to transform Suffolk County from a neutral intervenor to an opposing intervenor that would marshal local government's staff and resources against the plant. As Bredes explained:

> These included the problems with an evacuation plan, which was then just being formulated taking events at Three Mile Island into consideration. What kind of evacuation zone was sufficient? Is ten miles enough? Is twenty miles? How could anyone conceivably think of evacuating Long Island in the wake of a serious nuclear accident, when you have gridlock going in and out of the island to New York City on a normal day?

Bredes became the executive director of the newly formed Shoreham Opponents Coalition, which was to have a pivotal role in stopping the plant. Nineteen seventy-nine was an election year for county legislators, and the coalition held a series of rallies and demonstrations to focus voters' attention on who was running and their position on Shoreham. In that year, Peter Cohalan was elected, and he stayed neutral on Shoreham. But the coalition was able to influence the elections of Wayne Prospect, a Democrat, who was very influential in the fight against the plant, as well as Greg Flask, a Republican, who also came out against it. But the county still remained a neutral intervenor. Although the coalition was extremely frustrated at having so little to show for its efforts, Bredes continued to organize political support against the plant.

By 1981 Bredes found that the coalition's grassroots efforts were beginning to pay off, and "the public mood had changed and even politicians were more aware of the Shoreham issue." The coalition now reevaluated its strategy and launched what turned out to be a very effective campaign for ratepayers' rights. The campaign reframed the issue to focus on the economic impact of nuclear power at Shoreham. The coalition hired a utility economist from the Boston-based Energy Systems Research Group, who prepared an "alternative energy blueprint" that demonstrated that better use of energy conservation and efficiency could "more than offset the need for Shoreham."

Most important was that we decided to try to present our argument in a way that would be accepted by most people on Long Island, recognizing that most people have concerns about whether or not they can pay their bills and taxes, and that the rising cost of energy was affecting everyone.

The ratepayers' rights campaign designed a patriotic red, white, and blue stars and stripes logo and launched a very effective radio campaign that announced the campaign's phone number and asked people to call in for further information. By the end of the month, at least 100 calls a day were coming in to the office. The coalition used the calls as an organizing tool and developed a tremendous list of people who had objections to Shoreham. In 1981 the coalition was able to make Shoreham the central issue of the local election by investigating each candidate's stand and public comments on Shoreham and mailing that information to "thousands and thousands" of Long Islanders.

Bredes beamed with pride as the results came in. "We were able to unseat *every* pro-LILCO county legislator and replace him with someone who was anti-LILCO and anti-Shoreham." On the issue of Shoreham, the coalition and its supporters now effectively controlled 17 of the 18 Suffolk County legislators. Although Suffolk County's population was then about 1.4 million, its 18 districts were still relatively small and easy to organize. Tactically, Bredes recognized that her most effective "power lever" over LILCO was to make Shoreham a *local issue* by giving voters a say in the decision to stop the plant.

Sensing a distinct shift in the political winds and under a new mandate from the county legislature, Peter Cohalan, the Suffolk County executive and former supervisor of the town of Islip, now agreed that the county should become much more involved and for the first time actively oppose the licensing of Shoreham in the NRC proceedings on the plant. He launched a nationwide search for the best available law firm to spearhead the intervention. His search led to the county's hiring, with a great deal of fanfare, the Washington firm of Kirkpatrick and Lockhart, who appointed attorneys Herb Brown and Larry Lanther to coordinate the county's efforts. At first, Bredes and other local activists were suspicious of both the outside attorneys and the high cost of working with them.

But despite Bredes's initial suspicions, Brown and Lanther became the tactical architects of the county's legal fight against Shoreham. In one of the key strategic decisions made during the siege of Shoreham, the attorneys identified evacuation and emergency planning as the critical issue in which the county had a legitimate legal and political interest. Under continuous pressure from Bredes's Shoreham Opposition Coalition, in February 1983, Suffolk County voted to become an "imposing intervenor" and to challenge the evacuation plan. By the end of 1983, Suffolk County officially withdrew its support for the emergency evacuation plan proposed by LILCO to the NRC.

After Three Mile Island, the NRC had issued regulations that every nuclear plant had to have a fully designed and practical evacuation plan, approved by *all* relevant parties. As the official entities that controlled the county police department, the health department, the emergency planning department, and all of local government, all local counties surrounding a nuclear plant had to sign off on the evacuation plan submitted by the operating utility to the NRC as a precondition to the NRC's issuing an operating license for the power plant. Suffolk County's refusal to endorse the Shoreham evacuation plant threw down the gauntlet for a major political and legal battle between the county and LILCO.

For the coalition, the county's participation became the battering ram for the siege of Shoreham. Bredes now had a politically powerful and economically resourceful ally.

> What was most important was not only the county politically opposing the plant, but committing the resources. It took literally millions of dollars to hire this law firm, hire the experts. I think the budget towards the end of the fight when it was getting quite controversial was something like $12 million. While this spending was of course dwarfed by LILCO's expenditures, it was far more than any citizen group could ever marshal. We were doing well when we raised $100,000 a year.

Winning by the Tao   Commenting on planning a siege in his classic *The Art of War,* Sun Tzu quotes Wei Liaozi as saying, "Practicing martial arts, assess your opponents; cause them to lose spirit and direction so that even if the opposing army is intact it is useless—this is winning by the Tao." When the NRC accepted a revised LILCO evacuation plan that did not depend on Suffolk County participation, Bredes followed the Tao of the siege by turning an apparent defeat on the evacuation-planning issue into a victory by stopping Shoreham. She and her supporters did so by gaining the support of New York State governor Mario Cuomo and the State of New York Legislature, who entered the battle against LILCO to preserve home rule and assert Suffolk County's and New York State's rights against the federal government's drive to open Shoreham at all costs.

If Shoreham were a modern Troy, then attorney Herb Brown soon realized that LILCO's evacuation plan was its Achilles' heel. At first, the NRC did not know how to deal with the county's challenge to the evacuation plan. They simply insisted that Long Island *could be* evacuated.

Long Island houses eight million people living on a finger of an island that runs from Brooklyn, on the west end, to Montauk, on the east end. Its main street is a six-lane highway, the Long Island Expressway. At rush hour, the traffic going into, or out of, New York City—which sits about 60 miles east of Shoreham—backs up for two hours. And with an accident, such as an overturned or jackknifed truck, traffic can be stalled for six or seven hours. Evacuation was not an abstract issue, for everyone who lives on Long Island knows that at certain hours, traffic is "an intense problem."

LILCO issued a plan that had everyone west of Shoreham going west in case of an accident, while everyone to the east would stay at home so that they would not have to drive through the radioactive "plume" in case of a radiation release. The utility planned to put up barricades on the major roads leading west of the east end so that they could "prevent people from evacuating." In Bredes's view, "It was clearly so unworkable in a commonsense kind of way that I think that's what captured people's attention. That it was ridiculous to evacuate. And that was the issue that Suffolk County and the governor focused on."

Suffolk County had Kirkpatrick and Lockhart conduct a comprehensive study of the emergency-planning issue. Police officers, public health people, and sanitarians were brought in to testify on the viability of the plan. Essentially, they all doubted that the plan would work. By the end of 1983, Suffolk County officially withdrew its support for LILCO's evacuation plan, saying "we can't effectively protect people in an accident." Therefore, the county could not endorse the utility's evacuation plan. At this point, LILCO put together its own evacuation plan, to be staffed by the utility's emergency operation team.

Before the NRC, LILCO argued that if there were an accident and if the plan were to go into operation, regardless of what Suffolk County said, the county would participate in the evacuation plan because "that's their nature, that's what government does." Although this was a blatant challenge to home rule and a usurpation of local government powers, the NRC finally accepted LILCO's revised evacuation plan—and issued an operating license for Shoreham. Suffolk County was outraged. It filed further legal challenges in court and threatened to use its "police powers" against LILCO to prevent the plant from opening.

From a practical standpoint, the evacuation plan proved to be the Trojan horse of the siege of Shoreham. In the early eighties, it slowed down the entire licensing process, until the Chernobyl accident of 1986 brought the full significance of a viable emergency preparedness plan home to the people of Long Island and the governor. Under Governor Cuomo's direction, the State of New York now began seriously to explore a plan to purchase Shoreham from LILCO and established the public Long Island Power Authority (LIPA) to evaluate the issue.

The pressure of the federal government to open Shoreham burst into public view on April 14, 1986—just 12 days before the Chernobyl disaster in the former Soviet Union. Frank Petrone, the regional director of the Federal Emergency Management Agency (FEMA), resigned after refusing to remove a sentence he included in FEMA's February report on the LILCO evacuation drill. The line read that "since the plan cannot be implemented without state and local participation, FEMA cannot give reasonable assurance . . . that the public health and safety can be protected."

Petrone declared at a press conference that FEMA director Julius Becton told him to alter the report or be fired. Petrone also charged that FEMA had been under "tremendous pressure" from the NRC, the Department of Energy, other federal agencies, and the White House to assist in getting Shoreham licensed to operate. In his letter of resignation, Petrone wrote: "I believe the credibility of the agency is endangered when the national office moves to overturn critical regional decisions, particularly when the courts have ruled on their issues."[12]

Governor Cuomo praised Petrone's "courage and integrity." Suffolk County attorney Herb Brown called the situation "FEMAgate." Suffolk County legislator Wayne Prospect stated, "FEMA is exhibiting outright contempt for the people of Suffolk County."

Utility and federal arrogance had finally unleashed forces LILCO could not so easily contend with—Governor Mario Cuomo, the State of New York, and a citizens' initiative to take over LILCO and run it as a public company.

Governor Cuomo Buys Shoreham for One Dollar　By 1986 the cost of the plant had soared to $5.7 billion and was projected to reach between $7 billion and $8 billion if the plant were ever allowed to operate. LILCO's original cost estimates for the plant were in the $60 million to $75 million range, and thus overruns had already exceed 8,000 percent. And because of the imminent opening of Shoreham, Long Island consumers and businesses were expecting rate shocks that could have increased their utility bills by 80 percent. These increases would have made LILCO electricity the most expensive in the continental United States.

As costs and evacuation concerns mounted, a movement to get rid of LILCO tapped into a groundswell of public resentment. Citizens to Replace LILCO had recently placed a full-page ad in Long Island newspapers and was receiving a powerful public response. "THE PROBLEM ISN'T JUST SHOREHAM. THE PROBLEM IS LILCO!" it declared and went on to say, "Now LILCO wants you to foot the bill for their foulups" and pointed out that "Governor Cuomo called LILCO's proposals a scheme to save itself at public expense." The ad cited a publicly owned utility on Long Island whose customers paid less than half of what people who were "in LILCO's clutches" paid. The way to deal with LILCO was to "REPLACE LILCO WITH A LONG ISLAND POWER AUTHORITY."[13]

The sentiment against LILCO was deep and widespread. A November 1985 poll on Shoreham commissioned by *Newsday* found the opposition to the power plant had reached an all-time high of 71 percent, and 7 out of 10 Long Islanders believed that "Shoreham's owners, Long Island Light Co., should be taken over and run by local government as a publicly owned utility."

Although Governor Cuomo was not antinuclear per se, he understood that the opposition to Shoreham had galvanized a broad base of political support. He set up a special commission to look into the establishment of a Long Island Power Authority as a public authority to replace LILCO. The State of New York supported this overture by passing enabling legislation, which had the following preamble: "The legislature hereby finds and declares than an economic emergency exists in the Long Island Light Company franchise area. Mismanagement and imprudent decisions by LILCO have caused constantly escalating and intolerable costs of electricity in the franchise area thereby posing a serious threat to the economic well-being of the residents and commerce in the area."

Governor Cuomo sincerely wanted to be the public champion of the campaign to stop Shoreham. Yet, according to Bredes, "he didn't want to be the first governor in the United States since the New Deal of the 1930s to participate in the public takeover of a big private-investor utility, no matter how hated or suspect." So he compromised and approached LILCO with an offer "it could not refuse." In one hand, Cuomo carried the big stick of eminent domain and the threat of a LILCO takeover. In the other, Cuomo offered the utility the carrot of a "sweet deal" under which LILCO could use the rate-making process to be compensated for its investment in Shoreham, even though the plant would never open, would never generate electricity, and would never become "used and useful."

One antinuclear activist characterized the Cuomo settlement as "some piece of clout." Finally, in February 1989, the governor, working with LILCO, arranged a settlement that did not need the approval of the state legislature but was accepted by all parties. Acknowledging defeat, the NRC finally allowed the transfer of Shoreham to the Long Island Power Authority for one dollar. Part of LIPA's mandate was that it would never open Shoreham. Today the plant is being decommissioned as a nuclear facility, and LIPA continues to explore the options of converting the Shoreham facility to a natural gas plant or a coal plant with advanced scrubbers.

Bredes and her followers had hoped to defeat Shoreham without any payments to the utility. However, Bredes acknowledges, "I was the one who decided that we had to seize the opportunity to stop the plant and continue to fight on public power another day." At the same time, she notes bitterly that the settlement contained for LILCO "a guarantee of three years of rate increases at 5 percent per year, and a statement of willingness to most likely accept another seven years of rate increases at the same level. It was a very expensive settlement."

Over the course of her campaign against Shoreham, Bredes ran for office three times. She ran in the Democratic primary in 1987 and was narrowly defeated. In 1989 she ran as an independent pro-choice ticket and lost to a right-to-life Democrat. Finally she was elected to the Suffolk County legislature in a special election in 1992 to replace a strong environmentalist who had gone on to the New York state assembly.

Reflecting on the campaign for public power, Bredes now realizes that the power brokers of New York state, although they wanted to resolve the Shoreham debacle, did not want to open the Pandora's box of public power and municipally owned utilities. "Those of us who really wanted to see a takeover of LILCO realized later that the governor's commission was simply a ploy, an attempt to push LILCO to the bargaining table to settle the issue."

Bredes candidly admits:

> You know I was disappointed by the settlement. There was a group that was formed to oppose the settlement. I was part of that. But it split the movement against Shoreham. Yet Shoreham did not open, and that was the original goal. And while it didn't work perfectly and we certainly couldn't control all of the outcome as well as we wanted to, it did work. We did stop the nuclear plant at Shoreham!

By the late 1980s, Shoreham was not simply another canceled nuclear plant. The prolonged siege of Shoreham had become a pivotal battle between antinuclear and pronuclear forces. Shoreham had become a worldwide symbol for the nuclear industry. Its defeat was the death knell for LILCO's hopes of establishing a nuclear industrial park to serve the Northeast and for the nuclear industry's hopes of bouncing back quickly after the Chernobyl disaster.

For Suffolk County legislator Wayne Prospect, stopping Shoreham proved that "when people organize in a democracy, citizen power can defeat financial power." For others, the attempt by LILCO and the federal government to ramrod Shoreham into operation in spite of the will of local citizens and elected officials represented a serious "breakdown of constitutional government" and a fundamental threat to democracy in the United States.[14] Or, as Arthur McComb, a longtime Shoreham opponent, stated at an NRC hearing on Shoreham in 1983, this was an assault on the fundamental principle of states' rights and home rule:

> Why must we continue with this charade? Prejudgment is painfully clear. . . Home rule, due process, has been ignominiously massacred by our own federal bureaucracy, by non-resident, non-elective judges, on a licensing board appointed by appointees. . . . This three-judge licensing board of the NRC has made a farce of home rule, due process. This mockery has made fools of the people of New York State.[15]

Bredes's destiny was now irrevocably intertwined with Shoreham. Just as Shoreham died, Bredes was giving birth to her second son. She went into labor just as the critical vote on the settlement took place in June 1988.

Today, with her children in the car, she drives slowly out Route 347 into northern Long Island, past the prim two-story houses of suburban, Republican America. The trees are getting their first taste of autumn's paintbrush, and the dogwoods and cottonwoods are bursting with yellow and pink leaves.

Driving through the rolling farmlands, past brown fields and well-pruned orchards, she stops at the old LILCO sign that reads "Shoreham Facility. Service First." Utility lines stretch out into the distance from giant, three-armed high-voltage towers that rise above the landscape like H. G. Wells's invaders from Mars. As Bredes rounds the final curve, the choppy blue waters of Long Island Sound come into view, and the massive, abandoned plant sits silently by the shore, its gray containment building bordered with green trim. The parking lot is empty. Except for the chirping of the birds, the day is very quiet.

Nora Bredes laughs. Now in her mid-forties, with her blondish hair pulled back, she looks in the rearview mirror and sees "the face that launched a thousand ships, and burnt the topless towers" of Shoreham.

Financial Fiasco in the Northwest: Dan Leahy, Public Power Activist

We're not going to pay this son-of-a-bitchin' debt. Period.
—Dan Leahy, Olympia, Washington, 1983

In February 1982, when Dan Leahy arrived at the anti-utility rally in Grays Harbor County, Washington, he found the Hoquiam High School auditorium packed to the rafters. At the center of the stage stood Dorothy Lindsay, a Hoquiam homemaker. When Lindsay told the 5,000 residents who jammed the gym that "we're not going to pay this debt," she ignited the forest fire of the ratepayers' revolt that raged throughout the state of Washington and the Pacific Northwest during 1982 and 1983. The revolt culminated in a $2.25 billion bond default by the Washington Public Power Supply System (WPPSS)—now derisively labeled as "WHOOPS" by disgruntled electric customers.[16]

Only a few weeks earlier, Leahy had seen his dream of a citizens' movement to preserve public power in the Northwest spring to life as Lindsay and ratepayers like her throughout Washington confronted public utility district (PUD) commissioners about skyrocketing bills for WPPSS's five nuclear power plants. Costs for electricity had risen more than 600 percent in five years, and some Washington residents were facing the loss of their homes, farms, and businesses.

"Nothing could be done," the commissioners told Lindsay and her neighbors. Lindsay decided to organize. The rally she planned for the gym had taken on a life of its own. Now, with two PUD commissioners sitting behind her, Lindsay's voice boomed out over the microphone. "For years Washington residents have sat back and let others run their public power," she said. "Those days are over."

Dan Leahy liked what he heard. "There was this extraordinary woman, Dorothy Lindsay, who was the leader there. She was a gifted person, speaker, good presence, charisma, smarts, the whole package. When I saw her, I thought 'goddamn it, we're going to have a governor here.' "[17] Lindsay basically told the people of Grays Harbor County that they were not going to pay their pro rata share of the $2.25 billion WPPSS debt. As a result of that incendiary meeting, people in other Washington counties began organizing, and before long, 15 out of 39 Washington counties were in open rebellion against WPPSS.

As an energy activist working for the National Public Power Institute, Leahy saw a golden opportunity. He started visiting the organizers, primarily women, of the incipient ratepayers' revolt, offering advice on how to make their meetings more effective. The results were like "spontaneous combustion." These women did not even know Dorothy Lindsay. They saw her on TV and simply followed her lead. Leahy lived on the road for the next six months. He viewed these homemakers as the backbone of the rebellion.

> They were irate. They had been doing their best to be conservative-minded people. They had done all the things to their home that you're supposed to do. And all of a sudden they were being told that they owed this debt, that their PUD was in hock, and that they had to pay this—even if it meant losing their homes. This was absolute nonsense to them, and they were furious.

From February through June 1982, Leahy kept a calendar, trying to keep track of the spreading movement. Literally every day for the next four or five months, there was a major event. The ratepayers' revolt had begun. In time, the revolt would bring about the largest tax-exempt bond default to date in U.S. history, send shock waves through Wall Street, and threaten the creditworthiness and financial stability of the Pacific Northwest.

The catalyst for the revolt was a report in July 1981 by Merril Lynch, the prestigious Wall Street investment-banking firm, titled "WPPSS at the Crossroads." The report found that WPPSS nuclear units 4 and 5 were not proceeding as planned and declared that if WPPSS wanted to continue to float new utility bonds to continue construction on these plants, it would have to begin repaying interest during construction (IDC) on the $2.25 billion in bonds already outstanding.

In the face of this report, the PUDs already participating in WPPSS nuclear power projects attempted to "mothball the plants," for two years, until an anticipated report by the Northwest Power Planning Council would declare plants 4 and 5 to be "regional resources" required by the Bonneville Power Administration (BPA). This would allow the BPA to distribute the costs of WPPSS across the entire region, removing the burden from the local PUDs that had contracted for WPPSS's nuclear power. From Leahy's perspective,

> This boggled the mind of most people, because it would be extremely difficult to say that two of the most expensive nuclear power plants in history, now projected to cost $12 billion, and which were only 10 and 13 percent completed at the time, would be cheaper than buying conservation—which according to the Power Planning Council's mandate would be the most cost-effective resource.

Leahy began organizing citizens to lobby their elected PUD commissioners over the "mothball fight." Suddenly ratepayers had a tactic that could affect their destiny. Ratepayers began protesting to commissioners, saying "If you guys vote for this mothballing plan, we're going to recall the commission." By January 12, two major PUDs totaling 20 percent of the 88 participant shares in WPPSS had voted, "We're not going to mothball." This stunned WPPSS, and on January 22, 1982, the WPPSS board met and voted to terminate nuclear plants 4 and 5. The termination triggered bond covenants that gave utility customers who lived in the PUDs participating in WPPSS one year before they had to start repaying the $2.25 billion obligation.

After the termination, the *Seattle Times* began running stories that analyzed how much an average electric customer would have to pay. In many cases, Washington utility users were facing additional electric rate payments of $1,500 to $8,000 per year for the next 30 years. For the first time, Leahy was able to drive home the direct connection between the BPA, WPPSS, the debt, the PUDs, and runaway nuclear power costs to the residents he was trying to organize against WPPSS. With the crisis getting front-page attention in all the newspapers, Leahy now found a receptive audience throughout the cities and towns of Washington. "Right after termination, you had the newspapers saying that people owed all this debt for these cost overruns. This was *us!* It wasn't some entity. It was our PUD and these debts were ours," he exclaimed.

If the siege of Shoreham was about home rule versus the federal energy autocracy, then WPPSS was about "no utility taxation without representation." The consumer rebellion that precipitated the financial fiasco in the Northwest and WPPSS's $2.25 billion bond default on nuclear units 4 and 5 revealed a fundamental flaw in the use of the high electric growth demand forecasts of WPPSS and other utilities as a prudent basis on which to justify massive capital-intensive nuclear construction projects. When WPPSS defaulted on AAA-rated, municipally guaranteed utility bonds, it was the first time since the Great Depression that such a default had occurred and was the largest default in U.S. history. The default sent a shock wave through Wall Street that ultimately caused a reclassification of nuclear power plants as high-risk investments and shut off the essential flow of capital to the nuclear power industry.

Electric Power in the Pacific Northwest   From an electric power perspective, the Pacific Northwest is a well-defined region of some 275,000 square miles encompassing Idaho, Oregon, Washington, and parts of Montana west of the Continental Divide. These states are bound together by a natural, integrated electric supply-and-distribution system that, until the early 1970s, used renewable hydroelectric energy resources to supply virtually all the power needs of a population that numbered about eight million at the time of the ratepayers' revolt of 1982.[18]

This electrical self-sufficiency, which for decades generated the least-expensive power in the nation, grew out of the federal government's dam construction on the Columbia River and its tributaries, which contain about one-third of the nation's total hydroelectric potential. Under the mandate of Franklin D. Roosevelt's New Deal, the federal government used taxpayers' credit to finance and construct 30 of these dams. The government entrusted the marketing—but not the building—of the region's hydroelectric power to the Bonneville Power Administration (BPA). Today, BPA acts as a wholesale supplier to more than 120 utility customers, or PUDs, and also directly serves a smaller number of energy-intensive direct-service industries, such as aluminum companies and the pulp, paper, and lumber mills that cluster in the Northwest.

According to public power activists such as Leahy, the consumer rebellion against WPPSS's nuclear power plants was a continuation of the historic "fight over the Columbia River system and how the system is used. Because a lot of what the Pacific Northwest is about is who owns and controls the river system." From 1910 through the 1950s, the people of the Pacific Northwest were engaged in three power struggles that created an electrical energy system that was unique to the country and extremely beneficial to everyone in the Northwest. The first battle was fought over the ownership of the Grand Coulee Dam and other dams, which created massive irrigation projects for the region's farmers. The second battle was fought over how to control the Columbia River System and resulted in the establishment of the BPA, with a mandate that allowed only it to transmit and market—but not to construct and generate—power, with a preference for public customers and with a "postage stamp" rate and a federal transmission grid.

With the federally owned dams and the BPA in place, the third battle was fought over who would control the use of Northwestern power. This turned into another prolonged struggle between the public power entities (the public utility districts, the co-ops, and the municipalities) and the private investor-owned utilities. The battle was symbolized by the passage in the 1930s of the District Power Act, which allowed for the formation of municipally owned systems (PUDs), each with a countywide boundary and the direct election of PUD commissioners.

In Leahy's view, he was not just fighting a battle against WPPSS. He was protecting the "very progressive populist history of the state of Washington." What distinguished the electric power system of the Northwest was a century-long battle for public power. "What you had as a result of that long series of fights were the federally-owned dams; hydroelectric power transmitted and marketed by the BPA with no authority to construct or own; and a system of 110 or so preferred customers throughout the region, organized into mainly democratically-controlled municipal PUDs."

In the decades following its creation in 1937, BPA zealously followed its congressional mandate to "market federal power so as to encourage the widest possible diversified use at the lowest possible rates consistent with sound business principles."[19] As the real cost of BPA hydroelectricity, which effectively had no fuel cost, dropped steadily from the 1930s through the 1950s, the demand for electricity reached a steady annual growth rate of 7.0 percent a year.

Despite major engineering efforts, the Northwest's hydropower system could simply not support exponential increases of this magnitude, which saw regional consumption more than doubling every 10 years. The emerging power shortages were well foreseen by power planners, and by the mid-1960s, the utilities were gearing up to add substantial coal-fired and nuclear power plants to their supply grids. The utilities, including the PUDs, would jointly build these new thermal-fired plants. BPA would provide the peak power and reserve capacity and the transmission and distribution grid and would then pool the available low-cost hydro with the higher-cost thermal for sale at uniform rates.

However, at this stage, a false crisis in electric power produced a power plant siting plan than ran amok and nearly bankrupted the region. By 1974 BPA's Hydro-Thermal Power Program encompassed 16 large-scale coal and nuclear plants in various stages of planning or construction. Under the grand vision of BPA administrator Donald Hodel, even more ambitious plans were laid, under which, "between now and the year 2000, over 50,000 MW of additional thermal peaking capacity will have to be added to the region's resources."[20] This was a capacity equivalent to 50 average-sized nuclear power plants, which Hodel—who was later to serve as secretary of energy in the first Reagan administration—saw as the preferred thermal power source for the Northwest. These construction goals reflected aggressive expectations that regional electric loads would quadruple over the next 25 years, despite an increasing emphasis on conservation.

The Northwest's real crisis emerged from 1981 to 1983, starting with a collapse of confidence in the utilities' previously unassailable load growth forecasts. Between 1974 and 1981, annual estimates of expected 1990 electric loads had dropped seven consecutive times by a total of more than 8,700 reliable annual megawatts. It was under these unfavorable circumstances that WPPSS, in May 1981, released the revised construction budgets for its five nuclear units. An additional net increase of 38 percent brought the revised total bill to $23.8 billion, of which $11.8 billion represented costs attributable to Units 4 and 5, the two plants that were furthest from completion. As a result of financial setbacks and the ratepayers' revolt, the events over the next 24 months from 1981 to 1983 left the Hydro-Thermal Power Program in shambles and forced WPPSS into default. In the wake of the ratepayers' revolt, two of the WPPSS plants were terminated, two had construction suspended, and one was still under construction.

In total, throughout the region, four plants had been terminated, four were in "suspended animation," one was in operation, and three remained at least temporarily under construction. The entire utility system was assailed with litigation. The WPPSS battle alone had generated more than 60 lawsuits, and more were anticipated. BPA was facing uncontrollable electricity surpluses, rather than deficits, as regional consumption declined, and both wholesale and retail electrical prices were climbing sharply.

Ironically, at the same time, the Regional Council was completing its 20-year *Northwest Conservation and Electric Power Plan,* which called for the indefinite deferral of all new coal and nuclear plants. The plan's major conclusion was that "conservation could meet most of the region's anticipated needs for new electricity supplies."[21]

The Consumer Rebellion   In *Reveille for Radicals,* a clarion call for grassroots organizers, Saul Alinksy observed:

> A People's Organization is a conflict group. . . . A People's Organization is the banding together of large numbers of men and women to fight for those rights which insure a decent way of life. Most of this constant conflict will take place in orderly and conventionally approved legal procedures—but in all fights there come times when "the law spoke too softly to be heard in such noise of war."[22]

As Dan Leahy pulled his car into the parking lot to speak at the third rally of irate ratepayers for the day, he realized that the power struggles of the Northwest had finally erupted into full-scale warfare. It was time to break the law.

During the weeks that followed Dorothy Lindsay's call for a ratepayers' rebellion, Leahy had crisscrossed the state of Washington several times, organizing and speaking at house meetings and high schools to fan the flames of the consumer revolt that had risen throughout the WPPSS region, overturning the political establishment and throwing the power companies into chaos. During February alone, the conflagration spread through Clark County in the south, north of Seattle to Snohomish, and over the state borders into Oregon and Idaho. On one day, 300 consumers confronted power officials in Madison County. The next day, 1,400 people gathered at the Port Angeles High School in Clallam County. Two hundred miles inland, residents of Ellensburg packed Morgan Junior High School. Ranchers and housewives in Springfield staged a candlelight vigil and burned their utility bills. Wall Street executives threatened to cut off financing for the region's future public works projects if the debt wasn't paid. But across the continent from New York City, in the country kitchens and coffee shops of rural Washington, the disaster posed by "paying the debt" had already occurred.

Leahy's transformation from utility consultant to radical energy activist had come about slowly, but profoundly. When he returned home from graduate school to Wenatchee, Washington, in 1977, he was hired as a consultant for a large PUD that owned two dams on the Columbia River. His job was to develop the utility's public information program related to the Regional Power Bill. As Leahy studied the bill, he realized that it contained a devious strategy whereby "industry was going to utilize the Columbia River to bury the costs of nuclear power plants and raise the price of hydroelectricity to the public utility companies while keeping the costs low for private utilities and the direct-services industries, mainly the aluminum companies."

As his appreciation deepened of the historic struggle on the part of consumers, farmers, and labor unions to create "an extremely unique energy system in the Northwest," so did his anger at WPPSS's nuclear plans. In the process, Leahy became a radical organizer—that rare person in American life who cannot be fooled, bought, or intimidated and who breaks all the rules. With the support of his wife, he left his job as a utility consultant and began working as a full-time organizer for the National Public Power Institute.

As he surveyed the crowd of anxious and angry faces, he realized that the WPPSS debacle had created an organizer's dream and a utility executive's nightmare. The situation had forced all the secretive issues of utility financing and politics out into the public eye and created a receptive audience for his views on strengthening public power in the Northwest. Every PUD had become a conflict group.

For the umpteenth time, he explained how WPPSS's ambitions now threatened the audience's homes and the economic stability of the entire Pacific Northwest. As early as 1968, WPPSS had initiated plans to build 40 coal plants and 20 nuclear plants that would make WPPSS, headquartered in Richland, Washington, the "energy czar" of the Northwest. At the urging of the BPA—which had no authority to build or own power plants—118 PUDs and three private companies had joined into a WPPSS-led consortium and agreed to finance the first three nuclear plants (Units 1, 2, and 3). Eighty-eight public and cooperative systems pledged to finance and build two more (Units 4 and 5).

Throughout the 1970s, construction boondoggles and delays, chaos at the plant sites, and increased interest rates sent cost estimates for the project skyrocketing from $4 billion to more than $15 billion. By 1982 the cost estimate for finishing the five plants had nearly quintupled to $24 billion. As electric rates quadrupled, customers conserved and cut back on their electricity use, but rates continued to soar. In January 1982, WPPSS directors were forced to admit that at least two of the plants were no longer necessary, and the nuclear units at Satsop and Richland were canceled.

The total debt for funds already spent on the two unfinished reactors was more than $7 billion—of which $2.25 billion was now being called. In more than a hundred cities and towns across the Northwest, people were expected to pay off the debt in installments to the WPPSS bondholders over the next 30 years. In some towns, electric bills had already risen 600 percent. News of the plant cancellations was followed by announcements that a new 50 percent rate increase was imminent, with more to come. Jim Lazar, an Olympia economist, estimated that payment of the debt would cause the loss of 100,000 jobs in the Northwest. The situation had reached the breaking point.

Now came the tricky part, explaining the intricate economic strategies whereby WPPSS had burdened the ratepayers with a staggering 30-year debt obligation. It was the aluminum companies and the other large power users who forged ahead to build five reactors at once so that they could create a supply of cheap surplus power for the region. Although citizens and environmentalists had challenged the wisdom of overbuilding, BPA head Donald Hodel condemned them as "prophets of shortage" and echoed the industry's threats of brownouts, blackouts, and factory closings if the PUDs did not sign contracts to finance the WPPSS projects.

With WPPSS as the financing and construction arm of the nuclear plants, BPA would serve as the purchaser and distributor of the new power. "There's a lot of you sitting here tonight," Leahy explained, "who don't associate your PUD with WPPSS. To you, WPPSS is this entity out there building runaway nuclear power plants. Yet it was Don Hodel who convinced your PUD to back WPPSS by using its publicly owned, tax-exempt financing ability to build additional plant capacity for industrial customers. The irony of all this is that once the plants were built, the PUDs weren't even going to use the power but were going to turn them over to the big industrial users."

When people asked, "What can we do?" Leahy was ready. He knew that the two basic rules of organizing are "turn people on" and "give them something concrete to do to solve their problem." He explained that the public utility districts, which had taken on these massive debt obligations, were not meant to be "public interest" or "citizen activist" groups. They were meant to be "ownership groups." "You own the PUD. You are supposed to take responsibility for it. You can walk into a meeting and say, 'We'll recall you bastards if you go along with mothballing.' You can break the law and say, 'We're not going to pay this debt.' "

The Washington Supreme Court Ruling   For Leahy, the most significant ratepayer action was the intervention of the Ellensburg citizens' group, which joined the Chemical Bank lawsuit to argue that its PUD's contracts were illegal, and therefore ratepayers should not have to pay. "Without them, there would have been no legal basis for victory," Leahy explains. In April 1992, at the urging of the Ellensburg group, 12 co-ops filed a suit in Lewis County, saying, "I don't think we have to pay this thing. Give us a judgment on Units 4 and 5."

The case, which was quickly labeled the "Dirty Dozen Lawsuit," unnerved Wall Street. Chemical Bank, the trustee for the WPPSS bondholders, now filed a counteraction in Washington State district court saying, "We've heard rumors that you guys are thinking about not paying this, and we want the court to reaffirm that you owe it." Initially, district court judge Coleman ruled with WPPSS and Chemical Bank. "Yes," Leahy explains, "this is a power sales contract, the PUDs have the ability to enter into a power sales contract; they have the authority to do that, and they have to pay."

However, in July 1983, only 18 months after Dorothy Lindsay launched the ratepayers' revolt, the unexpected happened. The Washington State Supreme Court overturned Judge Coleman's decision and invalidated the PUD contracts. "No," Leahy says, interpreting the decision, "this is *not* a power sales contract. This is an agreement to enter into unlimited debt. Because the take-or-pay clause says, regardless of whether the plant's ever built or not, whether it's ever operated or not, you pay." The court had ruled that in contracting for WPPSS's nuclear projects, the Washington utilities had signed an agreement to take on debt, which they did not have the right to do.

Leahy liked to conclude his anti-WPPSS rallies by reading aloud the legal language of the "take-or-pay" contract in the PUD's lengthy participant's agreement. "Basically it says in very legalistic terms that regardless of whether the plant's ever built, ever operated, ever comes to fruition—you pay." "I mean," he observed, "if you read this in public, you get an incredible reaction." It's not that the plant has to be "used and useful," a criteria that many states have. "What I tried to stress, and I think a lot of anti-WPPSS organizers stressed, was 'it might be debt for somebody. But what WPPSS did was illegal, so it's not *your* debt.' "

Strategically, ratepayers were the only aggrieved party who would bring this issue to court. Chemical Bank, the bond trustee for Units 4 and 5, was suing WPPSS and the utilities—both of whom wanted to pay the debt. They wanted to keep raising funds to complete the nuclear plants. Plus none of the utilities would ever go to court and admit that they did not have the "authority," that they had floated "bogus bonds." Leahy believes that "no utility that ever wanted to float a bond again could do this, could say, 'well, we didn't have the authority,' without being sued for securities fraud. No, someone else had to say that, and it took the ratepayers to do that." Although the case raised many legal issues, the Washington State Supreme Court ruled only on this one, because it was a straightforward state issue—not a federal issue or a securities issue. WPPSS was a creation of the state legislature. The case hinged on whether a state-created entity had the authority to act. There was no appeal.

For Leahy, the surprising decision by the Washington State Supreme Court was ultimately a *political* decision that reflected a victory for the grassroots anti-WPPSS, antinuclear, anti–Wall Street movement that was sweeping the state.

> I have worked with labor unions, antiwar stuff. I've been in lots of situations where there's been tension and activity. But I have never seen anything like this. I think it had a significant political impact on the state. I think that the Washington State Supreme Court decision was a political decision. When Wall Street said it was a political decision, I agreed with them. It simply happened to be a political decision that *for*

once was in favor of the people, and not in favor of Wall Street, and that's why Wall Street was so upset.

By virtue of his participation in the ratepayers' revolt, Leahy believes that he has been true to the populist tradition of the Pacific Northwest and has honored the struggles of the populist public power organizers who had come before him.

> I think it had to do with the fact that people came out of their homes for a couple of nights a week, flooded their auditoriums, and said, "We're not going to pay this son-of-a-bitchin' debt. Period. We're not going to pay it." That effort alone was, I think, enough to tell the powers that be that they weren't going to get the people to pay for this one.

Impact of the Ratepayers' Revolt   As of May 1983, Northwest utilities and their ratepayers had committed more than $7 billion to 10,000 megawatts of canceled or mothballed power plants. For some utilities, major relief was granted by the Washington State Supreme Court decision in June 1983 that the most heavily committed PUD participants in WPPSS Units 4 and 5 had acted "without statutory authority" when they assumed debt obligations for power that might never be produced or delivered. The court reacted "with incredulity" to the provisions in the WPPSS contracts whose intent was "to require payment to WPPSS whether or not the projects are ever completed, operable, or operating," thus obligating the PUD participants to "pay approximately $7 billion for nuclear plants which will never generate any electricity."[23] In its decision, the state high court rejected financing guarantees that had been purported by the BPA and WPPSS to be a "mainstay of the nation's electric utility industry."

Trapped between the relentless pressure of industry and financial leaders to continue the projects and an inflamed citizen opposition, a torpor of indecision settled over government and utility leaders in Washington. The situation continued to polarize. As forecasts on future power requirements continued to drop, a third reactor was canceled. Bailout efforts in the Washington state legislature and the United States Congress failed. Although ratepayer election victories at the PUDs removed most of the incumbent commissioners responsible for the WPPSS debacle, and appeared to pave the way for the implementation of conservation and renewable-energy strategies for the future, it was too late to stop the financial meltdown that had been building up over the past decade.

By a stroke of the pen, the Washington high court had invalidated the contracts between the public utility districts and WPPSS, forcing WPPSS—the issuer of $2.25 billion in bonds for Units 4 and 5—into technical default and triggering loan provisions calling for full repayment of the bonds. The WPPSS default shocked Wall Street with the largest municipal bond default in the nation's history. Chemical Bank of New York, the bond trustee for the WPPSS offering, counterattacked by organizing some 75,000 bondholders and filing suits against 600 public officials for fraud. Other targets for lawsuits arising from the default included the bond underwriters, bond counsel, the two national bond-rating services (Moody's and Standard and Poor's), individual directors of the defaulting utilities, and a number of WPPSS consultants, engineers, and contractors.[24] As the innumerable lawsuits began to work themselves through the courts, ratepayers vowed that even if the debt were ever forced back on the region, they would "still refuse to pay."

In *Power Struggle: The Hundred-Year War over Electricity,* authors Richard Rudolph and Scott Ridley observe that Wall Street firms have long been the "silent partners in the power empire."[25] To a degree that few people realize, the money managers of Wall Street have shaped the course of the electric power industry by deciding which power projects merit financing. Simply put, power systems have been as much involved in "the generation of capital as in the generation of electricity."

For decades, private power companies have been known to Wall Street insiders as the "dividend machines"—representing the "most capital intensive business in the world," requiring three or four dollars of investment capital for every dollar of revenue generated. By the mid-1980s, U.S. private power companies, with assets approaching $350 billion, had absorbed a third of all industrial financing. Half of all new industrial stock issued each year came from private power companies. As much as half of all the investment-banking business for blue chip firms such as Morgan Guaranty, Merrill Lynch, Salomon Brothers, Kidder Peabody, and other major Wall Street houses came from power companies. Typically, financing charges for construction of large power plants can amount to 40 percent or more of total plant costs. In 1985 the 210 private power companies in the United States received nearly half of their $37 billion annual capital budget from outside financing, with approximately 75 percent of the industry capital historically coming from Wall Street.

Given this involvement, it is no wonder that Wall Street was more unsettled by the ratepayers' revolt at WPPSS in Washington than by the siege of Shoreham in New York. At Shoreham, the utility was made whole on its investment by Governor Cuomo and allowed to recoup its losses through future rate increases. At WPPSS, the very foundations of power plant financing were shaken by the legal reality of public power and the political reality of the consumer rebellion.

Yet both WPPSS and Shoreham were symptomatic of a larger crisis in the nuclear power industry as dozens of reactors across the nation were abandoned or canceled in the early 1980s. Industry observers note that as the growth of the power industry has stalled and the crisis surrounding nuclear construction has deepened toward a $100 billion to $200 billion damage bill, the workings of Wall Street firms at the local and regional levels to protect their interests have become starkly visible. For example, in Washington, Wall Street firms contributed funding to an initiative to stop the citizen ratepayers' movement. And on October 3, three months after the WPPSS default, Chemical Bank vice president Will Berls pledged to "take any action necessary to force consumers to pay for the canceled plants." Berls called the default a "national crisis" and joined in the chorus of utility executives who were seeking a "national bailout plan" for the faltering industry.

Although the national bailout never materialized, the events caused many Wall Street analysts to fundamentally reevaluate the risks involved in nuclear power plants. The highly visible and agonizing collapse of WPPSS was the turning point in Wall Street's support for nuclear power financing. After WPPSS, nuclear plants became classified as high-risk investments, and utilities could not find financing for future plants. As one utility executive put it, "Today, no capitalist would think of trying to build another nuclear power plant."

One analyst, Eileen Austin, blamed the WPPSS collapse on the failure of major public and private institutions to respond to a changing environment. Private power companies, encouraged by tax and accounting incentives, and public systems accepting dubious high-growth forecasts were overly eager to expand. Wall Street was only too willing to finance that expansion. The state regulatory bureaucracy and the federal government—which has been a main booster of nuclear power—did not provide adequate oversight.[26]

Writing about the electrical energy future of the Pacific Northwest, Natural Resources Defense Council attorney Ralph Cavanagh wryly observes that "Future historians will debate the precise moment at which the thermal power age passed unmourned into memory. Most will agree, however, that the electric utility sector's once limitless enthusiasm for erecting coal-fired and nuclear power plants was irretrievably spent by 1983."[27] We would expand on Cavanagh's thoughts by adding that in evaluating this change of policy, perceptive scholars will undoubtedly ascribe particular significance to the siege of Shoreham and the financial fiasco at WPPSS. The former created a $5.7 billion nuclear white elephant that today sits in mute testimony to the folly and arrogance of the nuclear industry. The latter resulted in a $2.25 billion bond default on a nuclear power project backed by utilities in four states, endorsed by the federal government, and sold to investors by some of Wall Street's most sophisticated investment firms. As a result, utilities throughout the Pacific Northwest will face a skeptical bond market for as long as investors remember WPPSS's legacy. In both cases, the nuclear industry grossly underestimated the "wild card" of what antinuclear activists and irate ratepayers will do when faced with the accident risks and economic rate shocks of the nuclear power industry.

Ironically, while the voter revolt in New York and the consumer rebellion in Washington painted the power companies as the enemy, a coalition of progressive utility executives and consumers in California was forging a conservation revolution that would soon prove that new nuclear plants were not necessary for that state's energy future.

Mobilizing Principle 2:
Define the Issue so as to Build Broad Coalition

A strategic strength demonstrated by antinuclear activists was their ability to continually reframe, redefine, and hone the nuclear power issue until it touched the core economic values of U.S. society. Initially, the nuclear issue was defined in broad, multifaceted terms to encompass opposition to nuclear weapons, protection of the environment, worker safety, and political democracy. However, paradoxically, as energy activists moved to "cut the issue" more narrowly in purely economic terms, they significantly broadened the original narrow base of antinuclear opposition into a mass national movement with diverse support from consumers and public officials. Moreover, the ratepayers' revolt weakened the nuclear industry's support in Washington and on Wall Street.

Chapter Four

The Conservation Revolution

California today is at the forefront of global environmental regulation. When we look back on the 1990s, we may say that the regulators and the legislators in California were at least as influential, if not more influential, than OPEC in determining the future state, and the future shape, of the world oil industry.

—*Daniel Yergin,* The Prize, *1991*

After the OPEC oil shocks of 1973 and 1979, electric utilities saw only two paths to securing the United States' energy independence in an era of uncertain oil supplies. These paths led either to an increased reliance on fossil fuels (coal or natural gas) or to increased use of nuclear power. This was a cruel dilemma, because along with electricity, the power industry generates some of the world's most serious environmental problems. The industry is the leading consumer of fossil fuels, including coal, the dirtiest of those fuels. As a result, power generation accounts for nearly one-third of global emissions of carbon dioxide (CO_2), the primary greenhouse gas, and generates nearly two-thirds of the sulfur dioxide (SO_2), the major factor in air pollution.

However, in the late seventies, an obscure group of antinuclear activists and energy analysts at the California-based Environmental Defense Fund (EDF) firmly took this dilemma by the horns when they reached an amazing conclusion. Their rethinking of California's energy future was grounded on the premise that renewable energy, particularly conservation, was not simply a visionary goal of environmental idealists. Using sophisticated computer models, EDF proved that electric utilities, their shareholders, and their customers would *all* benefit by reducing power use—by saving energy rather than building new base-load plants to meet future electric demand. EDF proposed to bring about a veritable "conservation revolution" by replacing "megawatts" with "negawatts."

At the time, the very idea of "generating electricity without using it" was perceived as both technically ridiculous and economically threatening by most utilities, whose profits were largely a function of the size of their installed power base.

If EDF's heretical ideas were to have any lasting impact, the maverick environmental organization would have to undertake the daunting task of persuading the giant U.S. utility industry to change its thinking. Electricity is a fundamental commodity of modern civilization, and electric utilities are core institutions. Generating and distributing electricity has become one of the world's largest businesses, with annual revenues estimated at more than $800 billion—roughly twice the size of the world automobile industry.[1] In the United States, the electric utilities have long been known for their bureaucratic inertia, political power, and fierce resistance to change.[2]

How could this renegade band of solar crusaders hope to change the direction of the utility industry in general, and particularly that of California's Pacific Gas and Electric (PG&E) and Southern California Edison (SCE), the first and second largest utilities in the nation, located in one of the most populous and fastest-growing states?

The answer was in "the trimtab factor."

When Harold Willens, a successful entrepreneur, founded Business Executives for National Security (BENS), he created an organization with an ambitious agenda.[3] The goals of BENS were to put the Pentagon on a businesslike basis, to stop the arms race, and to change the United States' relationship with the Soviet Union. Although the arms race had accelerated for nearly 40 years, Willens thought that the leverage of the business community could be the critical factor in changing the thinking of the president, Congress, and the defense establishment regarding the "nuclear weapons crisis."

In developing a political strategy that would mobilize bipartisan support for the BENS agenda from Fortune 1000 business leaders, Willens likened his approach to what R. Buckminster Fuller called the "trimtab factor":

The principle of the trimtab also applies to a ship's rudder. In explaining the trimtab factor, Buckminster Fuller used the image of a large ocean-going ship traveling at high speed through the water. The mass and momentum of such a vessel are enormous, and great force is required to turn its rudder and change the ship's direction. In the past, some large ships had, at the trailing edge of the main rudder, another tiny rudder—the trimtab. By exerting a small amount of pressure, one person could easily turn the trimtab. The trimtab turned the rudder, and the rudder turned the ship.[4]

In Willens's view, the trimtab factor demonstrates how the precise application of a small amount of leverage can produce a powerful effect. He built BENS, which was instrumental in bringing about President Reagan's new overtures to the Soviet Union, as an elite organization on the premise that business leaders were the trimtab that could change the direction of the U.S. ship of state. Just as BENS provided the trimtab factor for a transformation of U.S.-Soviet relations, so EDF became the trimtab factor for the conservation revolution at the California utilities. EDF's arguments before the California Energy Commission became the catalyst for rethinking utility energy futures, initially in California and eventually throughout much of the nation.

Fortunately for EDF, much like the Soviet Union at the end of the eighties, the United States power industry was ripe for transformation. During the seventies and eighties, a rising tide of new technologies, environmental concerns, and political conflicts was buffeting the electric power business, setting the stage for a major overhaul. Although the sudden collapse of the nuclear power industry did not alone cause the turmoil pervading the electric utility industry, it certainly exacerbated the issues.

Historically, the industry that Thomas Alva Edison founded had experienced a long period of growth and stability due to falling prices, rising demand, and growing profits and productivity. Regulation provided stability by limiting competition while controlling the worst monopoly abuses. This idyllic state of affairs lasted until the 1970s, when the effects of the oil price revolution and the malpractice of nuclear economics destabilized the basic structure of the utility business.

From the seventies onward, the cost of everything the utilities needed—capital, technology, fuel, and environmental controls—began to rise rapidly. The cost of building power plants and fueling them skyrocketed far beyond the expectations of conventional wisdom. The transition from declining to increasing costs was painful for the utility business and its customers. As the marginal cost of providing electricity now exceeded the average prices that regulators allowed utilities to charge, the historical business strategy of expansion and growth was undermined. Investors suffered as returns on investment dropped. Customers grew irate about rate increases. Utility regulators became unpopular political appointees. Once staid utility hearings on mundane topics such as electric rates and demand forecasts were turned into battlefields by disgruntled consumers, environmentalists, and antinuclear activists. In this volatile environment, electricity became a highly politicized industry, and the electric utilities stood at a crossroads.

It is no coincidence that the conservation movement was launched in California. As a "bellwether state," California has often led the nation in cultural trends, innovative public policies, and political movements. With nearly 30 million people in 1990, California is the world's sixth largest economy.[5] Primary energy consumption in California approached eight quads in 1992, putting California among the top 10 energy-consuming "nations" in the world, just behind France at number eight. California sits on vast oil reserves and is heavily dependent on petroleum, which accounted for nearly 60 percent of its energy sources in 1991. The other 40 percent were supplied by natural gas (27 percent), alternative energy (7 percent), coal (3 percent), and nuclear (3 percent).

Because vehicles consume three-fourths of all the oil and half of the energy used in the state, poor air quality has become a way of life for 80 percent of California's population. Los Angeles is the most polluted city in the nation. The South Coast Air Quality Management District (AQMD) estimated in the early nineties that the cost to health, forests, agriculture, and visibility from air pollution in the Los Angeles Air Basin amounted to more than $9 billion annually. Concerns about L.A. smog, oil drilling off the California coast, water quality, and water supply have also given rise in California to one of the most powerful and well-organized environmental movements in the nation.

It is therefore no surprise that California stands at the forefront of the global energy debate. For nearly two decades, the California Energy Commission (CEC), a unique institution created by Governor Ronald Reagan and subsequently staffed by Governor Jerry Brown, has blazed an energy path that has led to California's emergence "as one of the world's preeminent leaders in energy planning." During this time, the CEC's policies, which have had a dramatic impact on the state's utilities, have achieved economic benefits in excess of $100 billion. Today, as a result of the conservation revolution, "energy use per capita or per unit of economic output is about 30 percent lower in California than in the nation as a whole."[6]

Two remarkable utility executives have led California to the forefront of the conservation revolution. They are John E. Bryson, chairman and CEO of Southern California Edison (SCE), the giant utility that provides most of smoggy southern California with electric power, and S. David Freeman, who as general manager of the Sacramento Municipal Utility District (SMUD) is building the United States' "premier conservation power plant" in the capital of the Golden State.

The Green Crusader:
John Bryson, Southern California Edison

> *Many times there are* great *business opportunities in meeting environmental needs.*
> —*John E. Bryson, Chairman, SCE, 1991*

While our last two profiles in power laid siege to utilities in New York and Washington, John E. Bryson—whom *Fortune* magazine called "the green crusader"—breached the castle walls and found the holy grail of the antinuclear movement by igniting a veritable conservation revolution throughout the utilities industry. Since 1990 Bryson has served as chairman and chief executive officer of Edison International and its largest subsidiary, Southern California Edison Company (SCE), the nation's second largest utility.

SCE supplies power to 10 million people, covering an area of 50,000 square miles in southern California and serving all of the megalopolis's cities except for Los Angles and San Diego. Air pollution in this region was the highest in the country, violating federal standards two days out of three. Under Bryson's management, between 1991 and 1994, operating revenue at SCE increased from $7.3 billion to $7.8 billion, net income grew from $630 million to $639 million, and the ratio of earnings to fixed charges jumped from 2.92 to 3.43. Although sales of electricity have increased sharply by 10 percent (from 71,165 million kilowatt-hours in 1991 to 77,986 million kilowatt-hours in 1994),

SCE's total peak generation capacity has actually contracted (down from 20,875 megawatts in 1991 to 20,615 megawatts in 1994).[7]

Bryson has demonstrated that a major utility can increase sales and still make money, without building new plants or adding new capacity, while cutting air pollution. A graduate of Stanford University and Yale Law School, Bryson moves with patrician grace through the spacious hallways of SCE's headquarters at Rosemead, California, just east of Los Angeles. Six feet tall and trim, he exudes the confidence of a person who easily scaled the twin peaks of success in business and public service—while planting his unique banner of "corporate environmentalism" at each plateau in his career.

Pointing to the endless miles of tract houses and freeways that stretch to the horizon from his office windows, Bryson predicts that "in general well over half of future energy for the next two decades seems to be coming from a conservation direction."[8] Specifically, by the year 2010, SCE will need 6,400 more megawatts of power to supply its growing customer base. For some of this, Bryson will upgrade some older plants and purchase renewable energy from independent solar and wind producers. But 4,400 megawatts, or nearly 70 percent of the new demand, will be met through conservation—saving electricity that is now being used inefficiently. Twenty years ago, SCE would have relied exclusively on base-load power plants and would have built six new fossil fuel or nuclear plants to meet this demand.

Corporate Environmentalism   Bryson's career epitomizes the coming of age of the environmental movement. Over the past 25 years, he has successfully moved from the role of strident environmental activist to that of innovative utility regulator, and most recently to that of chief evangelist for corporate environmentalism at one of the nation's premier utilities.

After receiving his J.D. degree in 1969, he joined with six fellow members of the *Yale Law Journal* to found the Natural Resources Defense Council (NRDC), a contentious environmental group that sues business and government on behalf of environmental causes. After Bryson led a successful litigation to block plans to dam the American River in California, Governor Jerry Brown named him as chairman of the Water Resources Board in 1976 and president of the California Public Utilities Commission (CPUC) from 1979 to 1983.

As president of the CPUC, which establishes electric rates and profits for all California utilities, Bryson displayed a rare ability to combine environmental zeal with good business sense. His commission was one of the first, and certainly the most influential, in the nation to make a utility's earnings *independent* of how much electricity it sells. Before this innovation, as regulated monopolies, utilities' earnings were tied primarily to achieving a certain sales level or to how many "used and useful" assets they had built in to their "rate base."[9] In this context, utilities had no economic incentives to save energy because lowering future demand and avoiding the need to build new plants would lead to lower revenues. Under Bryson's leadership, the CPUC removed this conservation "penalty." Subsequently, in 1991, California took the next step of permitting utilities to include investments in energy-saving capital equipment in their rate base, thus enabling them to directly profit from conservation.

Bryson first joined SCE in 1984. His first mandate was to set up SCE's independent power subsidiary, Mission Energy Corporation, which has become one of the largest and most successful independent power producers in the world. After assuming the leadership of SCE in 1990, Bryson used his broad environmental and regulatory experience to implement his style of corporate environmentalism aggressively at all levels of utility management and power systems planning. By 1991 SCE had already invested more than $105 million in conservation, an amount that is projected to grow to $2 billion by the year 2000. As a result, the growth in customer demand for new power in the SCE grid will drop from 2.5 percent per year, the average during the 1980s, to almost 1 percent in the 1990s. Best of all, under the progressive regulatory framework that Bryson has forged, SCE will earn the CPUC's authorized rate of return of 13 percent on that investment. This framework has benefited all regulated California utilities, including Pacific Gas and Electric (PG&E), the nation's largest utility, which serves the San Francisco Bay Area and much of northern California. Richard Clarke, former chairman of PG&E, praises Bryson's ability to forge energy policy that recognizes the interests of utilities, consumers, and the environment. "Bryson stood above the zealots and visualized a balance of interest," Clarke states.[10]

Environmental and business interests are frequently incompatible, as in the cases of preserving wildlife habitat from the encroachment of logging companies and protecting coastal waters from oil drilling. But the economics of energy conservation create one of those rare situations that result in a win-win situation for all parties: utility shareholders, utility customers, and environmentalists alike. Reflecting on his initial success at SCE, Bryson notes, "Many times there are *great* business opportunities in meeting environmental needs."[11]

PG&E versus "the Greenie"   The first shot in the conservation revolution was fired across the bow of the PG&E from the modest offices of the Environmental Defense Fund, located in Berkeley, California. The shot came in the form of "the greenie," a 125-page technical document submitted to the CPUC in 1978, which made an irrefutable case that PG&E and its customers would be better off developing conservation, rather than building nine new nuclear and coal plants along the pristine coastline of northern California. The brief posed a fundamental question: "From the point of view of a profit-making utility company, what was the most economically efficient way to run an electricity business?"[12]

The greenie was developed by the core EDF staff of Zack Willey, a brilliant economist, Tom Graff, a public-interest lawyer, and David Roe, an attorney. Ironically, in 1879, David Roe's great-grandfather started what seems to have been the world's first central electricity company in San Francisco, using a dynamo he received as collateral on a bad debt. That company grew into what eventually became the largest utility in the United States, PG&E. In 1979, exactly 100 years after its humble beginnings, PG&E was fined $14 million by the California PUC for not aggressively pursuing conservation, at the request of EDF's lead attorney, David Roe. As Roe puts it in his book, *Dynamos and Virgins,* the utility was punished by the commission "for not putting enough faith in the ideas of a new generation of would-be electricity pioneers."[13]

California's environmental community was horrified by PG&E's 1979 plans to build 10 more power plants of the largest size, which would have added more capacity in the next 18 years than the company had built in the previous century. EDF's contrary idea called for a radical rearrangement of energy investing by applying Amory Lovins's global view of the soft energy path to the analysis of a specific profit-making utility—PG&E.

Willey's economic approach to the conservation problem was intentionally conventional. It accepted all of the principles that the electric industry preached. Utilities should grow at whatever rate matched the growth of customer demand; they should build what was cheapest and most reliable to meet that demand; they should use their own investment dollars, without relying on government help; and they should be allowed to charge customers accordingly. What was unique was that no utility on the verge of committing itself to build a new nuclear power plant had ever analyzed what the billion or so dollars required for that plant could produce if allocated to conservation and energy efficiency.

In praising the parsimony of EDF's arguments, Roe describes the years of research and analysis that went into forcing utility executives to "look at alternatives on strictly business grounds—to contemplate nothing more controversial than producing more energy for less money." The greenie was to become the ultimate antinuclear weapon, for instead of disagreeing with their principles, it showed utility planners that their coal and nuclear power plants were inferior choices, on their own terms. In making this argument, Roe believes that "a moment's pause was necessary in order to appreciate that, despite the enormous environmental implications, this argument about future power development would not mention the environment at all."[14]

When John Bryson, then the liberal environmental chairman of the California Utilities Commission, began to concur with the EDF strategy, Roe knew that EDF had effectively laid the groundwork for a fundamental change in the state's energy future. Underlining his preference for economic over regulatory-driven changes, Roe observed, "If you win something politically, it's only as good as the political alignments. You lose it when the politics changes. If you win something economically, it's there. And this is a wonderful example of that."

In reframing the energy debate in California, Roe acknowledges that EDF had created a powerful tool for both the antinuclear and environmental movements.

> As you can tell, all of this in some way is about nuclear power plants; certainly my personal motivation had a lot to do with what I saw as the environmental threat of nuclear power plants. Yet we never mentioned it. In fact, we never mentioned environmental threats at all. Obviously, I'm biased, but I think it was a more effective strategy to prevent construction of more nuclear power plants than a strategy that says, hey, this valve doesn't work and all that stuff. And I wouldn't want any of that work not to go on. But in a larger strategic sense, creating the alternatives and pushing toward the alternatives may even be more subversive than causing people to worry about the specific design.[15]

In presiding over this conflict between EDF and PG&E, one of Bryson's primary roles in redirecting California's energy debate was to create a regulatory framework in which constructive alliances between environmental groups and corporations could take place. Under consistent PUC pressure during the early eighties, PG&E chairman Richard Clarke scrapped the utility's plans to build several giant nuclear and coal plants. Like SCE, the giant utility began to plan an energy future based primarily on aggressive conservation programs, complemented by various renewable-energy systems such as cogeneration and windmills on the sites of regional businesses. In 1989 PG&E announced a $10 million study with the California offices of the NRDC to determine how to improve energy efficiency within the California region. The study uses the computer model first presented in the greenie, which PG&E now rents from EDF for $18,000 a year.

Of greatest significance is that the EDF-PG&E conflict, which was initially moderated by the Bryson-led CPUC, paved the way for bipartisan support in California that eventually enshrined the conservation revolution into regulatory policy. Under these initiatives, California enjoyed the benefits of energy efficiency and conservation programs throughout the early 1980s, until low energy prices and lackluster federal and state policies reduced incentives for utilities to invest in efficiency. As a result, utility conservation program spending dropped by 56 percent from 1983 to 1989. However, in 1990, in response to this retrenchment, the NRDC initiated a statewide "collaborative process" that brought together diverse groups—ratepayer organizations, utilities, environmentalists, and energy service companies—to produce an "Energy Efficiency Blueprint." This proposal offered a road map of how to realize the tremendous potential for improving energy efficiency in every sector of California's vast and diverse economy.

The blueprint proposed to reduce consumer gas and electric bills by holding down utility spending and by reducing the need for costly and often polluting power plants while creating a shareholder incentive program that would allow utilities to share in the "estimated dollar savings from these programs." Along with the rate-base treatment of conservation investments, these savings are significant because previously California utilities were reimbursed only for the actual amount spent on energy efficiency.

Small Is Beautiful . . . and Profitable   By 1991, PG&E's chairman, Richard A. Clarke, announced that the company's new conservation drive would meet 75 percent of new demand in the decade ahead. Whereas Clarke's announcement certainly ups the stakes in its long-standing "environmental beauty contest" with SCE, it should be noted that PG&E had to be dragged kicking and screaming into the conservation revolution. It had been more than a decade since EDF's greenie had irrefutably shown that "a shift to the alternatives would produce $472 million more in net earnings for the company than the ten–power plant plan, over the full time period that the company's internal projections covered."[16]

For utilities such as PG&E, which were dangerously overextended financially by long-term capital-intensive programs, the conservation revolution provided a wake-up call and a timely solution to a coming cash flow crisis that would have seriously impacted earnings and hurt investors. But utility executives, who were weaned with a "bigger is better" worldview, initially had a difficult time grasping that financial salvation could come in an accumulation of relatively small pieces, which could be quickly brought on-line and which kept planning flexible. Also difficult to grasp was that this "small is beautiful" world could be achieved by a surprisingly mundane collection of energy savers: specific pieces of efficiency hardware such as attic insulation and less wasteful air conditioners, specific cogeneration opportunities, more generators driven by geothermal steam, solar water heaters, and a modest number of windmills.

Nothing futuristic. Nothing experimental. Nothing technologically fancy. Simply put, sound business judgment argued in favor of a totally different way of meeting PG&E's future electric needs. The bottom line was that conservation and alternative energy could replace at least 9 out of the 10 big plants that the company had on the drawing boards. In California, as early as 1979, renewables were ready to get the same energy results as base-load plants. And at lower costs.

Renewables at SCE   While PG&E had to be prodded toward energy efficiency by outside forces during the decade of the eighties, SCE was already taking a leadership role. Although Bryson was not at Edison at that time, he recalls that

> In 1980 Southern California Edison's announcement that in the decade of the eighties all of its additional sources of power would either be from energy conservation or from alternative renewables was an enormous step, because it was kind of premature for this direction to be coming from a major utility. Up to that point, most of this kind of thinking was more evident in the activist and environmental community. So I

recall that when Edison announced this direction, I likened it to Nixon recognizing China.[17]

However, Bryson was destined to play a key role in every significant aspect of independent power, conservation, and renewable-energy development at SCE. He joined SCE in 1984 as a senior vice president for legal and financial affairs, hired away from the CPUC by then-SCE chairman Howard Allen, a visionary who recognized that the utility industry needed fresh thinking. Bryson had impeccable credentials for the job.

Bryson's first assignment was to lead the SCE team that created a new unregulated subsidiary for SCE, now called Mission Energy Company. Acting under the federal mandate established by the Public Utilities Regulatory Policy Act (PURPA) of 1978, Mission's goal was to build smaller power plants around the country and to sell electricity under competitive fixed-price contracts to other utilities. This qualifies Mission as an "independent power producer" (IPP), whose earnings are not regulated by the federal or state governments. Not saddled with the historical costs of inefficient or polluting plants, IPPs can generate both conventional and renewable energy and thus compete very effectively, especially because PURPA mandates that utilities purchase power from "qualified" IPPs at the "avoided cost" of building new power capacity.[18] As of 1992, the United States had 55,000 megawatts of IPP generators in operation—equivalent to 7 percent of the nation's power. That same year, the IPPs, for the first time, added more generating capacity throughout the United States than the utilities did.[19]

Since becoming chairman of SCE in 1990, Bryson has focused his Green crusade on a company-wide campaign to promote both renewable energy and conservation by aggressively implementing what energy planners call "demand-side management" (DSM) programs throughout the utility service area. DSM involves a variety of energy-saving technologies and replaces inefficient electric motors with more efficient ones—and offers rebates to customers who install efficient appliances.

According to SCE's annual report in 1991, its customers saved about four billion kilowatt-hours from its energy efficiency programs.[20] These programs cut customers' electric bills as well as air pollution. SCE anticipates that by the year 2000, new and expanded conservation programs will cut annual electric consumption an additional 10 billion kilowatt-hours, or enough to supply the energy needs of more than 1.5 million homes, reducing CO_2 emissions by 38 million tons.

In 1991 SCE spent more than $100 million on its 55 distinct energy efficiency programs, which reached more than 300,000 customers. Among these programs, the utility offered incentives to commercial and residential builders to construct homes and buildings that exceeded California's already stringent efficiency standards. These energy-saving measures included home insulation and greater use of advanced technologies such as energy-efficient lighting, electric motors, and heating and cooling systems.

In addition to its DSM programs, SCE has exceeded its 1980 commitment to add 2,000 megawatts of renewable (solar, wind, geothermal, biomass, and small hydro) and alternative (cogeneration) generating capacity during the 1980s (see figure 3). By 1990 SCE had exceeded its goal by two and one-half times. The addition of these resources helped reduce SCE's dependence on oil for electricity generation from 58 million barrels in 1977 to about 100,000 barrels in 1990. Likewise, nitrogen oxides emissions from SCE power plants in California's South Coast Air Basin were reduced 76 percent between 1980 and 1990.

Figure 3.
SCE Renewable Purchases under PURPA
(Contribution to Total Energy Requirement—
Millions of kWh)

	1981	1991
Geothermal	0	5,649
Biomass	0	1,607
Wind	0	1,542
Solar	0	732
Small hydro	106	188
Total renewable purchases	106	9,718

Source: Southern California Edison, *Renewable Energy: Technology Options for the Future* (Rosemead, Calif.: SCE, 1992), 2.

By 1991, as a result of these programs, SCE was already obtaining 20.7 percent of its energy from renewable sources, twice the national average of 10.2 percent. In addition, as a result of maximizing the conservation option, SCE anticipates that it will be able to keep its demand projection for its future energy sales to average annual growth rates of 1.4 percent from 1995 to 2000 and to 1.8 percent from 2000 to 2005.[21]

As summarized in figure 4, SCE's Energy Mix Projection for 1995, 2000, and 2005 demonstrates how Bryson plans to transform the company from a traditional utility corporation into an energy service company that accesses power from a diversity of sources in order to meet shareholder, customer, and environmental demands.

According to Bryson, "what has motivated this over a long period is the judgment about what's best for our customers. We have felt that the touchstone has to be how do you provide customer value, and to the extent we stray from that, we are not likely to be very successful at our business over a longer period of time."[22] Ultimately, Bryson led

---

Figure 4.
SCE Energy Mix (March 1995)—
Resource Projection (in GWh)

	1995 GWh	%	2000 GWh	%	2005 GWh	%
Total DSM[a]	4,767	5	7,404	7	8,381	8
Total Renewable Purchases[b]	28,326	32	28,700	29	28,663	26
Total Energy Sources	89,315	100	99,431	100	108,179	100

Source: Southern California Edison, "Energy Mix: March 1995, Resource Projection (GWh), 1995–2005" (Rosemead, Calif.: SCE, 1995).

[a]DSM refers to demand-side management conservation and efficiency energy sources.

[b]Includes purchases under PURPA of biomass, cogeneration, geothermal, hydro, solar, and wind from renewable and alternative resources owned by nonutility (non-SEC) producers.

SCE to the forefront of the conservation revolution on the conviction—reinforced by 20 years of experience in environmental advocacy and utility regulation—that conservation is good for the utility business, good for the consumer, and good for the environment. Bryson believes that conservation will become a nationwide trend among utilities:

> I think that electric utilities can't think meaningfully about their businesses without thinking of the environmental dimension, because all the public opinion polls show that consumers care about the environment. And those polls that focus on utilities show the public's concern about the environmental impact of utility operations. So there is a tremendous level of public support for rethinking how energy and electricity are used. And if efficiency offers opportunities for our customers to get greater value, as it clearly does, then we have to offer those products to our customers if we expect to stay relevant.[23]

Electrifying Southern California   Bryson has already made environmental concerns a part of the fundamental analysis in any major decision at SCE, not something that is considered after the fact. But he already has an even bolder vision for the Green agenda. In response to the pressing air quality problems of the southern California area and to the emerging threat of global warming, Bryson's ambitious goal in the long term is to displace the polluting effects of gasoline and diesel fuel by electrifying southern California. Bryson argues that SCE's power currently pollutes only half as much as nonelectric fuels because 20 percent of it is nuclear; 33 percent is renewable solar, wind, and water power; and the company's advanced gas turbines are more efficient than other fossil fuel turbines.

Bryson has pledged the utility to cutting emissions of carbon dioxide, a greenhouse gas, 10 percent by the year 2000 and 20 percent by 2010 from the 1988 base case year level. The company has already reduced other hazardous waste emissions from 16,000 tons annually in 1987 to 2,800 tons in 1991.[24] Once again, SCE is at the environmental leading edge of the private utility industry. Although most utilities have installed scrubbers that remove smokestack pollutants to comply with the requirements of the federal Clean Air Act of 1990, even advanced scrubbers will not remove CO_2. Only burning cleaner fossil fuels will do that, and SCE has pledged to do so.

SCE has also worked closely with southern California's South Coast Air Quality Management District (AQMD)—which enforces the strictest air quality standards in the nation—to cut nitrogen oxides (NO_x) emissions 86 percent by installing new pollution control equipment by 1987. NO_x are significant contributors to ozone and smog pollution in the Los Angeles area. The utility may spend up to $700 million on replacing many of its oil-burning generators with natural gas turbines, which release less of both CO_2 and NO_x.

But the ultimate antipollution question in Los Angeles—the city designed around the automobile—is how to replace oil. In 1990 California established an innovative policy precedent with its statewide Low-Emissions Vehicle (LEV) program, which mandated that by 1998, 2 percent of all vehicles sold in the state must be zero-emissions vehicles (ZEVs)—with that number increasing to 5 percent by 2001 and to 10 percent by 2003. However, this California legislation was bitterly opposed by the U.S. auto industry. With the next generation of electric vehicles (EVs) still costing two to three times more than conventional cars, Detroit pointed to the still-unresolved technological difficulties of manufacturing an electric car acceptable and affordable to buyers and noted that internal combustion engines were already 95 percent cleaner than they were 30 years ago. The auto industry further argued that it needed more time to develop and evaluate battery technology and "that the production of cleaner gasoline powered cars from 1998 to 2002 would exceed emissions reductions currently projected under existing ZEV requirements."[25]

Faced with mounting pressure from automakers, LEV technical experts, state lawmakers, and taxpayers afraid of higher utility bills, in March 1996, the California Air Resources Board (CARB)—the agency charged with enforcing the LEV program—voted unanimously to delay the implementation of a ZEV mandate on all new cars and trucks sold in the state. Although CARB suspended the 2 and 5 percent requirements for 1998 and 2001, respectively, it negotiated an implementation plan with the "big seven" automakers that kept in place the 10 percent quota for 2003, which will be equivalent to approximately 126,000 ZEVs.[26] Nevertheless, this legislative delay has not changed Detroit's or Japan's plans to bring an electric vehicle to market, despite the fact that the major automakers reluctantly jump-started their EV production plans primarily in response to the California regulations.

Although cars and buses powered by hydrogen fuel cells are still in the commercial testing stages, today only electric battery–powered vehicles can currently meet ZEV requirements. SCE claims that new electric vehicles are 97 percent cleaner than internal combustion vehicles, even counting emissions from Edison's power plants to recharge the vehicles' batteries. But recharging batteries can take hours, posing a major obstacle to commercializing electric cars. Bryson is also advocating the return to an electrified lightweight train system for Los Angles in order to reduce pollution further. Today, rail transports only 27,000 people per day over 22 miles of track in southern California. Bryson wants to dramatically expand the system. SCE is evaluating the possibility of building, owning, and profiting on the cable system that would power an expanded electric mass transit system throughout the southern California area.

Excited by this opportunity to increase the infrastructure of the utility industry dramatically by electrifying the United States' transportation system, SCE is working closely with General Motors to evaluate several solutions to this problem, including opening "solar electric service stations." There, ZEV motorists could swap spent car batteries for charged ones, a process that would take no longer than filling the gasoline tank does today. Bryson notes that SCE "has been involved in virtually every electric transportation initiative around the country and in the state in a major way."

As a direct result of California's ZEV mandate, which has been under serious consideration for adoption by 13 northeastern states from Virginia to Maine, some major automakers—Ford (Ecostar), General Motors (EV-1), Honda (EV Plus), and Toyota (RAV4)—are planning to sell (or lease) their first EVs to the public in 1997.[27] Introduced in December 1996, the General Motors (GM) EV-1 is available for lease at $399 per month from GM Saturn dealerships in southern California and Arizona.

The low-slung, sleek two-seater has a list price of $34,000. It features a virtually noiseless 137-horsepower AC induction motor and runs on a 312-volt lead-acid battery, which weighs 1,175 pounds, equal to 40 percent of the electric car's overall weight of 2,970 pounds. The vehicle is 169.7 inches long, 69.5 inches wide, and 50.5 inches high. It has an electronically regulated top speed of 80 miles per hour, accelerates from 0 to 60 miles per hour in less than nine seconds, and has a combined city and highway range of only 79 miles, limiting the vehicle to intraurban travel. Standard equipment on EV-1 includes dual airbags; air-conditioning; power windows, door locks, steering, and brakes; AM-FM stereo radio with a single-disc CD player; and cruise control.

So far, EVs represent the kind of regulatory-driven project that environmentalists love and Detroit hates. However, if the U.S. effort to build a competitive EV is successful, it will bring about phenomenal changes in the $500 billion global automobile industry. And the effort may well succeed. Despite the high prices of these early EVs, the cost of electric components and therefore of electric vehicles overall is projected to fall exponentially as volumes increase. Furthermore, new charging technologies may soon double or triple battery life; improved lead-acid batteries may increase EV range; and utilities may install multiple quick-charge stations that recharge batteries in 15 minutes (as opposed to the current time of 7 hours). This combination of technological improvements may resolve the EVs' power supply problems (related to limited vehicle range, short battery life, and long battery-recharging time), thereby making electric cars more acceptable to consumers.

"It's time to get electric vehicles out of the lab, into the showroom and on to the road," stated GM chairman John F. Smith when he announced plans to market EV1 in January 1996.[28] Because two-thirds of southern California's smog is caused by cars, trucks, and buses, Bryson relishes the thought that Detroit will ride to L.A.'s rescue. In July 1991, SCE and other utility members of the Electric Power Research Institute, the U.S. Department of Energy, and the Big Three automakers formed the U.S. Advanced Battery Consortium, which will invest $100 million annually until 2002 to improve the performance of electric vehicles.

At the same time, the 1991 AQMD Plan for the Los Angeles Basin anticipates 90 percent rail electrification and 30 percent bus electrification by the year 2010. The Los Angeles County Transportation Commission's 30-year plan devotes 80 percent of its $150 billion in secured funding to electric mass rail and bus transit. By participating in a number of public and private partnerships, such as Calstart, to encourage the development of an advanced electric transportation industry in southern California, SCE is positioning itself to be at the forefront of an all-electric transportation future.

Electric transportation offers SCE a unique opportunity to increase its electric infrastructure dramatically by replacing petroleum as the fuel of choice for transportation. The utility already has enough electric generating capacity through 2002, during off-peak evening hours, to meet potential customers' needs to recharge one million electric vehicles. Within SCE's grid, nighttime recharging would use power plants more efficiently and help reduce the average cost of electricity for all customers.

Bryson beams when discussing SCE's leadership role in an all-electric transportation future for the Los Angeles area. His face lights up with the mischievous grin of the rebellious law student who set sail 20 years ago under the green flag of environmentalism to challenge the corporate and government polluters. Today, with a twinkle in his eyes that seems to say "I told you so," Bryson stands tall at the helm of SCE, his hand firmly on the trimtab rudder of the conservation revolution.[29] As a rising corporate star in a new generation of corporate environmentalists, he steadily gazes at the next great business opportunity emerging on the horizon. After building his career by implementing the conservation revolution at the nation's second largest utility, Bryson now has his sights set on transforming SCE into an all-purpose electric service company that will electrify southern California and—in the process—replace the oil companies and dramatically reduce pollution.

America's Premier Conservation Power Plant: David Freeman, Sacramento Municipal Utility District

Our policy is to put Exxon out of business in this county sometime early in the next century.
                    —David Freeman, general manager, SMUD, 1992

S. David Freeman was the first person in the federal government working on conservation and energy policy, serving under Presidents Johnson and Nixon from 1967 to 1971. After advising the Senate Commerce Committee on the Automobile Fuel Economy Act, he played a key role in President Carter's national energy plan, which featured energy conservation. For seven years—three years as chairman of the board of directors—he served at the Tennessee Valley Authority, where he shut down seven nuclear plants and earned a reputation for turning around troubled utilities and setting industry standards for environmentally sound energy policies.

In June 1990, Freeman was appointed general manager of the Sacramento Municipal Utility District (SMUD). Why did this Washington energy czar agree to head a modest publicly owned utility system encompassing 900 miles of cropland surrounding California's capital city?

Freeman came to SMUD because an earlier voter rebellion had scrapped the Rancho Seco nuclear power plant and offered him an unfettered opportunity to test his theories about conservation and electric transportation.

In most utility circles, Freeman was regarded as an environmental extremist. But California in the early nineties served as a nurturing incubator for the innovative ideas he had been advocating in Washington over the past two decades.

For nearly 15 years, from 1974 to 1989, the residents of Sacramento County were wed to the troubled 900-megawatt Rancho Seco nuclear power plant. After a prolonged public debate, they abandoned it in 1989, voting overwhelmingly to shut down the unreliable plant, which was draining SMUD economically and driving up utility bills.

Today SMUD not only is nuclear free but is thriving as a world-renowned laboratory for energy conservation, renewable fuels, and electric transportation. Under Freeman's guidance, SMUD has become America's premier conservation power plant. Through the year 2010, SMUD will meet *all* of the region's electric growth requirements through aggressive conservation and efficiency programs and will replace Rancho Seco's 900 megawatts of power through a combination of renewable-energy programs. As a nuclear utility, SMUD lost $575 million in 1989. Without nuclear power, SMUD made $46 million in 1992.[30]

"There is life after nuclear power, and it's not a bad life," says Freeman.[31] As he saunters into his spacious office at SMUD headquarters, wearing brown leather cowboy boots and a blue denim shirt, Freeman today looks more like a rancher than a utility executive. His whitish hair, drooping mustache, and large, languid eyes exude the warm demeanor of a kindly professor who enjoys scolding industry and government on the subject of energy. His office is cluttered with solar cell arrays, drawings of electric-vehicle charging stations, and classic works on energy policy, from David Lillianthal's *TVA and Democracy,* to the Ford Foundation's *Energy Conservation,* to Freeman's own *Energy: The New Era,* published in 1974.

For Freeman, SMUD is a crucible for testing the visionary ideas that he believes are essential to the United States' ability to compete with Japan as a high-tech leader in the solar and hydrogen energy and transportation technologies that will dominate the next century.

A Clone of Three Mile Island In contrast to PG&E and SCE, which are private, investor-owned utilities regulated by the State of California, SMUD is owned by its customers, and the locally elected board of directors sets plant rates and policy. For this reason, SMUD was able to act quickly to invest its revenues in energy efficiency in order to replace Rancho Seco. SMUD's existence as a public utility district dates back to 1923 when it was established as a PUD under the federal Municipal Utility District Act.[32] The act authorized special districts to be formed with the authority to provide public services such as electricity, sewage, water, gas, and telephone. Only after the district received the authority to issue debt was it able to purchase the PG&E distribution system. SMUD's first big project, authorized in the 1950s and constructed in the 1960s, was the development of 640 megawatts of hydropower on the American River, providing an inexpensive and reliable resource for the district.

In 1968 the next major decision was made to build Rancho Seco. The decision came after senior managers visited the Oyster Creek nuclear plant in New Jersey. They came away favorably impressed and recommended the construction of Rancho Seco as "the most cost-effective new source of power."[33] At the same time, an agreement was signed between PG&E and SMUD under which PG&E would provide power reserves for Rancho Seco in exchange for excess power when it existed. This "energy banking" agreement, under which no funds would change hands, was essential because SMUD was the smallest U.S. utility that wholly owned a nuclear power plant and had no reserves within its grid to cover Rancho Seco in case of outages.

As in so many other cases during the "great nuclear bandwagon market" of the 1960s, the decision to purchase Rancho Seco was made without any systematic review of alternatives. It was then firmly believed that demand for electricity was going to grow at 7 percent per year for the foreseeable future. Like so many other cities, Sacramento was caught up in the whole "Atoms for Peace zeitgeist," and the SMUD Board of Directors thought that nuclear power would provide by far the cheapest source of electricity. At that time, elections for the SMUD board were rarely contested, and the incumbents were usually reelected. As in the Pacific Northwest before the WPPSS fiasco, there was very little reason for broader public scrutiny when hydroelectric plants were being developed because utility rates actually decreased throughout the mid- and early sixties. Construction on Rancho Seco began in 1968 and was completed in 1974.

Almost immediately after construction, the plant, which was a clone of the Three Mile Island reactor design manufactured by Babcock and Wilcox, began experiencing turbine problems, causing the plant to be shut down most of the time. The plant subsequently developed tube leaks and steam generator corrosion similar to that of Turkey Point, which resulted in further shutdowns. Over its 14-year lifetime, Rancho Seco operated at a dismal 39 percent of capacity. The turning point came when PG&E, which had been providing SMUD with far more energy than it was getting back during the 1980s, gave notice that it was going to terminate the energy-balancing agreement in the 1990s. This meant that SMUD would have to assume full responsibility for planning its own power supplies, for independently operating the plant, and for obtaining sufficient reserves to backstop the plant if it were shut down. Coming on top of Rancho Seco's mounting repair costs, this would place a staggering economic burden on SMUD.

After a 1985 shutdown, the public began to lose confidence. The *Sacramento Bee* called for a full study of "alternatives to continued operation of the plant." Community activists circulated a petition forcing an election on the plant. After three additional outages in 1988 and 1989, the last one coming on the anniversary of the TMI accident and resulting in major criticism from the NRC that the plant was not being operated safely, the community voted to close the plant in 1989. Edward A. Smelloff, who eventually became president of the SMUD Board of Directors, led a reform slate of directors, who threw out several pronuclear incumbents. "After the plant was closed, I was able to work with the swing member of the board, become president, and change the policy direction to make a major investment in energy efficiency, including a new general manager who would support that policy 100 percent," notes Smelloff.

The new general manager was David Freeman. Freeman observes that the decision to close Rancho Seco was an economic one, not one motivated by concerns about nuclear safety or by antinuclear sentiment. Because no U.S. utility has ordered a nuclear plant since 1987, and some utilities are abandoning existing plants rather than pay for their upkeep, Freeman believes, "It was the financial vice presidents of the utility industry that killed nuclear power, not Ralph Nader or Jane Fonda."

California's Unilateral Disarmament   California utilities "have all unilaterally disarmed," Freeman says. "We have all accepted the conservation revolution. We don't build power plants." That leaves California utilities with the choice of expanding power supplies through natural gas and renewable fuels such as solar energy and hydroelectric power or reducing demand by means of conservation and efficiency. "We are building SMUD's conservation power plant by buying power from our customers," Freeman states. Every major energy study, including those conducted specifically for SMUD, demonstrates that "conservation is the most reliable source of energy, and best of all, the price never goes up."

Freeman gives California governor Jerry Brown credit for establishing state technical support and the regulatory environment in which conservation projects could blossom during the seventies. The California Energy Commission promoted that mandate throughout the eighties and nineties, reinforced by public concern about the state's serious air quality problems and the general political sensitivity to environmental issues. In the late eighties, Ralph Cavanagh at the NRDC led the utilities into a collaborative effort that reestablished conservation as the utilities' top priority.

In this context, Freeman found that he was very rapidly able to move the utility from its position as "Peck's bad boy" to the state's leader in conservation and efficiency programs. After shutting down "the Ranch," he had no choice, Freeman commented. "Soon after I arrived, we decided that energy efficiency just fit us to a tee because we had unilaterally disarmed. We had to balance our energy budget by both reducing the demand and increasing supply simultaneously to replace 900 megawatts of power. And we have been doing that rather successfully."

Initially, SMUD's replacement for Rancho Seco has come from purchasing power from other utilities. SMUD's aggressive efficiency program is designed to offset any growth in electric demand indefinitely. Today SMUD is meeting 100 percent of its growth needs with efficiency and is, over time, replacing Rancho Seco with a group of smaller, diverse power plants: a wind plant, some high-efficiency natural gas plants, and in the future a combination of solar, geothermal, and other advanced energy technologies.

SMUD's Conservation Power Plant Freeman is especially proud of what he calls "SMUD's conservation power plant." It will eventually provide about 700 megawatts, which meets all of the utility's growth through the year 2010. Whereas SCE and PG&E are projecting that they will meet about 70 percent of their growth through conservation, SMUD is the first utility in the nation to meet 100 percent of its electric power growth demand through conservation and efficiency, making it "the nation's premier conservation utility."

Because SMUD is a public, voter-controlled utility, Freeman was able to act quickly and decisively to implement the ratepayers' mandate that he turn the utility around. "We're not regulated, and we don't have to fuss around with the PUC. We have a greater vested interest in the immediate outcome. In that sense, if we overshoot our mark and install 'too much' conservation, well, that's just fewer renewable power plants that we have to build," Freeman notes. The larger private utilities have to fit their efficiency programs into a more complex resource plan. Their planning process is complicated by needing approval from the triangle of interests comprising the ratepayer through the CPUC, the utility, and the utility's stockholders. "We don't have a triangle. Our ratepayers are our stockholders. If we save them money, they're happy. They are not worried about dividends. The dividends come in the form of more efficient refrigerators, lights, and air conditioners in their homes—which we help them buy and install."

Nevertheless, SMUD does have "a rigorous regard for getting our money's worth," based on strict economic criteria for how much the utility will pay per kilowatt-hour for efficiency. "I describe it very simply," Freeman reports.

We're buying from our customers the electricity that they would otherwise waste. And we are doing so through a variety of measures, in some cases through cash rebates on new appliances and in others by just going in and installing it, when it's cost-effective to do it that way. Our advantage as a utility is that we can finance this at our cost of money over a ten-year period, which is a key factor, because most consumers do not have the capital resources to go out and buy a more efficient air conditioner, and pay more money for it on the front end, even though it will save them money over its lifetime. Here, Adam Smith is just plain wrong. Every human being is not a perfect economic animal, making the most rational decisions. People have shortages of financing and shortages of information. We supply both.

Under this efficiency program, SMUD will provide up to $150 in cash rebates on a new refrigerator, depending on how efficient it is. In addition, the utility will pay $100 for the older refrigerator, which they recycle, "because we want that 'old kilowatt guzzler' eliminated," Freeman explains. "We don't want to encourage people to buy an efficient refrigerator, only to leave the old one running in the garage. That's not saving, and that's not smart." The same approach is used for air conditioners. One of the most innovative things that SMUD hopes to do is to give away trees, if they are planted at the right spots around the house to provide "ecological cooling."[34] "When I see a tree, I see a window air conditioner. It doesn't rust. It grows and grows, and fifteen years from now, it's a central air conditioner. So we have tried to be fairly innovative and practical at the same time," Freeman says.

SMUD describes its efficiency programs as "a plan to build a 700-megawatt power plant a piece at a time by reducing the energy use in Sacramento homes and businesses." For the $51.7 million spent on energy efficiency in 1993, the utility anticipates a demand reduction of 42 megawatts, forever. A comparable conventional mini–power plant could have been built for less, but SMUD's investment will "generate the same power year after year, with no cost for fuel, operations, or maintenance." By the year 2000, conservation will provide nearly 20 percent of SMUD's power resources, and renewables, including both geothermal and hydro, will provide an additional 54 percent of the system's resources.

According to Ed Smelloff, president of the SMUD board, "in two short years the publicly-owned Sacramento Municipal Utility District has rebounded from its nuclear nightmare, stabilizing double digit rate increases, recovering Wall Street's confidence for its previously plummeting bond ratings, and transforming a depressed work force into proud employees. Its plan to meet future electricity demand with efficiency improvements will actually *save* SMUD ratepayers more than $1 billion by the year 2010."[35]

Clean-Air Capital of the Nation   Freeman is confident that California's zero-emissions-vehicle legislation will have a significant impact in the next century. "Today, SMUD is perhaps more deeply committed to the electrification of the transportation system than any utility in the country," he observes. Freeman then wryly declares with obvious gusto, "Our policy is to put Exxon out of business in this county sometime in the next century." SMUD has pledged to deal with the air quality problem and to "clean the air of this region not only for ourselves, but for future generations as well."

Freeman believes that the air quality–transportation-utility issue must be approached as a whole system:

> We intend to electrify the entire transportation system. But we come into the equation with clean hands because we are going to have a clean source of electricity. It's not in my view good enough to simply say electric cars are an unmitigated good. You've got to combine it with reducing the pollution required in making electricity. By the turn of the century, our electric system will be 75 percent either efficiency or renewables, and only 25 percent natural gas. So we are going to have a very clean source of electric power, and we intend to use that electric power to help people get to work.

SMUD is in the process of strategically putting electric charging stations all around town to power a growing fleet of electric passenger

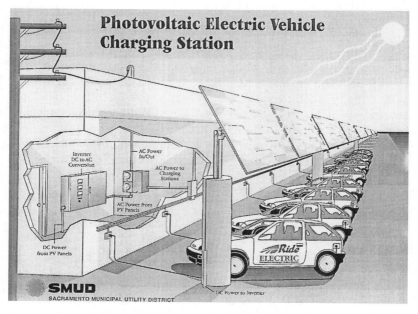

Figure 5. SMUD Photovoltaic Electric Vehicle Charging Station
Source: Sacramento Municipal Utility District, 1992.

vehicles, vans, and trolley buses. As figure 5 indicates, some of these charging stations will be powered by photovoltaic cells.

SMUD is also laying the foundation for a regional electrified transit agency, a process that requires a long-term commitment. Freeman expects that in 25 years electricity will be the dominant fuel for transportation in Sacramento County. "That is why we will hopefully be the clean-air capital of the country, maybe around 2010," he remarks.

The California Air Resources Board has mandated that by 1998, 2 percent of all vehicles sold in the state be zero-emission vehicles. At present, EVs are the only vehicles that can meet that emission standard. For SMUD, even the most formidable obstacles—range and price—to the mass commercialization of EVs are surmountable. First, by the mid-1990s, the typical EV is projected to travel about 80 to 120 miles on an eight-hour battery charge (increasing to 250 miles by the year 2000). Because the vast majority of people in the United States live in metropolitan areas and drive less than 30 miles per day, five days per week, range limits are not real limits at all. Recent studies indicate that the average distance of a daily commute in the United States is 24 miles; one-third of all fleet vehicles are driven less than 35 miles per day.

The price for the GM electric car, EV-1, which was first introduced in December 1996, is $34,000. Regarding this "sticker shock," SMUD believes that "prices will undoubtedly come down dramatically once mass production begins," just as they did in the early years of the U.S. auto industry when average prices dropped from nearly $35,000 per auto in 1890 to less than $10,000 by 1920.[36] Commercialization will be facilitated in California, where the major investor-owned utilities plan to spend more than $300 million for EVs and EV infrastructural development during the 1990s. The California Council on Science and Technology, in its 1992 Project California Report, estimated that the size of the market in the United States for EVs will grow to $8 billion in 2003 and to $24 billion by 2007.

Under Freeman's leadership, "SMUD plans to be an innovator and motivator in going beyond the 2 percent goal, making Sacramento a leader in the electric transportation movement." To meet this goal, the utility is testing and demonstrating electric vehicles in its own fleet and is in the process of converting its vehicles to electricity as quickly as possible. SMUD is exploring the formation of a partnership with Regional Transit to help finance and build the electric power supply system for electric buses to replace diesels. Most important, through its "EV Pioneer" program, SMUD is enlisting community support in order to develop a market and build the infrastructure necessary for the large-scale use of electric vehicles of all sizes—buses, vans, pickup trucks, and cars—throughout Sacramento by the late nineties.

"My vision is Bill Clinton driving down the streets of Tokyo in an American-made electric car in 1996," says Freeman.

The Arrogance of Ignorance   Nearly 30 years ago, in 1968, a group of activists who were fighting a power plant in New England sat in Freeman's Washington, D.C., offices and educated him about energy waste and conservation. He became one of the nation's earliest and most effective advocates for energy efficiency. Today Freeman is using his position as one of the United States' most innovative utility executives as the bully pulpit from which to lecture the nation on the "arrogance of its ignorance" regarding energy.

The reason behind this "energy mission" is that for Freeman, the utility industry's pivotal role in electrifying the U.S. transportation system goes beyond the obvious air quality and greenhouse effect issues and cuts to the heart of the nation's "real energy crisis," which is the nation's dependence on foreign oil for transportation. Our dependence has become a national addiction that will continue to threaten the United States' economy and national security. For this seasoned energy hand, EVs must become the next Apollo Project. "Folks," he chides, "almost thirty years ago NASA astronauts were driving electric vehicles on the moon. If we can put electric vehicles on the moon, we can certainly put them on the roads of Sacramento."[37]

Initially, the United States' dependence on foreign oil can be broken by electrifying the transportation system. However, by using natural gas as a bridge fuel, Freeman believes we can transition to a solar and hydrogen economy during the next century. In this scenario, rather than having chemical EV batteries, cars would be powered by hydrogen fuel cells. The United States could build "giant solar power plants in the desert" and use the electricity generated by photovoltaics for the electrolysis of seawater to generate oxygen and the hydrogen needed to power fuel cells. Unlike fusion power, which still requires major scientific breakthroughs, the transition to hydrogen requires a large developmental effort, and the main questions are economic, rather than technical. In Freeman's opinion, "If as many of us believe that we're in a race for the very survival of this high-energy civilization, then the economics are going to take care of themselves over time." The real obstacles to the solar and hydrogen economy, in Freeman's opinion, are "Exxon, Texaco, the nuclear power industries, the status quo, and most of the money in the world, which is lobbying for nuclear power, coal, and oil."

In this context, although the conservation revolution of California utilities is commendable, their efforts are still very modest. And Freeman believes we would be "extremely myopic" to think of energy as a California, or even a U.S., issue anymore. With world population exploding and with major regions of the world—such as Eastern Europe, the former Soviet Union, India, Brazil, and China—striving for industrialization and capitalism, it is difficult to expect them to conserve or not to burn "their damn coal" unless we can offer them a nonpolluting hydrogen future. In Freeman's view, "We're in a global environmental crisis and an emerging energy crisis of unknown proportion, and the only answer lies in the development of an alternative solar and hydrogen economy as a major federal initiative for high-tech industrialization."

Utilities are small players compared to the oil and automobile industries, who currently "will kill anything that would make cars more efficient." The solution, in Freeman's view, is for the president to form a new industrial partnership between the federal government and the utility, energy, and transportation industries while providing the economic incentives necessary to create a "USA Incorporated that can compete with Japan Incorporated." Without a federal initiative of epic proportions, we will not make the transition. The current market—or even the imposition of higher gasoline taxes—will simply not get us there. "I think the proof of my point," Freeman observes, "is that you have four-dollars-a-gallon gasoline in Europe, but you don't have electric cars. Let that sink in to the true believers in the free market."

"How crucial is this?" Freeman asks rhetorically.

> Crucial! I am not saying the fate of the world depends on it, because I've got reasons to believe that the Japanese or the Germans might do it. But it could very well be that the economic fate of the United States of America depends upon it. Because if we have to get out of the automobile and energy business, and end up buying these technologies from the Germans and the Japanese, then I don't know what the hell we are going to have to sell. And we are going to be hard-pressed to provide jobs. I think that this is the greatest industrial opportunity that America will have for a long time: to capture the automobile and energy industries of the future!

Both John Bryson at SCE and David Freeman at SMUD have proven the skeptics wrong in demonstrating that private and public California utilities can meet their growth requirements by replacing nuclear plants with conservation. Still, there is a profound irony associated with the conservation revolution in California. These visionary utility executives, who embraced the conservation canon of replacing utility plant expansion with "negawatts," are now poised to dramatically increase the penetration of the electric utilities into the vast, energy-intensive transportation sector. As a result, in the name of clean air and national security, the potential emerging collaboration between the electric industry and automobile manufacturers may lead to one of the greatest expansions of utility infrastructure in American history.

Impact of the Conservation Revolution   Enlightened leadership made SCE a pacesetter in implementing California's "Energy Efficiency Blueprint," proving that conservation is good for consumers, good for business, and good for the environment. At SMUD, citizen pressure converted a troubled nuclear utility into a model conservation and renewable power plant. Partially as a result of California's success, efficiency reforms are catching on at other utilities, including those in New England and the Pacific Northwest.

By implementing cost-effective measures in utility planning, pioneers such as Bryson and Freeman are at the forefront of a broader conservation and efficiency revolution that is sweeping much of the United States. At the beginning of the nineties, some 200 utilities were investing $2 billion into 1,300 conservation programs. By the year 2000, these programs should effectively replace demand for 24,000 megawatts, according to the Edison Electric Institute (EEI), an industry group. That is equivalent to 24 large power plants, or about 7 percent of current national peak demand.[38]

And that just begins to tap the conservation potential. Tough new national standards will lead to dramatically reduced consumption by refrigerators, washers, dryers, and other appliances. The tide of efficiency innovations now surging through the energy sector promises to reduce energy consumption and CO_2 emissions dramatically in six sectors that account for nearly half of all U.S. energy demand. These sectors are airplanes, cars and light trucks, electric motors, heating, cooling and ventilation, and refrigeration. A *Business Week* report entitled "Conservation Power" observes that "while Washington fiddles over a national energy strategy, these eclectic approaches are evolving into a de facto energy diet for America."[39]

As a result of the oil crises of the 1970s, a flurry of prestigious energy studies identified conservation as the United States' key resource for dealing with these crises.[40] Today a new generation of studies have not only reaffirmed that conclusion but also produced stunning projections for a viable clean-energy future. For example, according to *America's Energy Choices: Investing in a Strong Economy and a Clean Environment* (1991), "If current policies and energy-use trends continue, until 2030, national energy consumption will rise 41 percent, renewable energy will make only a modest contribution to our energy supply mix, petroleum consumption will increase by 16 percent, and carbon dioxide emissions will increase by 58 percent."[41] By comparison, in the report's most aggressive case—the Climate Stabilization scenario:

- National energy requirements in the year 2030 would be cut nearly in half, and renewable-energy sources would provide more than half of our energy supply.
- Our nation's petroleum consumption would steadily decrease to just one-third of current levels by 2030.
- Carbon dioxide emissions would be reduced by more than 70 percent by 2030.
- Consumers would save some $2.3 trillion in net fuel and electricity costs over the next 40 years.

Despite the practical benefits of building an energy-efficient economy, there are significant institutional barriers to such aggressive energy scenarios. Many governmental policies and marketplace incentives still encourage the wasteful use of fossil fuels and the inefficient allocation of energy resources. The greatest threat to further advances in conservation at the nation's utilities comes from "the mirage of retail wheeling," which in essence proposes to create a completely "open market for electricity" all the way from the power producer to the retail consumer. If enacted as proposed, it is highly likely that "retail wheeling would only partially realize the benefits of increased competition, and would severely undermine the long-term planning that has been so vital to the evolution of an efficient, environmentally sound electricity market."[42]

Regardless of the outcome of the retail-wheeling debate, the success to date of the conservation revolution represents a major victory for the antinuclear movement on several important fronts. First, over the past 20 years, the concepts of energy conservation and efficiency have been successfully implemented at leading utilities, demonstrating that these concepts were not impractical environmental pipe dreams. Second, progressive utility executives have proven that aggressive conservation programs can replace major large-scale base-load power plants as a cost-effective foundation for meeting long-term electric growth demands in the nation's most populous state. Third, in implementing the conservation option, major segments of the antinuclear movement have shown that they can effectively move from confrontation to collaboration with utility companies and regulatory agencies. And, fourth, a new generation of utility executives has emerged, bringing the lessons and principles of the antinuclear and environmental movements into the boardrooms of the nation's electric industry.

Mobilizing Principle 3:
Demonstrate Viable Alternative Solutions

In the early stages of the antinuclear and pro-safe-energy movement, energy activists could speak about alternatives to nuclear power only in theoretical terms. Such conceptual possibilities, no matter how meticulously documented, were easily debunked by nuclear power advocates, who pointed to the need for practical solutions to the United States' energy crisis. However, once major utilities (often under pressure from energy activists, independent power producers, and ultimately state public utility commissions) began successfully to integrate conservation and renewable energy into their power grids, then technical, regulatory, and public skepticism about conservation and renewable-energy alternatives to conventional power plants diminished.

Chapter Five

The Energy Entrepreneurs

Inventors must be poets so that they may have imagination.
—*Thomas A. Edison, 1925*

For all his love of poetry and fascination with the supernatural, Thomas A. Edison was "refreshingly modern," according to a biography by Neil Baldwin.[1] What distinguishes the man who "invented the century" from other early-twentieth-century scientists was his passion for imagining and building whole systems, not just disparate devices. Electric lighting illustrates his penchant for organic thinking. While designing the lightbulb, Edison was also creating an entire power infrastructure, the forerunner of the modern utility company. His Edison Electric Light Company, a predecessor of General Electric, made everything required to deliver illumination to the public, from lightbulbs to transmission lines to early coal-fired generators.

When asked to settle a dispute about what was his greatest invention—the phonograph or the lightbulb—Edison's response, scrawled in huge letters, was "Incandescent Electric Lighting and Power System."[2] One consistent sign of Edison's genius was his inclination to think globally long before achieving success locally (well before such thinking was fashionable). Edison wrote of the electric light endeavor, "All parts of the system must be constructed with reference to the other parts, since, in one sense, all the parts form one machine."[3]

Much like Edison, our next profiles in power are constructing innovative and integrated power systems. One, based on solar electric cells, will eventually allow us to "plug in to the sun" and "get off the grid." The other uses hydrogen—the most plentiful element in the universe—as the basis for a new, nonpolluting global energy infrastructure that can replace both oil and the internal combustion engine in the next century. Both of these energy entrepreneurs are designing renewable-energy systems that have vast potential for global commercialization.

The present generation of independent power producers (IPPs) and energy entrepreneurs benefits significantly from the wave of deregulation, restructuring, and competition that is sweeping through the utility industry in the 1990s. Utility deregulation, which began in earnest with the passage of PURPA in the late 1970s, has accelerated dramatically under the federal Energy Policy Act of 1992, which effectively dropped most remaining controls on the generation of electricity. However, whereas deregulation in the airline and telecommunications industries led mainly to increased competition and sometimes lower prices, the ultimate impact of utility deregulation may be a complete upheaval in the economics of electricity, perhaps to the point where it will be economically viable for individual homes and industries to unhook from the grid and make their own power.

Since the passage of the act, a vigorous debate has raged about how to restructure the industry. The most ambitious proposals call for the vertical dis-aggregation of the power business. Doing this would require utilities to divest their power plants, fostering competition at the wholesale generating level while permitting regulated monopolies to continue operating only in the transmission and distribution (T&D) area, where competition is counterproductive. In this context of increasing costs, exhaustion of central station economics of scale, environmental considerations, increasing competition, and the development of viable alternative technologies, the concept of a distributed utility (DU) is emerging as a replacement for the centralized utility (CU) of today.[4] In the DU model, modular and renewable electric generation technologies and specifically designed conservation programs can be "distributed throughout the transmission and distribution system and serve as an alternative to planned central generation investment and transmission and distribution system expansion."[5] In the extreme case, utilities will be out of the power-generating business altogether.

This transformation from the traditional utility model to a distributed model in which residential customers may eventually generate their own power—through rooftop solar systems and basement fuel cells—is analogous to the change from mainframes to personal computers that thoroughly revolutionized the computer industry. Such a transformation could improve efficiency and environmental quality by eliminating the need for both large base-load plants and additional power lines. As energy analyst Christopher Flavin points out, "A typical company with 50 power plants connected to its system today could see that figure reach 5,000 or even 50,000 by 2010. The change would be similar to that of a corporation that used three mainframe computers in 1980, and 30,000 personal computers in 1994."[6]

A significant factor in the decentralization of the utility industry is that the cost of renewable-energy technologies generated by IPPs has declined dramatically since the 1970s, and their reliability has been proven in numerous demonstration and commercialization programs. Globally, renewable-energy sources are far more abundant than fossil fuels, and renewables, in the form of biomass and hydro, already provide 25 percent of the world energy supply. As solar scientists Carl Weinberg and Robert Williams wrote in *Scientific American:* "Electricity from wind, solar-thermal and biomass technologies is likely to be cost-competitive in the 1990s; electricity from photovoltaics and liquid fuels from biomass should be so by the turn of the century."[7]

The dream of a safe and nonpolluting renewable-energy future is no longer the isolated rallying cry of eco–true believers. In 1995 the Union of Concerned Scientists (UCS) commissioned a study with three prestigious national energy and environmental groups that demonstrated that "if coupled with strong measures to use energy more efficiently, renewable energy could provide more than half of the U.S. energy supply by the year 2030."[8] The UCS publication *Renewables Are Ready: People Creating Renewable Energy Solutions* profiles the work of numerous grassroots renewable-energy ventures and argues that "by the end of the decade, renewable energy will have been carried by community activists and conscientious consumers from the realm of fantasy to an exciting and profitable reality."[9]

Lately this theme is being echoed by some of the world's most prestigious energy and economic thinkers. For example, the Royal Dutch/Shell Group has been one of the most successful forecasters in the energy business and the only group that anticipated both the 1973 oil price boom *and* the 1986 bust. In its "Energy in Transition" scenario, Shell projects that "renewables may make up a third of the supply of new electricity within three decades *even if electricity from fossil fuels continues to decline in cost,"* with the renewables industry growing to sales of $150 billion annually.[10] Likewise, in a 1995 article titled "The Future of Energy," the *Economist* suggests that a battle for world power has already begun on the fringes of the mighty $1-trillion-a-year fossil fuel industry that could force it into retreat in the coming century. The article concludes that "It is no longer reasonable to snigger at the dreams of those mad renewable-energy scientists."[11]

What are those mad scientists planning for in the early twenty-first century? Imagine a home that has maximized efficiency to reduce its power requirements by 30 to 70 percent and is also energy self-sufficient through a combination of solar electric panels on the roof (or even integrated into the building's roof and facades) and hydrogen fuels cells in the garage or basement. Such an energy self-sufficient home may completely reverse the current flow of power and money by generating its own electricity and selling it back to the national grid, or even by that time into a worldwide power grid. The grid may be all that is left of the utility business as we know it today, for in this "back to the future" world, the centralized electric utility may have "crumbled under its own weight."[12]

Two energy entrepreneurs have already staked a business claim to this vision of the future. However, they represent very different profiles in power. The first, John Schaeffer, a former hippie turned businessman, is building a renewable-energy retail chain and catalog company by helping consumers "get off the grid," mainly through solar electric power systems. The second, John Perry, a wealthy inventor-entrepreneur and friend of the Kennedy family, is drawing on his experience with the U.S. Space Program and Hydro-Lab to lay the technological foundations for the transition to a solar and hydrogen future.

Getting Off the Grid: John Schaeffer, Real Goods

We came to understand that knowledge, even more than solar products, was our most important product.
—*John Schaeffer, President, Real Goods Trading Corporation, 1995*

"I went to the woods because I wished to live deliberately, to front only the essential facts of life, and see if I could not learn what it had to teach, and not, when I came to die, discover that I had not lived," wrote Henry David Thoreau in 1854. Thoreau's "two year, two month" ascetic experiment at Walden Pond epitomized the self-reliant spirit of the anti-industrialists of the late nineteenth century.

As a sixties urban refugee in northern California, John Schaeffer embodies Thoreau's passion for independent living. But Schaeffer did not "turn on, tune in, and drop out." Instead, he dropped out, plugged in to the sun, and, in founding Real Goods (Real Goods Trading Corporation as of 1990) made a small fortune selling "products for creating a sustainable future." Whereas Thoreau sojourned in nature to escape the city, Schaeffer stayed in nature to plant a seed that may ultimately transform the city. As our fossil fuel–dependent civilization reaches its endgame, Real Goods' Solar Living Center, located in Hopland, California, offers an alternative model of a decentralized metaindustrial village—a high-tech, energy-independent, sustainable Walden of the future that portents the end of industrialism.

As a company, Real Goods represents a unique fusion of the sixties back-to-the-land movement, the pioneering spirit of the American frontier, advanced renewable technologies, and the dynamic nature of capital markets. But the Real Goods story is much more than a hippie version of the rags-to-riches saga and much more than a "high-tech commune meets Wall Street" twist to the American dream. In a broader context, Real Goods' success can be seen as a market referendum on the commercial viability of renewable technologies and a successful merger of environmentalism and capitalism.

With his long white hair, mustache, and goatee, Schaeffer is a mountain of a man who looks as if he would be more comfortable splitting rails than running a company. Dressed in blue jeans and a T-shirt, he laughs easily and frequently as he reflects on the humble origins of Real Goods, Inc. From a rural general store selling solar products to hippies in Mendocino County, Real Goods has grown into a $16 million public company whose stock is traded on the NASDAQ Small Cap Market. The corporate mission statement describes Real Goods as a company whose "merchandise provides tools that facilitate independent living and energy self-sufficiency."[13] Schaeffer proudly characterizes Real Goods as a Green enterprise that not only has helped pioneer the renewable-energy technology market but whose primary goal has been to educate the public through projects such as the annual Real Goods Tour of Independent Homes. In the tour's first three years of existence, nearly 25,000 people have toured hundreds of "off-the-grid" homes in the United States and Canada to experience first-hand the realities of a renewable-energy lifestyle. To further its educational mission, Real Goods designed and developed the Solar Living Center, a 12-acre environmental demonstration center for sustainable living, which opened in 1996 on Route 101 in northern California, just south of the company's headquarters in Ukiah.

In *Darkness and Scattered Light,* Jungian historian William Irwin Thompson conceptualizes the "metaindustrial village" as a new paradigm for the emerging postindustrial society. Thompson argues that a decentralization of industrial culture, accelerated by the computer and telecommunications revolutions that are ushering in the Information Age, and culminating in the return to what he calls the *metaindustrial,* is upon us.[14] This transformation away from urban centers will be accomplished, in part, through the implementation of renewable-energy and wireless telecommunications technologies, leading to the decentralization of power production and information distribution.

> The energy grid for metaindustrial culture will not be the center-periphery system of fossil fuels but the anarchic flow of wind and sun, a flow in which "the center is everywhere and the circumference nowhere." The culture of fossil fuels literally feeds off the past, off the world of the dinosaurs, but the culture of solar energy feeds off the light, and so the shift from the subterranean world of the coal mine and the oil well to the open horizons of wind and sun is really a shift in archetypes which will have profound repercussions in the collective unconscious.[15]

In important ways, Thompson's vision of a metaindustrial village complements Peter Drucker's description of the "Emerging Knowledge Society" and Alvin Toffler's "Third Wave." These models all describe a future in which knowledge has replaced natural resources as the world's most important commodity. Similarly, the knowledge of ecosystems and recycling technologies also drives Buckminster Fuller's vision of reengineering the industrial systems of "Spaceship Earth" to create the technological basis for a sustainable society. Real Goods is a prototypical knowledge-based company. As Schaeffer points out, "We came to understand that knowledge, even more than solar products, was our most important product."

"Getting off the grid" through the application of new knowledge has been John Schaeffer's corporate rallying cry ever since the birth of Real Goods nearly 20 years ago. It is through Schaeffer's remarkable success as an energy entrepreneur and his vision for independent living based on renewable technologies that Thoreau's ideals have been revivified in the late twentieth century.

The Real Goods Story   Real Goods was born of necessity. After graduating from the University of California at Berkeley in 1971 with a degree in anthropology, John Schaeffer moved up to Mendocino County. There he joined some friends at a 290-acre homestead for "urban refugees from New York, L.A., and the Bay Area," who moved there to live the "traditional back-to-the-land commune type scene."[16] They went to the woods to "live deliberately," Thoreau would have argued. In those woods, Schaeffer discovered "alternative energy" and the spark for his Real Goods vision.

The "eighteenth-century mentality" engendered by the practice of self-sufficiency was both romantic and fulfilling, Schaeffer recalls. "We milled all our own logs, built our houses, hauled our own rocks and gravel, and drilled our own wells." But after six or seven years, as the romance and novelty wore off, "people got a little tired and wanted to have a little more comfort." For Schaeffer, "it was the kerosene lamps that began to get old, and not having any refrigeration."

Almost by accident, Schaeffer "rediscovered" electricity, and with it the concept for a new business. "I discovered one day some 12-volt lightbulbs, which was the first thing that got me into this, in a hardware store, that were gathering dust. . . . so I thought 12-volt lightbulbs, what does that mean?" Before long, Schaeffer had strung up lighting throughout his house. By using his car and his 40-mile workday commute as a recharging station for his two batteries, Schaeffer created a makeshift independent power supply for his homestead in the wilderness. As Michael Potts, director of the Real Goods Institute for Independent Living, recalls, "He became the most popular person on the commune . . . whenever it was time for *Saturday Night Live*."[17]

After experimenting with the possibilities of self-sufficient power and realizing there was a need for "one store that sold all the products needed for independent living," Schaeffer opened his first store in Willis. "The first back-to-land store" he called it. The "New Age general store," his bankers tagged it. Schaeffer's first store carried everything for living out in the wilderness: "from gardening supplies to irrigation supplies, to clothing, to alternative energy supplies including batteries and converters." Real Goods was born.

"I remember the first Earth Day. I was in Berkeley in 1970, and back then it was just the total fringe wackos, who were looked at like idiots. Solar was equivalent to marijuana and acid . . . and now it's public policy," Schaeffer recalls. Ironically, the creation of remote, self-sufficient dwelling by the rural-revitalization and independent-living movements helped drive the U.S. market for solar electric, or photovoltaic (PV), power systems, which are manufactured by some of the world's largest energy companies. These companies include Advanced Photovoltaic Systems, Energy Conservation Devices, Kyocera, Siemens, Solarex, Texas Instruments, and Westinghouse.

In 1992 the U.S. PV market accounted for about one-fourth of the total world PV module shipments of 60 megawatts. According to the U.S. Department of Energy (DOE), PV system electricity prices are expected to drop, in 1990 dollars, from 25¢ to 50¢ per kilowatt-hour for remote stand-alone applications in 1991; to 12¢ to 20¢ per kilowatt-hour for high-value distributed-utility applications by 1995; and to 5¢ to 6¢ per kilowatt-hour for central grid–competitive applications by 2010 to 2030. During the same time frame, efficiency and reliability of PV cells will increase, and cumulative U.S.-installed PV capacity is projected to grow from 200 to 1,000 megawatts between 1995 and 2000 to 10,000 to 50,000 megawatts, the equivalent of 10 to 50 large power plants, between 2010 and 2030. For this reason, Bernard Gillespie, president of Mobil Solar Energy Corporation, believes that "It's not a question of whether photovoltaics will become a technology of choice—it's only a question of when."[18]

These advances in the PV industry have occurred despite the fact that the DOE's policies toward renewables over the last four decades have been less than favorable. From 1948 to 1994, only 10 percent of all federal R&D energy spending was allocated for renewable technology. "When Ronald Reagan was shown that Jimmy Carter's solar panels didn't work, he took them off the White House . . . discontinued the solar tax credit program," and reduced the federal government's R&D funding for renewable energy by 80 percent.[19]

While alternative energy was being mothballed by Reaganomics, Real Goods was operating three successful retail stores: one in Mendocino County, which made $750,000 in its first year; another in Ukiah; and a third in Santa Rosa. By 1984 these three stores, which catered mostly to the hippies and marijuana growers in the hills of northern California, were "doing $3 million a year." But the Real Goods vision was soon to be severely tested.

Although apparently successful, the company was severely undercapitalized. With a 15:1 debt-to-equity ratio, Real Goods could not get a loan to sustain its rapid growth. At the same time, Schaeffer was experiencing problems with his partner. Soon after selling out his half of the company—because his partner "would not sell out to him"—Schaeffer moved to Asia with his family and was suddenly "out" of the alternative-energy business. Six months later, Real Goods filed for bankruptcy.

Horace wrote that "the man who is tenacious of purpose in a rightful cause is not shaken from his firm resolve by the frenzy of his fellow citizens."[20] Driven by a burning desire to keep his dream alive, Schaeffer "came back to pick up the pieces." As he recalls, "the only thing left was the mailing list of 2,000 names." Scraping together his last $3,000, Schaeffer mailed out a "pretty ugly" 16-page catalog. To his amazement, within eight weeks, he had $30,000 in orders. In late 1986, Real Goods was rising from the ashes like a phoenix to realize its mission "to provide knowledge and products to redirect the world toward a sustainable future where all living things are recognized as interconnected."[21]

Between 1987 and 1991, Real Goods' revenues grew by more than 400 percent per year. Schaeffer was now convinced that "the proliferation of sensible energy use that was once envisioned as an environmentalist's fantasy was now happening routinely."

The $5 Million Pee   In achieving $4.2 million in sales in 1990, Real Goods had not only maxed out its $30,000 credit line at its bank but needed far more growth capital than the $100,000 loan pledged by a bank in neighboring Santa Rosa. With no sources of collateral and a debt-to-equity ratio of 11:1, going public became the company's only option for continued growth. In February 1991, a favorable article about Real Goods appeared in the *Wall Street Journal.* Schaeffer recalls the flood of calls that came in from all over the country "with all kinds of proposals." One man in particular, Drew Field, who had just written a book called *How to Take Your Company Public,* called and asked Schaeffer, "How would you like to do a direct initial public offering (IPO) and get $1 million or so in capital?" Although Schaeffer was skeptical, he invited Field up for lunch to discuss the IPO alternative. Although it still sounded "way to good to be true," Field had given Schaeffer his first insight into the power of public markets. Schaeffer began seriously to explore taking his backwoods company public.

The first question was simple: If we put stock on the market, will anybody buy it? To answer this, Real Goods conducted a poll of 2,000 of its best customers, people who had purchased more than $1,000 in products and had made purchases more than four times during the past year. To the surprise of everyone involved, the test mailing sent out to ascertain customer interest in a potential stock offering came back with pledges totaling $1.25 million.

At the time, the catalog industry, whose mailings had jumped from 5 billion pieces in 1980 to a staggering 13 billion pieces by 1990, was imploding under its own weight. But Schaeffer's idealism, products, and commitment to customers had created the catalog industry's equivalent of the goose that laid the golden egg. This was Real Goods' fanatically loyal customer base, which was connected to the company spiritually as well as financially.

In September 1991, Real Goods began the laborious process of going public. Within three and one-half months, its initial public offering was complete. At the end of the process, Real Goods had sold nearly 200,000 shares at $5 a share and raised $1 million in working capital. The response was so overwhelming, Schaeffer recalls, that "we had to send back $200,000 to $300,000 that came in after the deadline."

Now Real Goods was poised to become a "real company." Within two years after the IPO, Real Goods' sales had nearly doubled to almost $8 million. Schaeffer decided that another public offering was necessary. This time the offering fell under the SEC Regulation A rules and was opened up ("blue-skyed") in 47 states. Eight months and 600,000 shares later, Real Goods achieved its capital goal of raising $3.6 million. This time, the company "had to return almost $1 million" in past-deadline purchase requests.

Schaeffer recalls the events of the day of Real Goods' secondary public offering with amusement.

> We finally got on the Pacific Stock Exchange on April 11 of 1994, and, sure enough, the first day it came out, the four of us went down to the stock exchange and put on our suits and ties and went onto the floor. They closed the ticker tape as it went across for the first trade of RGT. It was $6 [per share], but it opened at $8 because there was so much demand. And actually—this is funny—I went to the bathroom, and it had gone up two points from the time I went to take a leak to the time I came out. Since I had two and a half million shares, and the stock jumped up two points, I always call that the "$5 million pee." It was the most exciting day of my life!

After two successful public offerings, Real Goods now has a solid financial base for growth under Schaeffer's philosophy of "aggressive conservatism." During the nineties, the influx of capital has resulted in dramatic net sales growth for the fledgling solar company: $2 million in 1990, $4 million in 1991, $6 million in 1992, nearly $8 million in 1993, almost $12 million in 1994, and more than $16 million in 1995. The company now has more than 600,000 customer names on its catalog mailing list; new retail stores were opened in Hopland, California, and Eugene, Oregon, in 1994; and the company is considering franchising the Real Goods concept to "spread our message to areas of the planet where mail order would not be feasible." Real Goods now sells thousands of products through its catalog, including solar panels and flashlights, energy-efficient coolers and lighting, recycled shoes and clothing made from organic cotton, and gardening equipment and natural pest controls. The catalog even offers electric cars and "the first solar robotic lawn mower."

Schaeffer is no longer living the simple life. As president of a fast-growth public environmental technology company, Schaeffer finds his greatest challenge to be balancing the diverse needs of his employees, his customers, and his shareholders within a spiritually oriented business philosophy wherein "all living things are recognized as interconnected." Schaeffer's unique blending of business and social activism is spelled out in the Real Goods mission statement, which states, "Using experimentation, invention, and creative solutions, we will strive to educate through our products, our communications, and our example, that a simple, self-reliant lifestyle is the best way of sustaining the planet's limited resources for future generations."

To fulfill this mission, Real Goods has instituted a number of innovative programs, such as the EcoDesk and the Billion Pound Goal. Through the EcoDesk, Real Goods internally audits itself to "get all departments involved and fully conscious of our waste stream, energy usage patterns, transportation, and recycling practices." Through the continued sale and implementation of its products, Real Goods is hoping to eliminate the production of one billion pounds of the greenhouse gas carbon dioxide from the atmosphere by the year 2000.

With Schaeffer's "rediscovery" of the lightbulb during his rural commune days, Real Goods was built on the concept of supplying customers with high-quality tools for independent living. The company was the first in the nation to retail solar electric panels nearly 18 years ago. To this day, the radical technology of "plugging in to the sun" has remained at the heart of Real Goods' sales strategy and corporate vision.

Plugging In to the Sun   Consider the following statistics. The earth receives as much energy from sunlight in only 20 days as is believed to be stored in the earth's entire reserves of coal, oil, and natural gas.[22] The equivalent of nearly 1,000 trillion barrels of oil strikes the earth's atmosphere in the form of sunlight, and the winds it produces, each year.[23] With more than 40,000 exajoules of sunlight falling on the U.S. landmass each year—an amount equivalent to 500 times current U.S. energy consumption—and with even the best estimates predicting the depletion of fossil fuel reserves within 50 years, it is clear that solar energy must play a paramount role in the coming energy millennium.[24]

But is solar energy economical? Or, restated in practical terms by Paul Maycock, former head of the U.S. Department of Energy's photovoltaics division from 1975 to 1981: "When can I get PV on a grid connected house that costs no more than the utility charges me?"[25] In exploring the viability of peak, intermediate, and base-load PV integration into the current energy landscape, both domestically and internationally, it is important to understand this technology in its historical context.

Humankind has always been fascinated by the power of the sun. The ancient Greeks incorporated it into their architecture by using what we now call "passive solar" design. By orienting their buildings toward the sun, they were able to capture its heat using thick masonry walls for absorption. Joseph Priestley and Antoine Lavoisier, the fathers of modern chemistry, used solar energy in many of their experiments, some of which led to the discovery of oxygen. And the first solar-powered steam engines were developed by Augustin Mouchot in the late 1800s using silver-plated reflectors.[26] But it was not until 1839 that French scientist Edmund Becquerel discovered that certain materials produce a spark when exposed to light. He called this the "photoelectric effect," and his discovery led to the development of the first solar cells by Bell Laboratories in New Jersey in 1954.

According to Michael Brower, author of *Cool Energy: Renewable Solutions to Environmental Problems,* PV cells are the most elegantly simple of all solar technologies.[27] Initially developed to power satellites in space, solar cells are now found in a variety of applications, including wristwatches and calculators. Since the late eighties, the Japanese have sold an average of 100 million of these devices annually, constituting nearly 7 percent of the total global PV market.

Similar to, but far less expensive than, computer chips, solar photovoltaic cells are semiconductor devices made of silicon. Sand contains silicon. Because much of the earth's surface is composed of sand, the raw materials for PV cells are abundant. The physics behind PVs is quite simple: When light photons strike certain substances, such as silicon, they have the ability to "knock loose" surface electrons. These negatively charged electrons and positively charged "holes" are then swept onto opposing metal contacts by the voltage created between two semiconductor materials. Closing the circuit between the two materials produces an electric current, typically .6 to 1.2 volts per cell. When wired in a parallel or series circuit, the resulting solar cell panel can produce modular amounts of current or voltage respectively.

The two primary PV technologies being used today are "crystalline" and "amorphous" silicon. Crystalline, or single-crystal, silicon cells were first developed for the space program back in the early 1950s and have been the cornerstone of computer microchip technology as well. They are created by growing large blocks, or cylinders, of silicon crystals and then slicing off thin wafers, which are used for cell production. Although they have the highest sunlight-to-electricity conversion efficiencies, nearly 23 percent in ideal laboratory conditions, they have historically been very expensive. This has been a contributing factor to PV technology's early cost prohibitiveness. However, concentrator technologies achieve lower costs by combining less expensive optical components with 34 percent conversion efficiencies.

In contrast, amorphous silicon is very cost-effective and is viewed by Schaeffer as "the wave of the future." Amorphous silicon is created by a diffusion process whereby the silicon material is vaporized and then deposited onto a glass or stainless steel substrate. The possibilities for usage are unlimited. Amorphous silicon can literally be incorporated into windows, roofing materials, building components, car sunroofs, and so on. One of the main drawbacks to this process, however, is the low sunlight-to-electricity conversion ratios, currently measured at only 10 percent in ideal conditions. But through continued research, amorphous silicon technology should be able to provide a viable, cost-effective alternative for PV's future. Other materials, such as gallium arsenide, copper indium diselenide, and cadmium telluride are also being researched in an attempt to find cost-effective silicon replacements for PV manufacturing.

"Photovoltaic (PV) power is a prime example of a good technology: permanent, sustainable, benign, modular, maintenance free, quiet, nonpolluting, and clean," states Schaeffer. By the year 2000, the U.S. Department of Energy predicts that the cumulative installed PV capacity of U.S. industry will reach 1,500 megawatts, nearly three times the current rate. Although the PV market is rapidly transforming—from remote stand-alone fringe applications, to distributed high-value utility applications, to direct competition with central utility power—many obstacles to the mass commercialization of PV power still remain. For one, cost comparisons between PV and grid-based energy production have always been skewed in favor of the latter. Schaeffer argues that

> When we deal with energy economics, the first hurdle we must get over stems from our uncertainty about the true costs of non-renewable resources. Should we do our calculations based upon the cost at the gas pump, and the electric meter, which are based upon short-term extraction and distribution costs? Or, should we take a longer view, and try to assess costs based upon the time it takes to reduce biomass to petroleum (500,000 years of more), and the time it takes to abate the pollution effects of imperfect combustion—or, for that matter, the half life of nuclear waste?[28]

Due to these "cost externalities," the high levels of government subsidies for fossil fuels and nuclear power, and millions of military dollars spent annually to keep the "Gulf spigots open and flowing," Schaeffer argues that "it is next to impossible to come up with an accurate and objective answer" for what nonrenewable power really costs.[29] But despite these historical obstacles, PV power is a technology "whose time has come."

According to the U.S. DOE, the present-day installed cost of PV is 25¢ to 50¢ per kilowatt-hour. This is projected to drop to 12¢ to 15¢ per kilowatt-hour by 1998. Thus, before the end of this century, PV will become an economically viable alternative to centrally generated grid-based power.[30] In fact, according to Shimon Awerbuch, a PV economics researcher, "utility-scale PV installation can expect to generate electricity competitively . . . in the range of $0.18–$0.21 per PV kilowatt-hour as compared to $0.16 for a conventionally generated kilowatt-hour." He concludes that "renewable generated electricity presently costs between 16 percent and 25 percent more than grid power," making solar power almost economical right now, without counting the "external" costs.[31]

As Carl Weinberg, former director of R&D at Pacific Gas and Electric Company (PG&E), states: "The rules of the present energy economy were established to favor systems now in place. . . . Hastening the transition to a sustainable energy economy requires a major shift in priorities."[32] With PV's 20 percent annual growth rate and the steady improvement in cell efficiency and manufacturing, this shift is under way. In fact, in northern California, where many homes have been built outside existing transmission lines, PG&E has already incorporated the use of integrated PV systems as part of its service. With the average cost for installing small local electric distribution lines running between $13,500 and $33,000 per kilometer, contrasted with the average cost of a 500-watt PV system (with enough power to run a home's lights, radio, television, and computer) of less than $15,000, PG&E has realized the viability of cost-effective solar alternatives.[33]

Some of the world's innovative energy companies, such as Siemens, Texas Instruments, SoCal Edison, and Westinghouse have devoted millions of dollars annually to PV R&D. This research, coupled with the new synergy between government and private-sector PV R&D stimulated by the Stevenson-Wydler Technology Innovation Act of 1980, the Federal Technology Transfer Act of 1986, and the National Competitiveness Technology Transfer Act of 1989, suggests that a major shift in solar electric technology and policy is occurring. From the PV-powered remote villages of Sri Lanka, to the building-integrated PV systems of Europe, to the solar-powered farming settlements of the Dominican Republic, to the off-the-grid alternatives available from innovative utilities such as Idaho Power Company, solar technology is here—and with it the sunrise of postindustrial society.

The Solar Living Center   "I imagine a transformation from the present post-industrial civilization to a new planetary, metaindustrial culture," Thompson prophesied in *Darkness and Scattered Light.* Without realizing it, Thompson may have predicted John Shaeffer's "most exciting project ever." In 1996, Real Goods held a grand opening celebration for a unique "demonstration center for sustainable living" called the Solar Living Center. Nestled on 12 acres of floodplain, just a few miles south of the company's Ukiah, California, headquarters, the center represents the culmination of Shaeffer's vision of an independent, sustainable, humanistic community, which inspired him to found Real Goods nearly 20 years ago. But the center also offers a living demonstration model of Thompson's metaindustrial village, a *meta*-industrial alternative to the *supra*-industrial future predicted by many social scientists.

Designed by alternative-technology architect Sim Van der Ryn, this nexus of research and learning offers an information age synthesis of alternative technology, virtual eco-reality, and New Age community. "When you come to Real Goods we want you to be overwhelmed with a sense of crossing into a more sensible world—a cool, green, comfortable world, a parallel universe that reflects everything for which Real Goods stands."[34]

The center site contains a 5,000-square-foot retail showroom designed like a "curved bird wing" to reflect the seasonal moods of the sun. This showroom, built with state-of-the-art nontoxic and alternative building materials such as rice straw and hemp—natural Hungarian cannabis hemp—will serve as a showcase for "the best materials and energy systems available in actual use." Part of this will be accomplished by enlisting corporate sponsors, who, in return for their financial backing, will have "a high-profile forum for showing off and demonstrating their projects" to the center's thousands of projected annual visitors. Thus the center will offer eco-tourists and holiday travelers passing through northern California's wine country an ecological alternative to the fossil fuel–dependent "World of Energy" found at Disney's EPCOT Center.

As expected, the center will be powered by large photovoltaic arrays (with the surplus energy metered back to PG&E via a line tie), as well as by other proposed forms of alternative power, including wind and hydrogen. Striving for complete environmental sustainability, Shaeffer and the Real Goods management team have envisioned a model eco-community that will incorporate all available wisdom and technology on sustainable building practices, renewable-energy systems, organic agriculture, and people-friendly office spaces. There will even be PV charging stations for electric cars, including the center's electric shuttle, which will transport visitors to and from "the discreetly hidden parking lot for the fossil fuel cars."

Along with advanced solar energy technology, the center will rely on a biological sewage treatment facility dubbed the "Living Machine." It is designed so that toxins and heavy metals are removed from human waste through a "biological process including the use of bulrushes, water hyacinths, lilies, and even brine shrimp. Raw waste is transformed into clear water in three to four days, vividly demonstrating that in a properly functioning ecosystem, there is no waste."

According to Schaeffer, the real "highlight and soul" of the project will be the innovative landscaping designs of Stephanie and Christopher Tebbutt, owners of Land and Place in Boonville, California. Their contribution includes the creation of a garden that, borrowing from the design of Stonehenge, will track the sun's journey across the sky and its effect on vegetation throughout the seasons. The site will reflect the diverse habitats of the world's four ecological zones (woodland, wetland, dryland, and grassland) and include an organic garden. A bed and breakfast inn, with a vegetarian restaurant, is planned for phase two of the center.

With the development of the Solar Living Center, John Schaeffer has come full circle from his hippie, counterculture, back-to-the-garden roots in the sixties and seventies, to his transformation into a successful energy entrepreneur in the eighties, to his creation of the high-tech commune of the future in the nineties. John Schaeffer's story has added a vital piece to the transformational landscape now upon us. Perhaps Schaeffer intuitively grasped Thompson's prediction that

> People are going to have to come together in new communities of caring and sharing; they are going to have to give up many of their energy-intensive ways to return to labor. What will be necessary in the movement away from suburban society will be a turn on the spiral in a rediscovery of the preindustrial village.[35]

And, perhaps, Schaeffer possesses just the combination of inventiveness and imagination that Edison so admired. If he does, then the Real Goods Solar Living Center may become more important as a model for the future than cities such as New York or Los Angeles because it represents the living seed for the transition from an inorganic supraindustrial to an organic metaindustrial civilization.

The Green Car and Hydrogen Power: John Perry, Energy Partners, Inc.

> *[An] inexhaustible source of heat and light from water.*
> —*Jules Verne,* The Mysterious Island, *1870*

"I have always been a tinkerer," proclaims John Perry, a highly successful high-tech entrepreneur and founder of Energy Partners, Inc., a Florida company on the cutting edge of hydrogen power.[36] "I built my first submarine in my garage back in the fifties, but fortunately it was a total flop, because if it had succeeded, I probably would have drowned." Perry's candidness is one of his greatest assets. "I'm a businessman," he states with pride, "and I know when I can find someone better to do it than I can." From his early accomplishments in modernizing the publishing business through one of the first commercial uses of computers in the composing room, to his achievements in the manned and unmanned submersibles industries, it is clear that Perry knows what it takes to succeed in business. "I guess you'd say the reason for my success is that I don't sit around and talk about it, I do it."

Perry has set his sights on the farthest reaches of the renewable energy frontier. Driven by the goal of becoming a global leader in hydrogen-powered fuel cell technology, Perry has taken Energy Partners to the gates of Jules Verne's wondrous vision: the hydrogen future.

Perry is a remarkable entrepreneur. Combining his passionate concern for the environment with his recognized business acumen in commercializing new technologies, he seeks nothing less than to shift the world energy currency gradually away from fossil fuels. His goal is to replace fossil fuels with a radically different medium of energy exchange—clean, renewable hydrogen power.

A native of Seattle, Washington, Perry graduated from Hotchkiss in 1935 and Yale in 1939. He also attended the Harvard School of Business Administration with one of our country's most dynamic presidents. "I sort of grew up with Jack Kennedy," Perry recalls. "I even dated his sister for a while." Growing up in the elite social circle of Palm Beach, Florida, made Perry keenly aware of the way in which social and political influence can accelerate the development of new technologies. Perry got his first business break in part because of his political connections.

After serving his country as a pilot in both the Anti-Submarine Services and the Air Transport Command in World War II, Perry came home and continued to work in both the public and the private sectors. In 1966 he was appointed by President Lyndon Johnson to the Commission on Marine Science, Oceaneering, and Resources, and also served as the chairman of the Technology Panel for the newly commissioned National Oceanic and Atmospheric Administration (NOAA). There, through his involvement with Hydro-Lab, John was first introduced to alternative power systems.

Now a permanent member of the Smithsonian Air and Space Museum's collection, Hydro-Lab was one of Perry Oceanographics's first creations. It was also the first submersible to use fuel cells, which are electrochemical power generators that convert the chemical energy of hydrogen directly into electricity. Commissioned by the Johnson administration and originally located off the Kennedy's Palm Beach mansion, Hydro-Lab was designed to simulate a weightless environment for the Apollo Space Program. Powered by an alkaline fuel cell, originally borrowed from Pratt and Whitney, Hydro-Lab achieved many underwater firsts. "One of the projects we did," Perry recalls, "was to put three aquanauts in it for four days in 55 feet of water, right off of Joe Kennedy's house in Palm Beach."

Before being decommissioned, Hydro-Lab spent many years underwater involved in research off the coast of the Bahamas at Perry's private island, where he has established an alternative-energy research center. Although Hydro-Lab's early success in fuel cell technology eventually became the inspiration for Energy Partners, it was in the area of underwater submersibles that Perry achieved his next business breakthrough. Through an earlier company, Perry Oceanographics, John Perry started building commercial submarines in the early sixties and became the leading producer of nonmilitary submarines in the world. As Perry recalls, he was the lone survivor because "there were a lot of billion-dollar companies that were getting in the act, but they were all building very expensive submarines for the Navy." This left a comfortable niche in the nonmilitary commercial market for Perry to fill. Primarily used in the offshore oil industry, Perry's submersibles were eventually replaced by the Perry-designed remote operated vehicles (ROVs). Soon Perry Oceanographics had become a world leader in ROV design and manufacturing.

With back-to-back successes in both the fuel cell–powered Hydro-Lab and the underwater submersibles industry, it was only a matter of time before Perry Oceanographics merged the two technologies. This high-tech marriage resulted in the first commercial submarine powered exclusively by a fuel cell and eventually gave birth to a successor company, Energy Partners, whose mission was the fulfillment of Perry's hydrogen vision.

Dubbed the PC-1401, Perry's submarine embodied 12 years of research on a variety of fuel cell technologies, including nearly $6 million spent in R&D from 1991 to 1995. Powered by a patented three-kilowatt closed-loop proton exchange membrane (PEM) fuel cell, which had already logged 16 successful underwater missions, the PC-1401 provided the technological foundation for Energy Partners' emergence as a leader in fuel cell technology. For Perry, the attractiveness of fuel cells had always been that "they were extremely quiet and safe." Because of the fuel cells' low heat and sonic signatures, military submarines all over the world may soon be using PEM fuel cell technology, similar to the prototypes tested by Energy Partners for the Australian Navy.

With this impressive string of high-tech ventures to his credit, Perry conceived Energy Partners' two most ambitious projects, the hydrogen-powered green car and the hydrogen gas station, as alternatives to the internal combustion engine.

The Decarbonization of Autocentricity　Modern energy history has recorded the progressive transition from coal to oil to, most recently, natural gas as the preferred fuel source. In essence, this history has been characterized by a single theme: *decarbonization*. Ultimately, complete decarbonization of the energy supply holds the key to a clean, inexhaustible energy future. As Jesse Ausubel points out in "Energy and Environment: The Light Path":

> For 200 years the world has been progressively lightening its energy diet by favoring hydrogen atoms over carbon in our hydrocarbon stew. . . . Coal has only one hydrogen for each carbon atom, oil two, and natural gas (methane), of course, is CH_4. If we are concerned about greenhouse gas emissions, smog and spills, decarbonization is the powerful, clear energy prescription. . . . The success of decarbonization will ultimately depend on production and use of pure hydrogen fuel (H_2).[37]

Because its combustion yields only energy and water vapor, hydrogen is the "immaterial material" and the most environmentally benign of all fuels. For this reason, Perry and many other energy experts see the "decarbonization of autocentricity" through the development of a hydrogen economy as the next great transition in energy history.

At the beginning of the twentieth century, 22 percent of the automobiles in the United States ran on gasoline, 38 percent ran on electricity, and 40 percent ran on steam power. In fact, at the First National Automobile Show in New York in 1900, electric vehicles were praised for being noiseless, odorless, and free from smoke. Yet today American motorists drive nearly two trillion miles per year, using one-half of all U.S. oil and spewing nearly two billion tons of CO_2—equivalent to one-third of the nation's CO_2 emissions and 8 percent of all global CO_2 emissions—into the atmosphere.

With a new car rolling off the assembly line somewhere in the world every second, and with more land being used in the United States for roads, highways, and parking lots than for housing (taking up an area roughly the size of Georgia), the internal combustion automobile has become the driving force of modern urban society. Unfortunately, as Robert Williams notes in "The Clean Machine," "The gasoline powered internal combustion engine, which has dominated personal transportation for three generations, has given us extraordinary mobility. But the technology has also polluted our air, forced us to rely on oil from the politically unstable Middle East, and intensified the long term threat of global warming."[38]

There is broad consensus among scientists that the burning of fossil fuels has created a substantial imbalance in the earth's atmosphere that may potentially alter its ability to sustain life on this planet.[39] Although safe levels of "greenhouse gases" are necessary to keep the earth warm and habitable by creating a blanket in our atmosphere, the overproduction of these same naturally occurring gases is the primary cause of global warming and the greenhouse effect. Caused by the buildup in the atmosphere of gases such as carbon dioxide, methane, and nitrous oxide, which absorb heat radiating from the earth's surface, global warming is considered one of the greatest potential threats to our planet in the next millennia.[40]

The burning of fossil fuels (coal, oil, and natural gas) is the main activity responsible for global warming and releases more than five billion tons of carbon, at least 70 percent of total carbon emissions, into the atmosphere. Because carbon dioxide, the most dangerous greenhouse gas, has increased 20 to 30 percent over the past 100 years, scientists are predicting that the average global temperatures could rise as much as nine degrees Fahrenheit by the year 2050. Studies suggest that concurrent with this temperature change, the rise in the planet's sea level may range between a low of 1.8 feet and an extreme high of 11.9 feet by 2100.[41] Even a low estimated rise in mean sea level would also cause massive shore erosion, destroy irreplaceable wetlands, and contaminate water supplies and drainage systems with seawater. In addition, researchers suggest that the long-term consequences of a large, rapid rise in temperature cannot confidently be predicted when juxtaposed with the fact that a temperature drop of only about five degrees Celsius accompanied the last Ice Age.

Even as the long-range environmental impacts of global warming continue to be widely debated in both scientific and political circles, it is clear that dealing with air pollution has become a political priority in the industrialized nations over the past two decades. One of the most ambitious plans for pollution control is the state of California's Low-Emissions Vehicle (LEV) program, signed into law in 1990. Simply stated, this program requires that 2 percent of all vehicles sold in California by 1998 be zero-emissions vehicles (ZEVs), increasing to 10 percent by 2003.[42] With as many as 13 northeastern states possibly preparing to follow California's lead (including New York and Massachusetts), the "2 percent law" has become one of the most significant pieces of environmental legislation to date in the transportation sector. (Please refer to chapter 4 for further discussion of how this legislation has impacted planning at two California utilities.)

As one of the most "autocentric" societies in the world, the United States is the leader in automobile-generated pollution. In the Los Angeles area alone, nearly 15 million gallons of gasoline are consumed daily. With the fate of the earth's energy future and global climate hanging in the balance, John Perry believes that "radical problems demand radical solutions." Perry argues that "to get rid of pollution" we must "get rid of the internal combustion engine." What are the alternatives?

On June 25, 1985, the world's leading solar-powered automobiles rallied to challenge the internal combustion engine. Marking the first ever race of alternative power, 58 odd-looking racing cars pulled out of Pomanshorn, Switzerland, on a 229-mile race to Lake Geneva. Dubbed the "tour de sol," this unique competition showcased the world's leading solar technology for automobiles. Although more than a decade ago solar vehicles averaged only 24 miles per hour, today they can achieve maximum speeds of 90 miles per hour and can go more than 200 miles on a cloudy day before recharging.[43] But are solar-electric or electric vehicles really the answer? Some think not.

According to Michael R. Seal, director of the Vehicle Research Institute at Washington University, "solar energy at the earth's surface equates to one kilowatt per square meter and the efficiency of the best solar cells allows them to collect only about one fifth of it," making them highly inefficient for power production for high-intensity applications such as transportation. "Even if you park in the sun all day in Arizona," he explains, "it's not going to bring in that much energy." Like other pragmatists, Seal asserts that "supplemental energy" is the most we can expect from the sun for transportation purposes.

In recent years, electric cars have received attention as a partial solution to the air pollution problem. For example, the California Air Resources Board reports that electric vehicles reduce hydrocarbons by 99 percent, nitrogen oxides by 80 percent, and carbon monoxide by 97 percent, compared to gasoline-powered vehicles. Unfortunately, electric vehicles may not provide the ideal replacement for the internal combustion engine. In a 1994 cover story entitled "Electric Cars: Will They Work? And Who Will Buy Them?" *Business Week* examined the feasibility of mass-market electric vehicle (EV) consumption. Citing California's ZEV law as the driving force behind this budding market, the article acknowledged a viable future for EVs but sounded a major note of caution: "The drive to build a worthy electric vehicle is every bit as challenging as the Apollo moon shots," *Business Week* observed, echoing a sentiment shared by the Big Three auto manufacturers.[44]

According to industry analysts, EVs still suffer from three main drawbacks when compared to gasoline-powered vehicles: they have shorter ranges, are substantially more expensive, and are extremely inefficient.[45] Although pundits claim that mass production of these vehicles will reduce costs in the long run, and that continued improvements in battery R&D will give EVs more starting power and greater ranges (up to 100 miles per charge), critics contend that widespread urban use may never be fully realized. Furthermore, Robert Williams points out that "total local emissions from the battery powered electric car system would not be reduced to low levels—at least not in the near term."[46]

The power necessary to recharge an EV's batteries will be produced largely by grid-based plants, displacing the majority of the vehicles' pollution redemption factors to the centralized power plants recharging them. In this case, for the power plants supporting battery-powered cars, while emissions of carbon monoxide and volatile organics would be near zero, power plant emissions of nitrogen oxides, sulfur dioxide, and particulates would be *higher* for battery cars than for gasoline-powered cars. In general, "system-wide greenhouse gas emissions for battery-powered cars would be more than half of those for gasoline cars, if the electricity were provided mainly at night by the average mix of coal and nuclear plants expected for the United States in the year 2000."[47]

As more energy is needed to power an ever-increasing EV fleet (projected to reach nearly one million vehicles by 2003), more and more fossil fuel and nuclear power plants will be necessary to generate the vehicles' increasing electricity needs. This, coupled with the enormous infrastructure necessary to establish a network of convenient recharging stations, severely limits the potential of EVs. Despite these limitations, U.S. Electricar, the nation's largest manufacturer of electric vehicles, reported in 1993 that over the next six years, the major California investor-owned utilities plan to invest $300 million in electric vehicle and infrastructure development.[48]

However, Perry believes that this development will not solve the real problem of shifting the full life cycle transportation system to clean power sources. In his view, widespread skepticism regarding the marketability of expensive electric cars with limited ranges, resistance to change by the major auto manufacturers, and ongoing pollution problems associated with an all-electric transportation system will ultimately facilitate the transition to the hydrogen future.

The Green Car   Perry observes that "When Thomas Edison created the light bulb, it wasn't the least expensive technology of its day. The kerosene lamp was the economical solution—but the light bulb was the better technology—and to mankind's credit it found market acceptance for its safety, convenience, and higher quality of light in spite of its initial higher cost." Similarly, scientists have long been searching for the "dream fuel," a clean, environmentally benign, nondepletable power solution that is economical, renewable, and capable of satisfying humanity's voracious energy appetite. Ever since Jules Verne envisioned an "inexhaustible source of heat and light from water," hydrogen, the simplest and most abundant element in the universe, has often been nominated as this fuel. Until now, hydrogen has been expensive both to store and to harness. But with recent advances in fuel cell technologies, former Clinton administration secretary of energy O'Leary has concluded that "hydrogen has great promise as a renewable source of energy for the 21st Century."[49] It is through the "rediscovery" of hydrogen and the development of the proton exchange membrane (PEM) fuel cell that Perry's company, Energy Partners, hopes to create a new energy paradigm.

In his seminal work *The Structure of Scientific Revolutions,* historian of science Thomas Kuhn investigates and ultimately deconstructs the myth of modern science.[50] Kuhn's analysis uncovers the hidden framework underlying scientific revolutions and the theories that encompass them. Through these paradigm shifts, as he calls them, Kuhn demonstrates how scientists have historically replaced one theory of nature with another, with each successive theory explaining more natural phenomena with greater levels of detail and accuracy than its predecessor, yet without any claims to inherent or absolute truth. Kuhn cites examples of this phenomenon throughout the history of science, such as the shift from Kepler's geocentric universe to Copernicus's heliocentric universe, from Priestley's theory of combustion to Lavoisier's, and from Newton's absolute universe to Einstein's relative universe. In all three examples, one scientific paradigm was pushed to its conceptual limits by the phenomena it was supposed to explain. Each successive, unexplainable "anomaly" contained the seeds for a new paradigm. For Kuhn, then, science is not the "steady, cumulative acquisition of knowledge" and detail about nature, but rather a "series of peaceful interludes punctuated" by a radical shift from one paradigm to another.

When viewed in this context, our addiction to fossil fuel technology can be seen as the last stage of a dying energy paradigm. The environmental implications of a mature fossil fuel–driven energy economy, the displaced environmental hazards that grid-based electric cars may bring, and even the temporary ad hoc solutions offered by hybrid vehicles cannot save the crumbling fossil fuel paradigm. A new energy paradigm is emerging, one in which both the medium and the mechanism for energy production are transformed. As with Edison's lightbulb, for energy entrepreneur John Perry, the hydrogen-powered fuel cell represents "a better technology."

More than 25 years ago, Perry had the foresight to envision the global potential of hydrogen power. Starting in 1969, he began to devote his time and considerable financial resources to the development of renewable-energy technologies and a global energy strategy. In a fascinating parallel with Jules Verne's *The Mysterious Island,* Perry established energy research facilities on his private island in the Bahamas for testing photovoltaics, windmills, and fuel cells. He also developed a system for making methanol from seawater and launched the first commercial submarine powered exclusively by a fuel cell power system. This resulted in a closed-loop system patent for integration of fuel cells into practical working applications for transportation, utilities, and military hardware.

Most recently, he established a company, Energy Partners, Inc., in south Florida to further his research into the development of a total energy supply system using hydrogen as the "energy currency of tomorrow." "The strategic objective of Energy Partners, Inc., is to become a global leader in the development and commercialization of hydrogen-powered fuel cell technologies." Over the past 25 years, Perry has made major contributions to the technological advances that today "make it possible that mass-produced fuel cells will be able to compete with internal combustion engines in automotive applications." For as energy expert Robert Williams argues, "By early in the 21st century, fuel cells could do to the internal combustion engine what those engines once did to the horse and buggy."[51]

According to Marshall Miller, fuel cell analyst at the University of California at Davis, "Fuel cell vehicles powered by hydrogen produced from water are the most promising transportation technology for the 21st Century."[52] Invented more than 150 years ago, fuel cell technology is the cornerstone of the emerging solar and hydrogen energy future. Fuel cells are electrochemical power generators that convert the chemical energy of a fuel (usually hydrogen or methanol) directly into electricity. Like batteries or PV cells, fuel cells are modular and can increase their power output by adding additional cells or membranes (typically less than one millimeter thick) to the fuel cell stack. When supplied with fuel (hydrogen) and an oxidant (air), fuel cells represent an energy conversion technology that produces electricity (about .75 volts at load per cell), with pure water and heat (approximately 66 degrees Celsius) as by-products. With these characteristics, fuel cells represent a quantum leap in energy technology. These electrochemical engines have no moving parts, create only a fraction of the pollution, and produce more than twice the energy conversion efficiency of internal combustion engines. As Helmut Weale, head of the Daimler-Benz AG research division that produced the first Mercedes-Benz fuel cell–powered van, exclaimed, "We are at the beginning of a new era of technology, comparable to the days when Gottlieb Daimler and Karl Benz were constructing their first vehicles powered by internal combustion engines."[53]

Energy Partners has already devoted more than $5 million to the rapid research and development of fuel cell technology, most recently focusing on the hydrogen-fueled PEM fuel cell and fuel cell power system. Many researchers believe that this type of fuel cell promises to be both compact and inexpensive enough for practical automobile and other transportation applications. First developed for onboard power during the Gemini space mission of the 1960s, the PEM fuel cell offers a potential combination of long life, low maintenance, and higher efficiency (60 to 70 percent for hydrogen fuel cells versus 25 percent for gasoline engines). A fuel cell engine would comprise several stacks of fuel cell membrane assemblies connected electrically in a series. A typical passenger car would require a fuel cell stack weighing about 125 pounds and occupying a space not much larger than the gas tank of a conventional car. According to research by Mark DeLuchi, "the total 'life cycle cost' of owning and operating a fuel-cell vehicle would be comparable to or less than that of an internal combustion engine car—for fuels available in both the medium term (years 2005 to 2020) and for the longer term—because of relatively low repair costs. In all cases, fuel-cell vehicles would have lower life cycle costs than battery-powered cars."[54]

In fact, by storing hydrogen in porous carbon, James Schwarz of Syracuse University's Laboratory for Advanced Storage Systems of Hydrogen believes he has found a way to make hydrogen storage both cheap and efficient. In 1993 Schwarz predicted a day when a person will drive into a gas station and ask for a fill-up of hydrogen. Cooled hydrogen will be pumped into two car roof tanks containing specially treated carbons capable of adsorbing large amounts of hydrogen gas, which would be delivered as needed to the fuel cells by computers. Using this technology, hydrogen-powered cars would be able to drive 300 miles before refueling.

During the 1990s, Perry's dream of one day completely replacing the internal combustion engine, or the "infernal combustion engine," as he calls it, began to take shape. In 1993 he introduced Energy Partners' first PEM hydrogen-powered demonstration vehicle, called the Green Car. Powered by three seven-kilowatt, low-pressure, air-breathing patented PEM fuel cell stacks, the Green Car demonstrates that PEM fuel cells are a viable transportation technology. Because fuel cell–powered cars are more than twice as efficient as standard gasoline-powered internal combustion engines, hydrogen could be almost twice as expensive as gasoline and still provide equivalent energy service. As opposed to the EV, the Green Car is truly a zero-emissions vehicle (ZEV), it is arguable that hydrogen is already competitive with gasoline, if pollution costs of the latter are taken into consideration. Although the Green Car was an excellent "proof-of-concept" project, the vehicle prototype was expensive, costing Energy Partners about $150,000, and is already "obsolete right now." Recently, the company has developed a prototype 10-passenger van, called a "transporter," which is being showcased to potential customers around the country.

Although Perry believes that large-scale applications of fuel cell power systems in the transportation industry are still a decade away, Energy Partners sees the independent power producers (IPPs) as an immediate market for hydrogen-powered fuel cells. There are nearly 2,000 municipally owned or cooperatively owned public utility companies in the United States, representing some 90,000 megawatts of power, or 15 percent of the entire U.S. electric utilities market. This figure is expected to double by the year 2001. With a shortage of generating capacity anticipated by the end of the decade, coupled with the problems of siting and building new central power plants, IPP applications represent a primary commercial focus for commercializing Energy Partners' stationary fuel cell power systems.

Perry has built his career by "doing the impossible." He dismisses the naysayers and critics who have superciliously dismissed fuel cell technology. "*Life* magazine came out here and said 'it's impossible,'" Perry says in a huff. "I think that's bullshit. I think if you work at it, persist and do it right, and you're honest about it, then you'll get there. So that's what I'm trying to do. And, believe me, I'll get there."

The Solar and Hydrogen Cycle   Through a combination of mobile and stationary fuel cell power systems,

> Energy Partners has developed a long term strategy aimed at gradually shifting the energy currency away from fossil fuels and towards clean, renewable hydrogen. The [Hydrogen] "Gas Station" concept is simple in nature and relies on readily available technology and resources. The basic premise is to produce hydrogen fuel at a centrally located facility and supply it to individual residences and vehicle fuel stations for use in fuel cell power systems and catalytic combustion units.[55]

Using hydrogen as "the energy currency of tomorrow," Energy Partners envisions a complete hydrogen-powered society, as described in figure 6.

In visualizing a solar and hydrogen future, Perry asks us to join him in imagining a better society, an environmental Camelot, if you will. Imagine a society free from all fossil fuel pollution. A quiet society, free from the sounds of internal combustion engines and motors. A society that has no need for imported fuels, no dangers from oil spills, and no energy dependence on foreign governments. A society that exists in harmony with the natural cycles of the sun, the wind, and the ocean. This vision has motivated Perry for a quarter of a century. And this vision is the inspiration for his most ambitious proposal to date: the Total Energy Supply–Hydrogen Gas Station.

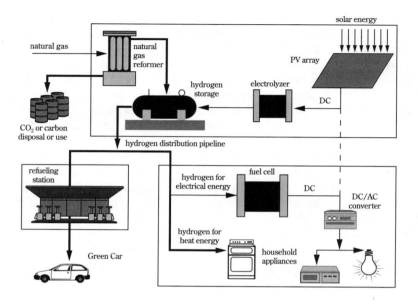

Figure 6. Energy Partners' Hydrogen "Gas Station": Using Hydrogen as the Energy Currency of Tomorrow
Source: Energy Partners, *Total Energy Supply: The "Gas Station" Demonstration Program* (West Palm Beach, Fla.: Energy Partners, 1993), 1–2.

Much like Edison, Perry does not simply tinker with new technologies. He envisions and implements total systems, whether they are for publishing, for submarines, or—most recently—for the redesign of the global energy system. "I fail every now and then," Perry remarks, "but I fail in the direction that doesn't matter. So I end up getting a total systems approach, which is what I learned in the Army when I was a pilot in World War II. They hammered it into our heads all the time. . . . you've got to see the whole system. There's no use in delivering a goddamn airplane if you don't have a bomb on it."

The "bomb" in Perry's total energy system is not the hydrogen bomb. It's simply a hydrogen-powered fuel cell, used to power vehicles and buildings. Elegant in design and already operating on Perry's private island in the Bahamas, the Gas Station concept uses both fuel cell technology and, ultimately, the natural solar and hydrogen cycles present in nature. The Gas Station's basic premise is to produce hydrogen fuel at centrally located facilities for use in mobile and stationary fuel cell power systems.[56]

Perry ultimately envisions large photovoltaic arrays supplying the power for the electrolysis of water. After being converted into electricity by PVs, sunlight will supply the current necessary to split water (H_2O) into its component parts of hydrogen (H_2) and oxygen (O). The hydrogen can then be stored in tanks to power homes, buildings, and factories or pumped via pipelines into the Gas Station for Green Car refueling. The process is cyclical, and the formula is simple:

Sunlight + PVs = Electricity + Water = Hydrogen + Fuel Cells =
Electricity, with heat and water as by-products

With electricity production present in two places in the equation, photovoltaics and hydrogen fuel cell technology combine to power a global energy system by plugging in to the solar and hydrogen cycles present in nature. As Peter Lehman and Christine Parra explain:

The solar hydrogen cycle is a natural process. Solar electricity is used to split water drawn from the environment into hydrogen and oxygen. The hydrogen fuel can be stored indefinitely and transported easily by pipeline. It can be used for heating by utilizing flameless, catalytic combustion, and for electricity production via fuel cells. The cycle is completed when the hydrogen is used and all the water originally consumed returns to the environment.[57]

Perry is pragmatic about what it will take eventually to commercialize fuel cell technology on a large scale and to build the massive infrastructure necessary for the transition to a solar and hydrogen society in the twenty-first century. "It's going to take a manufacturing facility backed by a large company that will see this as a way to make money . . . and that will be able to turn these things [fuel cells] out with proper quality and the lowest cost, competitive to combustion engines." For Energy Partners, the greater barrier to commercialization of fuel cell technology is cost. "No new technology is required; rather, the challenge is to advance manufacturing technology to a level which will reduce the cost of the fuel cell to a target of $1,500 per kilowatt for a complete PEM fuel cell power system," thereby making fuel cell system costs competitive with the installed costs of available conventional and alternative-energy systems.

For this to happen, Perry believes that fuel cell technology will have to be adopted and championed by the Big Three U.S. auto manufacturers and by other worldwide transportation industry leaders. This "migration to hydrogen technology" is already under way. Energy Partners is currently working on two projects with the Ford Motor Company. And Ballard Power Systems, Inc., a Canadian-based developer of PEM fuel cell technology, is collaborating with both General Motors in the United States and Mercedes-Benz in Germany. The project with Daimler-Benz AG is for the joint development of a compact, high-power-density Ballard Fuel Cell that was showcased in 1994 in Europe's first fuel cell–powered minivan, called the Necar. The Ballard program with General Motors is part of a U.S. Department of Energy project for a methanol fuel cell automobile.

GM scientists have already evaluated the cost and performance results of using Ballard PEM fuel cells in a Cadillac Fleetwood, Buick Regal, Chevrolet four-door Cavalier, and Chevy Lumina minivan. In each case, the vehicle was modeled to use methanol as a fuel with a processor converting the methanol into a hydrogen-rich gas that would mix with oxygen to produce power. According to the GM report, "a 60-kilowatt engine and fuel-processing equipment could be built in quantity for approximately $46 a kilowatt, or about $3,000, the approximate cost of a current internal combustion engine."[58]

Ballard, which today is Energy Partners' major competitor, is using PEM fuel cell technology originally developed by Perry. It was in the late 1960s that Perry borrowed an experimental fuel cell from Pratt and Whitney and put it into the U.S. Hydro-Lab project. Then, in the late 1980s, he put the first fuel cell into a submarine. Later, Energy Partners helped develop the first fuel cell for the Ballard group. As Perry recalls, "They built it and sent it down to us for testing, and we refined and tested it and sent it back to them 12 times before they got it right. It was the same cell we used in submarines, still sitting right out back. It's the PEM system that we built."

After receiving major infusions of capital through private placements from 1991 to 1993 and a $15 million public offering in 1993, Ballard has emerged as a world leader in the "development and commercialization of environmentally clean, reliable and cost-effective fuel cell based power generation systems . . . innovative power solutions for stationary and transportation applications."[59] Ballard's corporate goals for 1994 to 1995 were ambitious and included

Technology—commencement of pilot plant production of Ballard's low-cost proton exchange membrane;

Transportation systems—demonstration of a zero-emissions engine minivan and transit bus for transit fleets powered by Ballard Fuel Cells; and

Stationary systems—installation of a 30-kilowatt fuel cell power plant supplying power to an industrial facility and design development of a 250-kilowatt fuel processor for a commercial prototype natural gas power plant.[60]

As these goals are achieved, both Energy Partners and Ballard come closer to convincing the doubters that by 1998 customers around the world will begin to use fuel cell power systems on a large commercial scale. While focusing on the technical obstacles at hand, Perry continues to look toward the future. He predicts that in less than a century, our entire global infrastructure for power generation and distribution will be based on hydrogen. Through solar- and wind-generated electrolysis of fresh and sea water, we will draw on an inexhaustible supply of hydrogen, pump and ship it around the world to power fuel cells, and return the nonpolluting by-product—water—to the wells and aquifers to be used again. With the dawn of the solar and hydrogen age, the solar and hydrogen cycle will become a practical reality.

To the skeptics, Perry defiantly shouts his motto, "Nothing is impossible!" It is a motto that embodies his philosophy of life and business. It represents a lesson he learned in college, one that has inspired him throughout his career as an inventor and energy entrepreneur.

> I was a student at Yale. I think I was in my second or third year. There was a lecturer, Alexander P. Disaversky, who was recognized as the world's foremost authority on aerodynamics. And this friend of mine, who was with me most of my life here in business, named Bill Attaberry, and I went and listened for two hours while that guy explained why you could never exceed the speed of sound. Today, when I take the Concorde to Europe, I love to see the pilot's instruments where it says "Mach 2." So, to this day I say "Nothing is impossible."

Like Jules Verne a century ago, John Perry has retreated to his "mysterious island" to perfect a hydrogen-powered energy system that will usher in the dawn of the solar and hydrogen age.

Impact of the Energy Entrepreneurs   Were Jules Verne (1828–1905), the preeminent futurist of the last century, alive today, he would be delighted. It took the Apollo Program to accelerate the development of both solar electric panels and hydrogen fuel cells so that these energy technologies could journey from space back to earth as prime renewable power sources of the future.

Although PVs will not become commercially grid-competitive until the end of the decade, and hydrogen not until early in the next century, these energy systems represent the cutting edge of a host of renewable-energy technologies—most of which are available and competitive today. These renewable technologies include biomass, geothermal, hydropower, solar thermal, and wind, which have the advantages, in comparison to nuclear and coal plants, of relatively short construction lead times and of making up 92 percent of the "accessible energy resource base" available in the United States.[61]

Despite considerable obstacles and a nearly sevenfold decrease in federal R&D funding throughout the 1980s, renewable-energy technologies have thrived and are now ready to offer the United States significant energy options for the future.[62] With aggressive energy efficiency and conservation programs reducing U.S. electric demand by as much as 30 percent, there is a growing consensus that renewable energy could provide as much as 50 to 70 percent of all U.S. energy needs by about the year 2030.[63]

This generation of energy entrepreneurs has been indispensable to the antinuclear movement's efforts to reconceptualize the energy debate in all forums—at the plant, utility, state, regional, and national levels—as more than a gloomy choice of building either additional nuclear or fossil fuel plants. In demonstrating the technical and economic viability of a nonnuclear future that minimizes the United States' reliance on fossil fuels, the energy entrepreneurs have been able to color in the antinuclear movement's irresistible vision of an alternative-energy future. The application of Jeffersonian ideals of decentralized democracy to energy policy has inspired a broad coalition of citizens, business leaders, and public officials to complement the efforts of antinuclear activists working toward a safe-energy future. The viability of renewable energy has also reframed the antinuclear debate from its original narrow focus *against* nuclear power to a broader agenda *for* renewable energy as a positive solution to the United States' energy dilemma.

The nuclear industry and its advocates continue to argue that renewable-energy technologies are "idealistic" and "futuristic," whereas nuclear power provides the only proven nonpolluting solution to global warming. Representative of this view is the observation of Dr. Hans Blix, director general of the International Atomic Energy Agency, that "we need to escape from the greenhouse, but we need also to escape from the dreamhouse! Let us respect those who withdraw to the countryside to cultivate biodynamic carrots and get their electricity from a windmill. But don't let us believe that they have the recipes for the rest of us."[64] The emergence of a sophisticated independent power and renewable-energy industry has allowed the supporters of the antinuclear movement to avoid being labeled as Luddites or anti-progress eco-extremists by their opponents.

Conversely, the antinuclear movement has been instrumental in accelerating the process of utility deregulation, which was essential for the expansion of the renewable-energy industry. With electric generation representing nearly 45 percent of U.S. energy use, utilities obviously represent a major market opportunity for renewables. Although the utilities escaped the early 1970s era of deregulation that swept through the airline, telephone, banking, and transportation industries, the nuclear power debacles of the 1970s and 1980s made the once irreproachable power industry vulnerable to public and governmental scrutiny. Once the utilities became mired in nuclear power failures, the declining cost advantage of being a monopoly abruptly ended. As utility managers began to make significant economic errors on nuclear power projects, they were perceived no longer as benign technocrats but as callous monopolists willing to take inordinate risks with the public's money. Of course, the nascent procompetition utility deregulation lobby was tremendously strengthened by the entry of major engineering firms (Bechtel, Black and Veatch), manufacturing firms (GE, Westinghouse), and energy firms (ARCO, Siemens) into the independent power business.

Certainly, renewable energy and deregulation have made strange bedfellows. But with the retail wheel of utility deregulation still in spin, increased competition for utilities may turn out to be a double-edged sword for energy activists. For decades, antinukers and environmentalists have been pounding on the utilities in regulatory hearings and with lawsuits to make the utilities operate without polluting. As a result, many power companies now attempt to operate cleanly. However, just as most utilities appear to have incorporated environmental costs into their operations, deregulation may cause environmental protection to be sacrificed on the altar of profits in an increasingly competitive environment. As a result, the antinuclear and environmental movements, which once saw the utilities as the enemy, are now making alliances with progressive utilities as the institutions most able to incorporate conservation, efficiency, and environmental costs into long-range power planning and financing.

Furthermore, deregulation may even help revive nuclear power, creating the opportunity for consortia of plant manufacturers and builders to construct their own independent plants, unregulated by state power commissions, and sell their power on the open market. In a high-risk business, divorced from utility economics and regulation, a new generation of "inherently safe" nuclear plants may once again be perceived as viable investments with the risks borne by shareholders instead of ratepayers.

Ultimately, energy entrepreneurs such as Perry and Schaeffer have taken the world to the brink of a complete energy revolution. Indisputably, their modern quest for the holy grail of inexhaustible, nonpolluting power was made possible by the visionary recasting of the entire energy debate into a new paradigm offering a choice between the "hard path" and the "soft path."

Our next profiles in power, Amory and Hunter Lovins, are the couple who single-handedly redefined the global energy debate.

Mobilizing Principle 4:
Combine Economics with Environmentalism

Energy activists won major victories when nuclear power became the most expensive conventional energy option just as energy efficiency was emerging as the least-expensive way to meet the United States' future electric demand. The conservation revolution is therefore one of those rare ecologically sensitive arenas where there are significant opportunities to earn profits while simultaneously meeting environmental objectives. There is no doubt that the merger of sound business principles and reduced utility rates with the environmental benefits of energy efficiency and clean air has created significant incentives for utilities to support renewable energy over new conventional nuclear power or fossil fuel plants. Likewise, by founding innovative renewable-energy businesses, energy entrepreneurs are positioning themselves to capture a share of the vast emerging industry for advanced energy and environmental technologies.

Chapter Six

The Dawn of the Solar Age

Perhaps every science must start with metaphor and end with algebra.
—Max Black, philosopher

In 1996, Joseph Romm and Charles Curtis, high-level officials in the U.S. Department of Energy, wrote an article entitled "Mideast Oil Forever?"[1] The article contains an urgent plea to stop congressional budget cutters from ending the United States' leadership in renewable-energy technologies that could "generate hundreds of thousands of high-wage jobs, reduce damage to the environment, and limit our costly, dangerous dependency on oil from the unstable Persian Gulf region."[2] Romm and Curtis ask us to

> Imagine a world in which the Persian Gulf controlled two thirds of the world's oil for export, with $200 billion a year in oil revenues streaming into that unstable and politically troubled region, and America was importing nearly 60 percent of its oil, resulting in a $100-billion-a-year outflow that undermined efforts to reduce our trade deficit. That's a scenario out of the 1970s which can never happen again, right? No, that's the "reference case" projection for ten years from now from the federal Energy Information Administration.[3]

The authors then invite us to imagine another world, one in which fossil fuels have become a "sunset industry" entering a slow, steady decline toward oblivion; renewable-energy sources account for more than one-third of all new electricity generation; the "renewables industry" has annual sales of $150 billion; and the fastest-growing new power source worldwide is inexhaustible, nonpolluting energy from the sun. This is not an environmentalist's fantasy. It is a major oil company's—the Royal Dutch/Shell Group—planning scenario for three to four decades from now, or about 2030.

This alternative future was first envisioned by physicist Amory B. Lovins, who proposed a new metaphor for U.S. energy strategy called the "soft energy path." This radical reconceptualization of the energy issue as a fundamental choice between "the hard path" and "the soft path" was originally presented two decades ago in Lovins's seminal article "Energy Strategy: The Road Not Taken," which first appeared in *Foreign Affairs* in 1976, soon after the first global oil shock of the Middle Eastern crisis of 1973 to 1974.[4]

According to sociologist Robert Nisbet, "metaphor is our means of effecting instantaneous fusion of two separated realms of experience into one illuminating, iconic, encapsulating image."[5] Metaphors transform thinking by offering a conceptual way of proceeding from the known to the unknown.

Lovins created a new energy metaphor by a brilliant fusion of physics, economics, and energy policy. He suggested that we could generate more with less by dramatically conserving energy, at a time when the conventional wisdom, both in the traditional energy industry and in the environmental community, was that in response to the energy crisis, the United States had to generate more of everything— more coal and nuclear plants, more renewable-energy sources.

Furthermore, Lovins's predictions were dramatic. At the height of the energy crisis, with the pundits crying that "the sky is falling," Lovins had the audacity to argue that conservation could reduce energy needs so dramatically that oil would not run out and energy prices would plummet as well. He projected that by 2025 *all* U.S. gross primary energy use could derive from a combination of "soft technologies," primarily conservation and a mixture of appropriate renewable technologies. Unlike President Carter, who declared the energy crisis to be "the moral equivalent of war," Lovins was not asking Americans to sacrifice or to give up "hot showers and cold beers."

Lovins was suggesting that the United States could comfortably support its industrial base and current lifestyle by using just 30 percent of current electricity-generating capacity and that the conservation investment needed to produce those savings was available at a long-term cost of less than one ¢ per kilowatt-hour. Compared to average new generating capacity costs of about six ¢ per kilowatt-hour, investments in decreasing the demand for electricity are obviously "best energy buys," even without any consideration of the decrease in pollution and the increase in national security they provide.

Today, the projections Lovins made in the 1970s appear to have been conservative. After two decades of advances in efficiency and renewable technology, Lovins calculates that if America as a whole achieves electric efficiency at the actual rate implemented in southern California during the 1980s, then national power demand would fall by several percentage points even as gross national product (GNP) rises. Although gasoline sells for less in real-dollar terms than it did in the 1960s, since Lovins's article was published, total U.S. energy use per constant dollar of GNP has declined 23 percent.[6] Still, Lovins believes we can do much better. In 1992 he argued that "although we've already cut the [national] energy bill $150 billion a year, we're still wasting twice that much. We could substitute efficiency [technology] that's on the market, works better and cost less than waste is costing and save about $300 billion a year—slightly more than the entire military budget of $10,000 a second."[7]

Lovins's soft-path metaphor reframed the entire energy debate. Both his essay and *Soft Energy Paths,* the book that elaborated his ideas, provided a brilliant synthesis of cost and technical data, offering an irresistible utopian vision of a nonnuclear, non–fossil fuel future.[8] Moreover, his soft path provided the first significant challenge to the nuclear and utility industries' claims of technical invincibility and economic credibility in defense of hard-path centralized technologies. Most significantly, Lovins's work laid the foundations for the transition from the "age of oil" to the dawn of the solar age.

Over the past two decades, global leaders have been chastened by economic recessions caused by Middle East oil shocks and by the threat of climate change due to the acceleration of greenhouse gases caused by the increased use of oil and coal. As a result, the world energy economy is poised on the brink of a power shift as fundamental as the changeover from "king coal" to "black gold" at the beginning of the twentieth century.

Our final profiles in power are the harbingers of the coming energy revolution. Amory and Hunter Lovins, cofounders of the Rocky Mountain Institute in Colorado, are the revolution's Thomas Jeffersons, advocating the United States' independence from fossil fuels and from the political tinderbox of the Middle East. Christopher Flavin, senior energy expert at the Washington-based Worldwatch Institute, is the revolution's Paul Revere, circling the globe as a peripatetic town crier for the new energy technologies that are ushering in the dawn of the solar and hydrogen era.

The Soft Energy Path:
Amory and Hunter Lovins, Rocky Mountain Institute

> *Two roads diverged in a wood, and I—*
> *I took the one less traveled by,*
> *And that has made all the difference.*
> *—Robert Frost,* The Road Not Taken, *1916*

"If you had a list of the top ten energy experts in the world, Amory would have the top five spots," says Charles Komanoff, reflecting on the universal admiration Amory Lovins commands among energy experts around the world. Typically, in the country-and-western song, it's the rodeo-loving drifter who keeps riding off into the sunset, leaving the woman to tend the hearth. But in the case of Amory and his wife, Hunter Lovins, the cowgirl and the physicist have reversed roles.

"Amory is a four-eyed, classical music–loving physicist, and I'm a hell-bent-for-leather, Jack Daniels–drinking cowgirl. What we've come to is simply to love each other a lot, respect each other's lifestyles, and work together," says Hunter, an attorney, environmental educator, and former rodeo rider.[9] Wearing a black cowboy hat and jeans with a thick Champion rodeo belt, Hunter administers the Rocky Mountain Institute while Amory directs its research and circles the globe carrying his efficiency message to heads of state and corporations. Together, Amory and Hunter Lovins have teamed up to build a successful marriage, to develop the Rocky Mountain Institute into a prestigious resource conservation think tank, and to become the world's preeminent ambassadors for an alternative-energy future.

The Road Not Taken?   "It's nice to see so many folks whose activities make me look terribly reasonable," quips Amory Lovins as he begins his keynote address to the "Conference for a Nuclear-Free 1990s," convened by a coalition of antinuclear groups in Washington,

D.C., in April 1991.[10] This modern Prometheus then rattles off a barrage of facts documenting how much energy the United States has "stolen from the gods" since the nation began to follow the "road not taken" down the soft energy path he introduced nearly 15 years ago:

- Efficient use of electricity can save four times as much electricity as all U.S. nuclear plants make at about $1/7$ the cost of just running them, even if building them cost nothing, and about $1/20$ of the cost of building and running them.
- The French nuclear program effectively bankrupted the national utility. Nuclear power has been rejected in all market economies and thrives only under central planning. It has consumed probably a trillion dollars but delivers less energy than wood. Since 1979 it has added only 8 percent as much energy supply as savings have.
- Five national labs project that renewables in the year 2030 could cost-effectively deliver 70 to 125 percent as much electricity as the nation uses today.

"It seems to me that at the crux of the nuclear debate is how nuclear power relates to what we could do instead," Amory preaches. The staunchly antinuclear audience treats Amory like a messiah who has come to lead them out of the plutonium-endangered wilderness. Without doubt, Amory is the person most directly responsible for giving the antinuclear movement something to work *for*—a safe-energy future—as opposed to waging a series of seemingly endless campaigns *against* nuclear power plants. His thick eyeglasses and mustache are reminiscent of Charlie Chaplin, and Amory injects a full measure of comic relief into his speech about the value of energy conservation. But all joking aside, waving a calculator in one hand and a highly efficient lightbulb in the other, Amory epitomizes the "revenge of the nerds" in the nineties. Amory Lovins is to energy what Bill Gates is to computers. Both men have completely reconceptualized their industries.

In an age when the term *genius* has been grossly overused, Amory has been universally recognized as a child prodigy. He began composing complex music at the age of 11. He was taking college math courses while still in high school. He was an Oxford don at 21. After carrying his energy gospel to more than 20 countries and being awarded five honorary degrees, Amory and his wife Hunter were awarded the 1983 Right Livelihood Award, which is considered by many to be an alternative Nobel Prize.

What is so unique about this person whom *Newsweek* called "one of the West's most influential energy thinkers"? Partially, it is the lucidity with which he presents his radical ideas on energy. This has earned him the respect even of critics who hold opposing views. Dr. Alvin Weinberg, the pronuclear former director of the Oak Ridge Laboratory, called Amory "the most articulate writer on energy in the world today." The *Wall Street Journal* listed him among the "top 39 people in the world most likely to change the course of business in the 1990s."

It was David Brower, founder of Friends of the Earth, who first encouraged Amory to use his training as a physicist and experience as an outdoorsman to challenge the conventional thinking on energy. Praising the young scientist, Brower observed, "Where most of us use 10 percent of our brainpower, Amory uses 90. He is extraordinarily dedicated. He's insightful, intuitive, great with numbers. He sees the linkages better than almost anybody. He's an absolute genius."[11]

In the seventies, Amory predicted that the strategy of building more central fossil fuel and nuclear plants would "fall of its own weight" because it was too slow, difficult, and costly. "But," he observes, "it is where you get to, if the questions you ask are simply where to get more energy, from any source, at any price." For Amory, it is a basic scientific dictum that "the question you ask determines the answer you get." So "if you want to foresee how people will behave in a competitive marketplace, then you have to ask a different question." The right question: "What do we want all of this energy for?" Deriding nuclear plants as the energy equivalent of "cutting butter with a chain saw," Amory focused on the end use of energy rather than on the supply of energy. For each end use, he suggested that we had to ask "how much energy, of what kind, from what source, and at what scale is going to do this task in the cheapest way?"

Hunter Lovins attributes Amory's conceptual breakthroughs on the energy issue to "helicopter thinking."

> He has that kind of lateral-thinking mind. While most people pursue things logically and linearly, Amory suddenly hops sideways in unpredictable directions and makes connections that most people just don't see. He also has a tendency to try to go back to first principles. I think that's due to his training in physics. When he's dealing with an issue, he tries to understand its root causes and he tries in particular to under-

stand the questions to ask. Rather than searching for answers to questions that other people have posed, accepting the definition of the problem as others have set it, he tries to go back a step further and understand what are the appropriate questions. That frequently leads you in very different directions and much more productive directions. That's in a sense what he did with his soft-path thesis.

Insurmountable Opportunities　It was the publication of the *Foreign Affairs* article, followed by the book *Soft Energy Paths,* that launched Amory as an international energy expert. Nearly everyone was saying that "we are running out of energy and, therefore, we need more—of any type, at any cost." Amory proclaimed that "the emperor has no clothes" when he innocently suggested that "it was cost effective to save large quantities of energy." Lovins argued that we can use existing energy far more wisely and get far more bang for our energy dollar. "We understand too little the wise use of power. We're like somebody who can't keep the bathtub hot because the water keeps running out. Before we buy a bigger water heater, we ought to get a plug."

Amory ended his "Energy Strategy" article with a plea for action. "These choices may seem abstract, but they are sharp, imminent and practical. We stand at a crossroads: without decisive action our options will slip away. . . . Delay in widely deploying diverse soft technologies pushes them so far into the future that there is no longer a credible fossil-fuel bridge to them: they must be well under way before the worst part of the oil-and-gas decline. . . . We shall not have another chance to get there."[12]

As figure 7 shows, by following the soft path until 2025, nuclear, oil, gas, and coal are replaced by hydropower, biomass, solar, wind, conservation, and, above all, efficiency. Because the soft path changed forever the thinking of the energy industry and the international energy debate, Lovins's ideas sparked a firestorm of criticism. Energy experts crucified Lovins as an idealist, eco-extremist, tree hugger, and impractical dreamer. With absolute confidence in his thesis, Amory stood his ground and challenged his critics to prove him wrong. "All knowledge starts as heresy," he chided them.

Soft Energy Paths was immediately hailed as a seminal work. It joined an elite handful of contemporary works that have fundamentally changed the way we think about our world. These include Rachel Carson's *Silent Spring,* which first exposed the environmental and

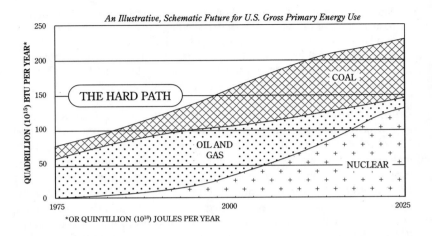

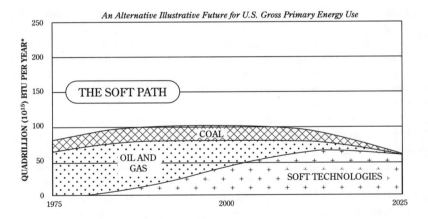

Figure 7. Energy Strategy: The Hard Path and the Soft Path
Source: Adapted from Amory B. Lovins, "Energy Strategy: The Road Not Taken?" *Foreign Affairs,* October 1976, 68, 77.

public health dangers of pesticides and chemicals; Jonathan Schell's *The Fate of the Earth,* which argued that nuclear war could mean "the end of history"; and Bill McKibben's *The End of Nature,* which forces us to confront the full implications of climate change. Fortunately, during the eighties and early nineties, while the U.S. government was spending billions of dollars to rush down the hard path, many consumers and industry leaders opted for the soft path. By 1991, Amory's energy efficiency scenario had become a reality. The road not taken had become an energy superhighway. "The revolution already happened," he proclaimed. "Sorry if you missed it."

In explaining the soft path, Amory is fond of quoting Pogo's observation that "we are confronted by insurmountable opportunities." Amory argues that following the soft path could "inhibit nuclear proliferation, abate acid rain and marine oil spills, save wild rivers, rescue troubled utilities, cut electric rates, forestall the CO_2 threat to the global climate, make farms and industries more profitable, rebuild distressed local economies, and save enough money to pay off the National Debt by the year 2000."[13] So why do we officially ignore these choices?

He believes that the answer is found in our past spendthrift production of real "energy gluttons" such as the modern refrigerator. In telling the "parable of the refrigerator," Amory reminds us of the

> pre–world War II refrigerators that had the motor on top. Those motors were close to 90 percent efficient. These days refrigerator motors are more like 60 percent efficient. They're also underneath, so the heat rises to where the food is. Thus, with the blessings of modern technology, refrigerators now easily spend half their effort taking away the heat from there own motors! . . . You can try if you like, but it's hard to come up with a dumber way of using electricity.[14]

When we consider that refrigerators are one of the biggest residential electricity users and that nationally "they use the equivalent of about *half* the output of *all* nuclear power plants," the parable makes us aware of the cumulative impact of energy inefficiency in American homes. Fortunately, in response to California efficiency legislation, manufacturers responded by progressively reducing the energy it takes to run a refrigerator from 1,800 kilowatt-hours per year in 1975 to only 550 by 1981.[15] Aside from refrigerators, additional big savings can be achieved by installing compact fluorescent lightbulbs, which last for a decade and provide soft light for a fraction of the energy used by standard incandescent bulbs. If a utility subsidizes the cost of thousands of these bulbs, it can eventually avoid building additional power plants, and the bulbs pay for themselves in lower power costs.

Likewise, if the U.S. government were to raise the average automobile's fuel consumption from 26.5 miles per gallon (the current standard) to just 32 miles per gallon, the resulting gasoline savings would equal the nation's entire annual oil imports from the Persian Gulf. "We sent soldiers in tanks that get eight miles a gallon to defend the Gulf, because we won't force Detroit to build cars that get an additional six miles per gallon," complains Amory.

The soft path teaches that "each of us has a small oil, gas, and electric 'well' right in our house, one that can be tapped fairly cheaply." Millions of small individual choices in the marketplace—weatherizing buildings, replacing lighting, driving more efficient cars, improving industrial motors—have provided "over a hundred times as much new energy as all of the new oil and gas wells, coal mines, and power plants built in the same period."

In summary, Lovins calculates that between 1976 and 1986, by following the soft energy path, the United States generated "seven times as much new energy from savings as from all net increases in new energy supply." As the visionary who created a new energy industry for America, Lovins proudly notes that "Another way of saying this is that the energy saving America achieved since 1973 . . . accounts for, in effect, a new energy source, two-fifths bigger than the entire domestic oil industry, which took a century to build. Oil has dwindling reserves, rising costs, and falling output, while efficiency has expanding reserves, falling costs, and rising output. What sounds like the better buy?"

Welcome to the Eco-Ark   When Hunter first heard of Amory's writings, she was working with a California group called TreePeople, involved with environmental education and outreach to children and senior citizens. Upon reading the *Foreign Affairs* article, her first thought was "this is really something different, but it's written in Martian." Hunter translated "Energy Strategy" into "basic English" so that she could share the essay with the other community activists, and she set out to meet its author. She was introduced to Amory in 1978 by the chief economist of the Atlantic Richfield oil company. A year later, Hunter and Amory were married. As Hunter puts it, "We decided it would be productive to join up."

Over the next two years, as policy advisers to Friends of the Earth, Amory and Hunter visited nearly 30 countries. They were constantly on the road, giving speeches, attending conferences, and defending the soft-path theory. Around 1981, Hunter recalls, "we got talking about settling down. . . . we literally lived aboard an airplane, just going from one place to another, to another." But Amory was concerned that if they settled down, they would limit their ability to spread the conservation message, to keep "cross-pollinating grapevines." Hunter suggested that they establish an institute that would demonstrate Amory's ideas and also function as a research center from which they could continue their educational work.

> I said, look, why don't we gather together a group of people, like-minded folk who want to do this kind of work, and create a small, close, tightly run little institute. Amory's response was "Horrors, I'll be an administrator." I said, "No, you won't be an administrator. I'll administrate and you direct the research." So, here we are.

Where they are is in the heart of the Old Snowmass Valley, a rural area 16 miles west of Aspen, on the western edge of the Colorado Rockies. This is pristine, alpine country, surrounded by the cleanest monitored air in Colorado, one of the largest migratory elk herds in North America, and wilderness with mountain peaks rising higher than 14,000 feet. It was here, in 1982, that the Lovinses decided to build the eco-ark that would serve as their home, demonstration bioshelter, and offices for the Rocky Mountain Institute (RMI). Built with a curved black Dakota sandstone rock face and set into a hillside, the "building is passive solar, superinsulated and semiunderground."[16] The biosphere is located at 7,100 feet, where temperatures drop below negative 40 degrees Fahrenheit nearly every winter and rise to the mid-80s in summer.

The building was designed as an energy efficiency showcase using then state-of-the art technology. Nearly 10 years latter, the efficiency is still impressive. The monthly home electric bill is about five dollars, but the PV panels on the roof generate enough surplus electricity that the utility pays the institute for the power it sends back into the grid. The biosphere represents the Lovinses' vision of a solar age when private homes, instead of consuming energy, will become mini–power plants that are net exporters of electricity.

"We could do much better today," notes Hunter as she points out some of the major features of the biosphere, which include argon-filled windows (twice the efficiency of triple glazing); a 1,500-gallon storage tank for solar hot water; a solar clothes-drying closet (saves 95 percent); an air-to-heat exchanger (saves 80 percent); a three-liter toilet (saves up to 90 percent); superefficient office equipment, including copiers and printers (saves 90 to 97 percent); cantilevered greenhouse arches (which shade the ends of the building in summer); numerous quadrupled-efficiency lightbulbs throughout the building; drip irrigation for the garden and the greenhouse; a passive water heater; a superinsulated roof; R-11 glass storm doors (four times as much insulation as triple glazing); active solar water heating; and rooftop photovoltaic panels (10 adjustable-tilt, 220 peak-watt panels that make solar electricity). Typically, the solar cells produce from one-fifth to more than one-third of the total electricity used by the building, depending on the weather.

As a result of these technologies, Hunter believes that the RMI dwelling is "one of the most efficient buildings in the world today." In round numbers, the RMI is saving 99 percent of space- and water-heating energy, 90 percent of household electricity, and more than 50 percent of household water. Using available 1983 technologies, the resulting $19-a-day energy savings repaid the extra cost of the efficient equipment in the first 10 months and will pay for the entire building in 40-odd years. Although many buildings save heat, the RMI also saves just as much electricity—the costliest form of energy. The building uses on average only 0.3 watts of power per square foot because it doesn't use electricity for space or water heating, air-conditioning, cooking, heating air to dry clothes, or (mostly) refrigeration. With these normal big energy uses removed, all that is left is power for the superefficient lights and appliances, which costs about $5 a month at 7.5¢ per kilowatt. In comparison, it is not uncommon for local all-electric houses of comparable size (4,000 square feet) in the Aspen area to have a $1,000-a-month winter electric bill.

This combined home, indoor farm, and office was designed by the Lovinses as a living biosphere, an eco-ark for an age of limited resources. But the house also demonstrates that resource-efficient buildings can be both beautiful and comfortable. In fact, the home is full of the modern amenities associated with luxury living in Colorado and California, including a hot tub heated with a Freon-charged heat-pipe solar panel.

Best of all, the building provides a pleasant work space where the Lovinses and the staff of the RMI feel happy and productive. It is in this positive setting of pleasing architectural curves, natural light, good indoor air quality, the lack of mechanical noise, the sound of the waterfall, the sights of the plants and the scent of the oxygen they produce, and the virtual lack of electromagnetic "smog" that the work of the Rocky Mountain Institute is carried out.

The Rocky Mountain Institute   Although the Lovinses' ideas offered a positive solution to the energy problem, many federal government and energy experts still regarded them as "overly idealistic" and "too good to be true." To this, the Lovinses reply that "Washington will be the last to know." All the more reason to establish an independent research institute to educate the public, industry, and local communities on the vast potential of resource conservation. In defining the RMI's mission, Hunter notes that they selected policy issues on which they had expertise or in which "the expertise we had might be applied and came up with five program areas: energy, water, agriculture, economic development, and global security."

Within this context, there are two main reasons for the Lovinses' phenomenal success. First, they don't try to push their values on anyone, and they base all their arguments on sound scientific research and economic analysis. Rather than preach an environmental ethic or an alternative lifestyle, they help individuals, communities, and businesses evaluate alternative technologies and do the math to answer the key question: "How can I get the best return for my dollar investment?" Second, instead of confronting people who hold opposing views, the Lovinses use what Hunter calls a gentle form of "aikido politics." Their cooperative and naturally friendly approach has depolarized the antagonism that has characterized the "energy wars" of the past two decades and won over many converts—even among the public utility companies.

Today, more than half of the RMI's $1 million in annual revenue comes from providing state-of-the art information on energy efficiency to utilities, governments, and more than 200 organizations in more than 32 nations. Many of these are subscribers to RMI's Competitek service, which provides "current and detailed technical reports on advanced techniques for electric efficiency." Already, energy efficiency has been institutionalized by California utilities such as PG&E, Southern California Edison, and SMUD. RMI collaborates closely with environmental groups that are working to spread the conservation revolution, such as the Environmental Defense Fund and the Natural Resources Defense Council in California and the Pacific Northwest, the Conservation Law Fund in New England, and the Land and Water Fund of the Rockies in Colorado.

For Amory, "to debate what sort of new power plant to build—should it be coal, or nuclear, or even solar—is like debating the best buy in brandy to burn in your car, or the best buy in Chippendales to burn in your stove. *It's simply the wrong question.* It's asking where to get more of a particularly costly form of energy. The real competitors with new power plants today are things like weatherstripping, insulation, greenhouses, heat exchangers, window shutters, and shades and coating." Small, familiar things that save energy.

With the proven ability to save almost "three quarters of the electricity at under two cents a kilowatt-hour and four-fifths of the oil and gas at under five dollars a barrel," Hunter believes that it is only a matter of time until all of the utilities, not only the forward-thinking ones, jump on the conservation bandwagon. "No one can afford to build a new plant," she notes. "It doesn't matter whether you're the ex-Soviet government or a tiny little county in Iowa. Basically, if they continue to build power plants they will go broke. . . . So over time all utilities are going to start moving in this direction. That is dictated by the economics."

Like the desert-dwelling Fremen in Frank Herbert's 1965 novel *Dune,* Amory and Hunter Lovins display a genuine reverence for water. The bioshelter does not simply conserve energy but conserves water as well. The "mini-use" showers, originally designed for naval vessels, deliver a strong shower with up to one-fifteenth as much water as standard showerheads. The three-liter Swedish Ifoe toilets use up to 90 percent less water than conventional toilets. RMI predicts that there will be "an integrated water-land-energy crisis in the 1990s" because—especially in the West—we are misusing water the same way we did energy throughout the 1950s and 1960s. When this next crisis emerges, the Lovinses believe that the nation will arrive at what they describe as "a teachable moment" on integrated resources.[17]

In the meantime, the RMI has developed a number of creative outreach programs that help communities analyze how to conserve their vital resource bases. For example, the RMI developed an analysis showing how Aspen could give away advanced water-saving devices to all its householders *at a net savings of $5 million*—because the energy saved in hot water will more than pay for the project. In addition, the institute has consolidated its work on energy and water and agriculture to build an "economic renewal project which seeks to provide a small rural community with a methodology that will allow it to begin building a sustainable, locally based economy for itself." "As we see it," Hunter explains, "there are three steps toward community economic renewal." The first is to stop the outflow of money in all areas, especially for wasted energy or water resources. The second is to determine what resources the community already has and what it can market to the outside. The third is to carefully evaluate any new economic activity. Will a new industry be a savior or an albatross? "Our ultimate goal at the RMI," Hunter states, "is to develop a stand-alone model that we can ship out across the nation to help communities with bootstrap self-renewal."

For Amory and Hunter Lovins, resource and economic self-sufficiency are intimately linked to global security.

The World's Energy Minister   In 1982, the Lovinses were commissioned by the Pentagon to do a study, published as *Brittle Power: Energy Strategy for National Security*.[18] In that study, they reported that U.S. dependence on centralized fossil fuel and nuclear power plants was a national security hazard. "The energy that runs America is brittle—easily shattered by accident or malice," they concluded, "and prone to sudden, massive failures with catastrophic consequences." For example, the United States has reached a point where "a few people could probably black out most of the country. . . . A terrorist squad could seriously disrupt much of the oil supply to the nation. . . . A few people could release enough radiation to make much of the U.S. uninhabitable." The RMI estimates that fully one-third of the U.S. military budget is spent on getting or keeping access to foreign oil and minerals.[19]

As a result, the Lovinses believe that energy independence and economic renewal are vital links in the chain of true national and global security. As Hunter puts it, "I'd like to be able to drive my truck wherever I want and not have to worry about whether some clown in the Middle East is going to blow up my fuel supply."

Although the RMI has focused on building the solar age from the ground up, as the world's foremost energy minister, Amory has definite views on what the White House and the Department of Energy could do to "displace all of the oil imported from the Persian Gulf, thereby improving American security."[20] First, the president should focus a national energy strategy on "least-cost, best buys." In addition, the federal government should eliminate taxpayer-funded subsidies that artificially lower energy prices and should promote higher efficiency standards on all electricity-consuming equipment and on gasoline-consuming vehicles.

The antienvironmental and anticonservation legacies of the Reagan and Bush administrations make these policies even more important today. For example, Reagan came into office promising to eliminate the DOE and rolled back efficiency standards for light vehicles from 27.5 miles per gallon to 26 miles per gallon. According to the Lovinses, this contributed to "a doubling of oil imports from the Persian Gulf and wasting more oil than the Reagan-Bush administrations hoped to find under the Arctic National Wildlife Refuge. The rollback also contributed to Japan's growing share of the U.S. car market."[21] In addition, these administrations also spent "tens of billions of dollars" protecting the flow of Middle Eastern oil. By adding the military costs of U.S. forces in or committed to the Persian Gulf—estimated at $40 billion per year—to oil's commodity price, each imported barrel costs about $80, even in peacetime.

The United States could dramatically improve its energy policy in three areas:[22]

1. *Electric efficiency.* Maximize electric efficiency to reduce the use of electricity, which costs Americans $180 billion per year and the world more than $500 billion per year. Although electricity-saving technologies are neither big nor glamorous, the thousand or so best electricity-saving innovations now on the market, "if fully used throughout the United States would displace over *half* of all the electricity the country now uses."

2. *Fuel savings.* Increase the gas mileage of the U.S. vehicle fleet by another 10 miles per gallon, or nearly 50 percent more than today's standards, by the year 2005, which would save 2 million barrels of oil per day and "would displace all oil we import from the Persian Gulf." For this reason, the Lovinses believe that efficient vehicles are much more important than electric cars, which will have maximum impact only in high-smog cities while offering central plant utilities an expansion niche market.

3. *Renewable energy.* Replace current federal support for nuclear power with support for renewable energy. According to one government estimate, nuclear power has already cost more than $1 trillion, if all the taxpayer-provided R&D is included (which is more than the cost of the Vietnam War and the space program combined), to deliver little more than half as much energy as wood. "A study by five national laboratories recently concluded that increasing R&D budgets by the cost

of building one nuclear power plant ($160 million a year for 20 years) could, by the year 2030, enable renewable energy to provide about half of the total energy and all the electricity used in the United States in 1989, including the equivalent of 9 million barrels of oil per day, directly replacing oil and natural gas."

In conclusion, the Lovinses argue that "cutting waste reduces environmental impact, improves security by lowering oil imports from politically unstable regions, puts more money in consumers' pockets, and need not compromise our standard of living." At the same time, "improving energy productivity rescues the trade and federal budget deficits, eases interest rates by virtue of lowered federal borrowing, and preserves vital resources for international development and future generations."

From a global perspective, Hunter firmly believes that the soft-path approach offers the only hope that the "industrial paradigm has to survive." Efficiency is the only reliable strategy we have to forestall absolutely hitting the "limits of growth." "In a sense," Hunter states, "we are the real cornucopia."

It is a little planet, and we need to learn more about its carrying capacity. Efficiency can buy us time to learn more about sustainability and to get some of these problems under control. Energy is not going to be the limiting factor, but two billion Chinese driving Buicks is not a future that makes sense, even if they're highly efficient Buicks. So, it's not the population growth in the developing world that's the problem; it's the population growth of the "high users" group. Efficiency of all sorts can give the industrialized world a much better standard of living, a much greater return on its investment. But it's absolutely crucial for the developing world. Without it, they cannot afford to develop, and their development process will ruin it for everyone on the planet.

Ultimately, the Lovinses have a great faith in populism, the democratic process, and the free market. They support the assumption of Jeffersonian democracy that most people are pretty smart and that, given the right information, incentives, and opportunity, will choose wisely for themselves. The Lovinses believe that out of the United States' current "large-scale national experiment in energy" will emerge "a realization that we need to build solutions to the energy problem mainly from the local to the regional and then to the national level." When all the nations of the world follow this path, then "international and global security based on economic sustainability will emerge at some point, because the security of any of us depends on the security of all of us." By having the courage to travel the road less taken, Amory and Hunter Lovins have spearheaded an efficiency revolution that has already taken the United States a long way down the soft path and to the gateway of the solar age. Their gospel has been spread worldwide by Christopher Flavin of the Worldwatch Institute, who has become an international apostle for the coming worldwide energy revolution.

The Coming Energy Revolution: Christopher Flavin, the Worldwatch Institute

The end of the fossil fuel age is now in sight. As the world lurches from one energy crisis to another, fossil fuel dependence threatens at every turn to derail the global economy or disrupt its environmental support systems. If we are to ensure a healthy and prosperous world for future generations, only a few decades remain to redirect the energy economy.
—*Christopher Flavin and Nicholas Lenssen,*
Beyond the Petroleum Age, *1990*

Near the conclusion of *Power Surge: Guide to the Coming Energy Revolution,* authors Christopher Flavin and Nicholas Lenssen take us "through the looking glass." They ask us to consider a scenario that could jolt world governments out of their lethargy on energy policy and accelerate the development of a sustainable energy future.

The date is early September 1998, and many parts of the world have just experienced one of the most brutal summers in memory. A severe drought and heat wave have cut the North American grain harvest to 20 percent below normal, following a 10 percent-shortfall the year before. . . . By mid-September, the prices of corn and wheat have tripled, and a consumer revolt forces the U.S. government to restrict grain exports and halt food aid. Rising grain prices cause a dramatic worsening of the famines that first appeared in parts of Africa and South Asia in the mid-nineties.

Then in late September, with newspapers still full of news of the food crisis, a Class 5 hurricane steams out of the Caribbean and slams into New York City. A week later a similar storm strikes New Orleans. . . . A week later a cyclone strikes south of Dacca, the capital of Bangladesh. . . .

In mid-October, one of the most dramatic scientific press conferences ever held takes place in a Geneva ballroom. Called by the Intergovernmental Panel on Climate Change (IPCC) and attended by 130 leading climate scientists, the message is simple and disturbing: advances in the understanding of atmospheric dynamics show that rising concentrations of carbon dioxide have increased the frequency and severity of catastrophic droughts and storms. . . . Headlines the next day proclaim: "Unnatural Disasters Threaten Millions." The world's stock exchanges, still reeling from the calamities of the previous month, plunge again.[23]

Although Flavin is the first to admit that the chances of this literally happening are "practically nil," he also believes that the future themes of megastorms, global droughts, and food shortages are "broadly plausible." It could be argued that making energy forecasts, in general, and linking them to climate change is a risky business. No one can say with certainty that another oil crisis will occur within the next decade, that global warming will accelerate dramatically because of increased greenhouse gas emissions, or that a shift to a renewable-energy future is imminent. But, as we near the end of the century, Flavin believes that each of these events seems "very plausible, if not likely."

Flavin uses this hypothetical anecdote to rivet our attention on the extreme case while urging us to contemplate the kind of energy scenario that might emerge "if the need for change becomes more urgent." He then asks us to consider, as he has done for the past decade, "what sort of energy path might unfold if the world decides to take the overriding goal of the Rio climate treaty seriously—stabilizing atmospheric concentrations of carbon dioxide by the middle of the twenty-first century."[24] For Flavin, this was a question worth asking, and one that he was uniquely qualified to answer.

Flavin developed an early passion for ecology. Born and raised in California, he "had an environmental consciousness built in through his family and upbringing." Growing up in San Francisco and then moving to the Monterrey Peninsula, he spent a lot of time outdoors, hiking and gaining an appreciation for the beauty of nature. After attending Williams College in the early 1970s, where he specialized in environmental studies, Flavin eventually earned a degree in biology at Amherst. But it was the oil crisis of the early seventies and President Carter's energy policies that gave Flavin "the energy bug" that has guided his career for the past two decades.

After initially working with Dennis Hayes at the Solar Energy Research Institute, Flavin gradually broadened his approach to the energy equation and for the last decade has focused primarily on renewable technologies. "I've worked on everything from the oil market to nuclear power. I really spent a good part of my time over the years on renewable technology and sustainable energy," he reports. Today, from his position as vice president for research at the prestigious Worldwatch Institute, Flavin has had the opportunity "to track the whole broad range of global network conferences and other advances in energy technology."

At first glance, Flavin looks more like an exuberant college student than a seasoned energy pundit whose energy writings, through the Worldwatch Institute's papers and annual *State of the World* report, are translated into 27 languages.[25] As a founder of the Washington-based Business Council for a Sustainable Energy Future, Flavin sits at the nexus of a global network of researchers, policy makers, entrepreneurs, and innovators who are bringing about the coming energy revolution.

"We wrote *Power Surge*," Flavin explains, "basically to say the world is changing very rapidly and most people are not aware of it because they don't have the time or the inclination to go look. So, we'll do the looking for them . . . and present some evidence of what is really going on." What is going on, according to Flavin, is that "outside of a few pockets of innovation, planners and analysts at the world's leading energy institutions seem trapped in the stagnation and confusion that began with repeated failures in the seventies and eighties to develop a viable energy strategy." From his vantage point at the Worldwatch Institute, Flavin perceives a global shift away from imported oil and environmentally damaging coal over the next few decades.

Driven by the consensus that the earth's climate must be stabilized and by major investment opportunities in the emerging renewable-energy industry, global energy markets are at the beginning stages of a watershed transition to more efficient, less-polluting, decentralized, and renewable power systems. This energy revolution will include a new generation of lightweight, superefficient electric cars that can be refueled at home; the rapid conversion of coal and nuclear plants to highly efficient gas turbines; a new generation of mass-produced wind and solar generators that are cost competitive with fossil fuel power plants; modular fuel cells and rooftop solar electric panels that will eventually allow people to generate their own electricity; and the gradual emergence of hydrogen as the world's main energy medium, ultimately supplanting both oil and natural gas.[26]

Like the Lovinses, Flavin has devoted his life to confronting the energy establishment and to challenging the way we think about energy. "You've got to be in these issues for the long haul," he explains. "Changing the global energy system is a half-century business at least—it's the work of a lifetime, literally." Just as the Rocky Mountain Institute is having a major impact on energy efficiency in the United States, the Worldwatch Institute, under Flavin's direction in the energy arena, is playing a major role in reshaping the global renewable-energy future. The two main forces driving this transformation are the "oil shocks" and the "eco shocks" of the past two decades.[27]

The Middle East Tinderbox　Throughout modern history, new technologies have been the precursors to energy transitions. Until the nineteenth century, human societies relied on water, wind, and wood to meet their energy needs. The Industrial Revolution and the invention of the steam engine made it possible to use a new source of energy, coal. Although the world never "ran out" of wind or wood, technological change enabled society to embrace the new energy medium of coal and exploit its hidden potential. Today Flavin perceives a similar situation occurring, given the mismatch between the highly efficient silicon-based information age and its inefficient infrastructure powered almost entirely by outdated coal and oil.

The Industrial Revolution was well under way, with its energy requirements being met adequately by solid fuels such as wood and coal, long before the petroleum era ever began. The first primitive automobiles took to the road during a highly publicized race between Paris and Bordeaux in the 1890s, ultimately proving the advantages of the internal combustion engine. Once again, Flavin notes, "the age of oil was ushered in at the turn of the century less by the discovery of petroleum, which had been found much earlier, than by the development of practical internal combustion engines that made oil useful."

Similarly, coal-based electricity was driven not by the discovery and abundance of coal but by the technology, such as the steam engine, that harnessed its potential. Consequently, when Thomas Edison connected the first coal-fired boiler to a steam engine and a dynamo and lit 158 Edison lightbulbs at the Pearl Street Station in New York City on September 6, 1882, he not only started the world's first electric power company but introduced technology that would prove to be pivotal in shaping life in the twentieth century. It was through that demonstration project, more than a century ago, that the Edison Electric Illuminating Company made converts of its carefully chosen first customers, J. P. Morgan and the *New York Times,* ushering in the "age of electricity." Electric power has not only transformed life and work but has fostered a global enterprise with annual revenues estimated at more than $800 billion.

In the case of oil and coal, technology was the driving force behind their commercialization. As in paradigm shifts of the past, Flavin sees energy innovations such as photovoltaic desert power stations, wind farms, and hydrogen fuel cells (which he calls "the silicon chips of the hydrogen future") as the technological precursors to the energy revolution. But, unlike past energy transitions, the present one is being accelerated by geopolitical factors that are independent of technology change.

On October 6, 1973, the eve of Yom Kippur, Judaism's holiest holiday, Egyptian and Syrian jets attacked Israeli positions near the Golan Heights, along the Suez Canal, and in the Sinai Desert. Three weeks later, nearly 20,000 lives had been lost, 2,800 tanks destroyed, and the fragile stability in the volatile Middle East once again shattered. The Yom Kippur war ended the era of oil-fueled economic growth that characterized the decades following World War II and ushered in the oil crisis of 1973 to 1974. Oil prices rose from $3 a barrel to $13, precipitating soaring inflation, slower economic growth, high rates of unemployment, and a worldwide economic recession.

Several years later, in January 1979, after nearly a yearlong struggle between secular and fundamentalist Shiite Muslims in Iran, the Peacock Shah fled Tehran and his throne. This sparked a series of tumultuous events leading to strikes by Iran's oil field workers that subsequently cut off exports from what was then the world's second largest exporter of oil. World oil prices nearly tripled, spurring an even deeper recession than that caused by the oil crisis of 1973, and "it was not until 1986 that prices fell to less than $20 per barrel"—which was still 50 percent higher than the average market price.

In Flavin's view, the oil shocks of the 1970s led to many U.S. government–funded "crash efforts to commercialize everything from breeder reactors to solar power." But the greatest lesson of the Iranian Revolution was the extent of the West's dependence on fossil fuels in general and on oil in particular. Not only was the world addicted to cheap oil, but the largest liquor store "was in a very dangerous neighborhood." The sobering reality that the world could no longer continue indefinitely along a path of petroleum dependence without suffering the consequences of political and price instability had now become all too clear. Nevertheless, it was not until Saddam Hussein invaded Kuwait, and the United States military might replaced the British "east of Suez," that the full costs of Middle East oil dependence were realized.

"When Iraq's tanks rumbled into Kuwait in August of 1990, the world suffered its third oil shock in 17 years. The invasion, which immediately raised Iraq's share of world oil reserves from 10 to nearly 20 percent, caused a 170 percent increase in oil prices in three months, and led to near panic in world financial markets," Flavin observes. Like its two predecessors in the seventies, the oil shock of the early nineties precipitated by the Persian Gulf War underscored the brittleness of the West's insatiable demand for free-flowing Middle Eastern oil. Just as significantly, the aftermath of the Gulf War focused the world's attention on an equally dramatic connection: the environmental impact of petroleum dependency.

The Greenhouse Effect   During the past two decades, eco-shock images have been indelibly etched into humanity's consciousness: European forest death caused by coal-burning power plants in 1982, the Chernobyl nuclear explosion of 1986, the Exxon Valdez oil spill of 1989, and the continual burning of the Brazilian rain forests over the past decade. But even though the global community was becoming inured to eco-trauma, nothing had prepared it for the fallout of the Gulf War.

Before being driven out of Kuwait, Iraqi troops released nearly three million barrels of oil into the Persian Gulf, and even more into the desert, unleashing perhaps the worst environmental devastation the world has ever seen. Flavin likens this disaster to a "scene out of Dante's Inferno," as pillars of flame and oily smoke from the more than 500 oil wells set ablaze by retreating Iraqi soldiers choked the capital city of Kuwait. "For close to a year, the Kuwaiti oil fields burned, at their peak consuming 6 million barrels of oil a day and releasing 10 times as much pollution as all U.S. power and industrial plants combined." But as Flavin argues, "the Gulf War's transition from an energy and military crisis to an ecological calamity was symbolic." By the early nineties, energy markets were already being shaped more by environmental crises and responses than by the economics and politics of oil.

Only recently has environmentalism become a potent force in world energy markets. True, as early as 1306, King Edward I of England banned the burning of coal in London in order to reduce the heavy air pollution already choking the city. His decree was noble in principle but did very little to deter the onset of the Industrial Revolution in Britain. The unbreathable air and blackened buildings that London became known for by the late nineteenth century were a direct result of the growth of the coal industry that fueled the Industrial Revolution until World War I.

It was only about a hundred years ago, in 1896, that the Swedish chemist Svante Arrhenius first proposed that humanity's industrial activities might disrupt the earth's atmosphere. Theorizing that the rapid increase in the use of coal in Europe since the onset of the Industrial Revolution would cause a gradual rise in global temperatures, Arrhenius discouraged coal's use and proliferation. Unfortunately, Arrhenius was ahead of his time, and the lone voice of the modern era's first environmentalist went unheard. His prophetic discoveries fell on deaf ears. Only now are we forced to confront the climatic reality discovered by Arrhenius nearly a century ago.

According to the World Health Organization (WHO), an estimated 1.3 billion people worldwide, most of them in developing countries, now live in areas that do not meet WHO pollution standards for atmospheric particulates. These pollutants are responsible for 300,000 to 700,000 premature deaths annually. Particulates are generated by the rapid growth of heavy industry and the quintupling of automobile use outside the Western nations from nearly 22 million in 1970 to nearly 109 million in 1991.

In Los Angeles, with its basin geography, heavy population, and overdependence on fossil fuel–driven internal combustion automobiles, a scenario similar to London's is unfolding. Because of a climatic phenomenon called an inversion, in which a layer of warm air traps carbon emissions in the lower atmosphere, L.A.'s air quality ranks among the worst in the world. By 1953 local governments had already passed their first air pollution laws, which were shortly followed by state-level standards that eventually served as a model for the U.S. Clean Air Act of 1970. By 1990, with pollution still spiraling out of control, California passed the "world's toughest auto emissions standards to date," the ZEV law. Although California's struggle to control its "yellow haze" has become a paragon for environmentalists worldwide, the greatest example of fossil fuel combustion–based pollution and its environmental and social implications is found in the deplorable conditions of Third World cities such as Mexico City.

Mexico City has the worst air in the world, with concentrations of carbon monoxide, ozone, and particulates exceeding legal limits nearly every day it does not rain. In 1993 residents enjoyed only 31 days of safe, breathable air. With many other cities around the world, such as São Paulo, Tokyo, and Bombay, where breathing the air is now "equivalent to smoking 10 cigarettes a day," following in the footsteps of London, L.A., and Mexico City, nonpolluting energy alternatives have become paramount in today's energy debate. Flavin predicts that "some sort of an environmental shock" will probably be the spark that ushers in the renewable soft energy paradigm advocated by both the Rocky Mountain and the Worldwatch Institutes.

Over the past 25 years, several developments have pushed climate and energy policy into the political limelight. These include the discovery of a rapidly expanding ozone hole over Antarctica, caused primarily by the release of CFCs into the atmosphere; the increasing awareness of the greenhouse effect and its link to increased fossil fuel combustion; and the sobering reality that Middle East oil dependence had become a form of "energy roulette" for the West. Yet real change in energy policy has been slow to occur. Even most so-called energy experts, Flavin laments, do not have the foresight to see an energy future beyond "only minor changes to existing paradigms . . . yielding only slightly more efficient, marginally cleaner versions of today's fossil-based energy economy." With the oil and coal companies denying that they face a long period of decline, and with auto and electric power industries reluctant to accept the massive new investments and restructuring that a change of course might suggest, the fundamental question of the global energy debate becomes "How do we get from here to there?"

Flavin believes that June 23, 1988, may have been one of the most significant days in the history of the world energy economy. On that day, James Hansen, the director of NASA's Goddard Institute for Space Studies and a leading atmospheric scientist, testified at a U.S. Senate committee hearing that "rapid climate change was likely in the decades ahead as a result of human activities."[28] Until the late eighties, most of the concern regarding the environmental impact of 100 years of unfettered carbon-based pollution came primarily from the "fringe" environmentalists. Until then, technological optimism ruled the day, and the expression "if we can go to the moon, surely we can . . ."

was commonplace with regard to nuclear energy and technological solutions to environmental problems.

At about the same time that this "sober government scientist" was
publicly stating his conclusions about the greenhouse effect, the United
Nations formed the Intergovernmental Panel on Climate Change
(IPCC). Through the panel, 150 of the world's leading climate scientists
began investigating the earth's environmental fate. Basing their predictions on computer models indicating that a rapid rise in global temperatures would occur by the late twenty-first century, the IPCC declared:
"We are now conducting an unregulated experiment with the earth's
only atmosphere, and the burden of proof should lie with those who believe there is no problem."

In the panel's latest report, *Climate Change 1995: The IPCC Second
Assessment,* 2,500 contributing scientists from 60 countries evaluated
more than 20,000 papers in a variety of research fields, including cli-
matology, economics, and oceanography. The IPCC report represents
a level of comprehensive worldwide review rarely attempted in any
scientific field, and therefore, according to the Union of Concerned
Scientists, "the IPCC's 1995 report literally represents the state of human understanding on climate change to date."[29] Among the most significant conclusions reached by the report are that

- the average surface temperature over the globe has risen by
  0.5 to 1.1 degrees Fahrenheit since the late 1880s;
- the 10 warmest years on record since 1860 have occurred in
  the last 15 years, despite a 3-year global cooling caused by
  the 1991 eruption of Mount Pinatubo;
- the world's oceans show the secondary effects of this warming trend, with a 4- to 10-inch rise in global sea levels in the
  last hundred years, resulting from expansion of warmed
  ocean water; and
- the burning of fossil fuels, initially coal and later petroleum
  products, since the advent of the Industrial Revolution has increased the atmospheric concentration of greenhouse
  gases—particularly carbon dioxide by 30 percent, nitrous oxide by 15 percent, and methane by 145 percent—to levels
  higher than in preindustrial times.

The *Second Assessment* concluded with the consensus that "the balance of evidence suggests that there is a discernible human influence

on global climate." Based on these trends, the 1995 report predicted that this global warming trend will accelerate, causing a global average temperature increase of 1.8 to 6.3 degrees Fahrenheit over the next 100 years. The effects, particularly on the members of the Alliance of Small Island States, could be devastating: "melting of polar glaciers and ice sheets and the thermal expansion of the oceans due to increasing global temperature could further raise sea levels by 6–38 inches."[30]

At the initial Framework Convention on Climate Change held in Rio de Janeiro in 1992, four years after Hansen's testimony and the initial IPCC warnings, governments from around the world pledged that the long-term goal to stabilize greenhouse gas concentrations in the atmosphere "at a level that would prevent dangerous anthropogenic interference with the climate system" was of paramount international importance. But government mandate alone has historically been unable to effect the fundamental changes necessary for a sustainable energy future. With entrenched utility and automobile lobbies exercising political resistance, along with continued government subsidies masking the true costs of a fossil fuel–driven energy economy, a more ambitious plan was necessary.

The Worldwatch Institute provided that plan by constructing a viable model for a sustainable energy future and provided a global road map showing how we get "from here to there."

Toward a Sustainable Energy Future   In response to the combined fossil fuel and greenhouse effect dilemmas, Flavin has devoted much of his thinking to the development of viable scenarios for a sustainable energy future. Under his direction, the Worldwatch Institute has developed two models for a solar economy in which carbon dioxide emissions are dramatically reduced.

The first "40-year plan" was presented in 1990 in a Worldwatch paper titled *Beyond the Petroleum Age: Designing a Solar Economy*.[31] The plan reports world energy use and carbon emissions for 1989 with projections for the year 2030 (see figure 8). At that time, scientists believed that global emissions of carbon dioxide must be cut by 60 to 80 percent in order to stabilize CO_2 concentration in the atmosphere. The proposed Worldwatch carbon budget for the year 2030 is 2.5 billion tons—roughly a 55 percent cut from current levels of 6 billion tons.

In order to achieve these ambitious targets, the use of coal, the most carbon-intensive fuel, must be cut by about 90 percent, the use of

Figure 8.
World Energy Use and Carbon Emissions,
1989, with Goals for 2030

Energy Source	1989		2030	
	Energy (mtoe)[a]	Carbon (million tons)	Energy (mtoe)[a]	Carbon (million tons)
Oil	3,098	2,393	1,500	1,160
Coal	2,231	2,396	240	430
Natural gas	1,707	975	1,750	1,000
Renewables[b]	1,813	*	7,000	*
Nuclear[b]	451	*	0	0
Total	9,300	5,764	10,490	2,590

Source: Christopher Flavin and Nicholas Lenssen, *Beyond the Petroleum Age: Designing a Solar Economy,* Worldwatch Paper 100 (Washington, D.C.: Worldwatch Institute, 1990), 15; the data in this figure were compiled by the Worldwatch Institute, based on British Petroleum, *Statistical Review of World Energy* (London: 1990); J. M. O. Scurlock and D. O. Hall, "The Contribution of Biomass to Global Energy Use," *Biomass,* no. 21, 1990; Gregg Marland et al., *Estimates of CO$_2$ Emissions from Fossil Fuel Burning and Cement Manufacturing, Based on the United Nations Energy Statistics and the U.S. Bureau of Mines Cement Manufacturing Data* (Oak Ridge, Tenn.: Oak Ridge National Laboratory, 1989).

[a]Million tons of oil equivalent.

[b]Under certain circumstances, both renewable energy and nuclear energy can result in net positive carbon emissions. An asterisk (*) indicates the possibility of some emissions.

oil cut in half, and nuclear power phased out because it is not economically or socially sustainable. Such a future would be possible only if energy efficiency were highly utilized, so that the world produces goods and services with one-third to one-half the energy it now uses. However, even with greatly improved efficiency, total energy needs by 2030 will still be slightly higher than those of 1990 because of both population and economic growth. According to Flavin, the only way to create a sustainable economy, stabilize the greenhouse effect, and meet global energy needs is for the world to quadruple its renewable energy output. This would entail expanding the use of energy from biomass (biological sources such as wood or agricultural wastes) and hydropower, but more importantly would require large contributions from solar, wind, and geothermal sources. The technologies to harness these resources are now ready for widespread use—if they receive effective support in the years ahead.[32]

In *Power Surge,* his most recent book, Flavin contemplates what the world energy system would look like if we took the goal of stabilizing the earth's climate seriously. The result of this "what if" exercise is the Worldwatch Institute's "Sustainable Future," a 100-year projection for global energy use and atmospheric carbon dioxide concentrations. In contrast to the "Business as Usual Case" forecasts of IPCC, wherein "carbon dioxide concentrations rise from the 1993 level of 357 parts per million to about 700 parts per million at the end of the next century," the Worldwatch model shows "carbon dioxide concentrations leveling off by mid-century at about 450 parts per million and then declining gradually in the following decades." Furthermore, the IPCC case projects that fossil fuels will still be used for approximately two-thirds of global energy by 2050 and 2100. In the Worldwatch case, fossil fuels account for only one-half of global energy use by 2050 and only one-tenth by 2100.[33]

Under this scenario, wind power, solar photovoltaics, and solar thermal energy would each provide as much energy in 2050 as nuclear power does today. In order to continually decrease the use of fossil fuels after 2025, a 75 percent increase in the use of renewable energy would be needed between 2025 and 2050. At that point, renewables would have replaced oil as the world's second largest energy source, providing more than half of the world's primary energy by 2050, with the share rising as high as 90 percent by 2100.

Flavin's most optimistic conclusion is that all of this is doable: "Although an energy system this different is hard for most people to envision, we see no technical or economic barriers to such a transition." In fact, this transformation can take place with a projected annual growth in new renewable-energy technologies of around 20 to 30 percent, which "is actually slower than the growth rates of nuclear power in the sixties and seventies, or of personal computers in the eighties. Under this scenario, the renewable-energy industry would have annual revenues of roughly $200 billion (1993 dollars) in 2025—twice the 1993 revenues of Exxon."[34]

In Flavin's view, the foundations of a sustainable energy future have already been well established. Since 1973, renewable energy has nearly doubled its contribution to the nation's energy grid, and today renewables provide almost 10 percent of domestic energy production. Although, as Flavin explains, "back in the late seventies we had the oil crisis, and governments and industries definitely accelerated" alternative energy R&D, very little happened because the "basic technology was not ready to go." Many noble strides were made in wind, hydropower, biomass, and PV technology. But "looking back it is hard to believe that anybody really thought that a wind machine, which hadn't even been operating in a field for more than a month or two, would really get up . . . and be made operational." It was through a new generation of private entrepreneurs, grassroots activists, and policy innovators, "driven by the challenges of creating a less environmentally destructive energy system and lured by the market opportunities that beckon," that the alternative-energy revolution was conceived and renewable technology was born. Whereas a decade ago alternative technologies "were somewhat immature," today Flavin sees that "you have got mature industries . . . with a track record" waiting to be implemented.

"One can argue even today, but certainly five to ten years from now, technology will be so ready to go that if government and private sector really started to step on the accelerator, there would be a real response." Citing such technologies as wind turbines, photovoltaic arrays, natural gas power plants, and hydrogen fuel cells, Flavin sees technology as one of the driving factors for the coming energy transition. "You just see so much change and so much new technology out there," he explains, that "I feel even more bullish about the likelihood of rapid change in the future. . . . There's something happening, sort of a dynamic occurring that I believe has sort of a logic and a momentum of its own these days, and I don't tend to think that things like the Republicans' turn in Washington, or other sorts of political developments, are going to do all that much." On the topic of federal policy, Flavin fully concurs with the Lovinses' observation that "there are many in Washington who will be the last to know that the energy problem is being solved from the bottom up, not from the top down." Although many promising technologies will play vital roles in the coming energy revolution, Flavin essentially sees wind power, natural gas, and the solar and hydrogen systems integrating PV and fuel cell technology as the primary resources behind the transition to a sustainable energy future.

Wind
- Wind turbines installed on .6 percent of the land area of the 48 contiguous states, mainly in the Great Plains, could meet 20 percent of current U.S. power needs.
- With improvements in both design and efficiency, and with environmental costs factored in to both coal and natural gas power plants, wind power is likely to become one of the least expensive sources of electricity, projected at around $.03 per kilowatt-hour by 2030.
- In Worldwatch's energy projection for 2030, wind power stations will provide roughly 1,500 gigawatts of base power worldwide and would be deployed across resource-rich areas such as the U.S. Great Plains, the Thar Desert in India, La Ventosa in Mexico, and the Sahara of North Africa.

Natural Gas
- Because of its lower carbon content, natural gas produces 30 percent less carbon dioxide per unit of energy than oil and 43 percent less than coal. And with virtually no ash production, and smaller quantities of volatile hydrocarbons, carbon monoxide, and nitrogen oxides in its combustion than that of oil or coal, natural gas is most likely to become the dominant global fuel early in next century.
- The Worldwatch Institute predicts that natural gas will account for almost one-fifth of the world's energy needs, producing almost one-half of its total carbon emissions by 2030. However, the role natural gas will ultimately play is one of a transition fuel establishing a bridge from the fossil fuel to the solar and hydrogen era.

Solar and Hydrogen Power Systems
- In its most basic terms, the earth is made up of 70 percent water and is struck by nearly 5.4 million exajoules of solar energy each year. After atmospheric reflection and wind conversion are taken into account, 2.5 million exajoules remain to irradiate the earth's surface—more than 6,000 times the amount of energy used by all human beings worldwide in 1990.
- As natural gas supplies level off or are phased out to further reduce carbon emissions, the fuel most likely to fill the

dominant power-supplying niche is hydrogen, combined with oxygen in hydrogen power fuel cells to produce heat or electricity.

- In fact, with a solar photovoltaic and hydrogen fuel cell infrastructure in place, "all current U.S. energy needs could be met with just 1 percent of today's U.S. water supply."[35]

However, Flavin is the first to acknowledge that it will take a major commitment and foresight on the part of the United States and world governments to make the transition to the solar and hydrogen future. "Fuel cells basically suffer from the fact that they don't fit into any existing market," he comments, "making them unprofitable for the present. . . . The marketing schemes of the big power generation businesses, like General Electric and the others, have been historically geared toward utilities and big units." Even if PV and fuel cell technology could completely transform the way we use energy, it would require a fully decentralized power system and a vastly different infrastructure than exists today. Flavin believes we are now poised at that turning point.

Impact of the New Energy Paradigm   In *Power Surge,* Flavin has meticulously drawn a blueprint for the coming energy revolution. Although no one can predict the exact timing of this transformation, Flavin believes it is imminent. Drawing on two decades of experience in the energy arena, he observes that "things go on, changing very slowly, and gradually, and then they will suddenly jump up to a different level." Citing the personal computer revolution as an example, Flavin envisions a similar technology-driven accelerating shift in energy. Borrowing a concept from his study of biology and the reworking of evolutionary theory by Harvard biologist Steven Jay Gould, Flavin describes this process as "punctuated equilibrium." Through his research, Gould postulated an alternative theory of evolution that states that most evolutionary changes occur in sudden bursts driven in part by external environmental influences that force species to evolve quickly in order to survive. According to Gould, evolution is often marked by "long periods of stasis, followed by brief eruptions of radical change." Applying this model to changes in energy policy, Flavin has learned that "you can plug away for a long time and think you're not making any progress, and then suddenly it changes, seemingly all at once. But really, it was all the work that people have been doing over an extended period of time that made the rapid change possible."

Two events could significantly accelerate the emergence of a new energy paradigm. The first is the decentralization of the utility industry; the second is a major shift in worldwide government support in favor of renewable energy. "The key factor to the energy revolution and shifting energy paradigm would be to vertically separate the industry," Flavin argues. One of the primary problems with the current system is that "utilities have been able to own both the generation and the transmission and distribution systems," creating a monopoly on power that is "a system ripe for abuse." Citing recent examples in the telecommunications and computer industries as models for the utility deregulation he envisions, Flavin believes the best way to minimize regulation and get the maximum degree of innovation at all levels of the power business is to require that separate companies operate the generation, transmission, and distribution of electric power—and, at some point in the future, of hydrogen power.

The second factor would entail a fundamental shift in the way that governments routinely provide major subsidies to traditional energy sources, keeping prices artificially low, encouraging waste, and skewing actual energy costs in favor of conventional fossil fuel and nuclear power systems by ignoring "back-end" environmental costs. In 1991 alone, direct fossil fuel subsidies totaled $220 billion worldwide. In the United States, energy industries received federal subsidies valued at more than $36 billion in 1989 alone, with a 60 percent–30 percent split between fossil and nuclear. In addition to reducing and eliminating fossil and nuclear subsidies, changes in government R&D must follow suit.

Finally, if we are to make the sweeping changes necessary worldwide, then a renewed effort to channel international energy assistance to developing countries is needed to help the development of sustainable energy systems. Since 1948 nearly four-fifths of the $57 billion the World Bank has loaned for energy projects to Third World countries has gone to their power supplies, and less than 1 percent of the $67 billion lent by all the development banks in the 1980s for energy projects went to improving end-use energy efficiency and renewable technology. Clearly, major changes in investment priorities are needed to help achieve the ambitious goals set by the Rocky Mountain Institute and the Worldwatch Institute.

Flavin sits in his modest office in the spacious headquarters of the Worldwatch Institute near Dupont Circle, reflecting on his work. He has indeed taken the burden of the world's energy future on his shoulders. Yet, unlike Atlas, he bears the burden lightly. Speaking with Christopher Flavin is an uplifting experience. It is like asking a question about a future, which many have come to fear, and hearing a cheery, confident voice reply that "the future will be just fine."

Having circled the globe tracking the new energy trends, Flavin finds hundreds of reasons to be cautiously optimistic about the fate of the earth. In the conclusion of *Power Surge,* he wrote:

> The road ahead will not be without obstacles and detours. The investments required for achieving a sustainable energy system are sizable, the economic forces to be overcome well organized, and the challenges to human ingenuity enormous. Still, when economic historians look back on the mid-nineties, they may well decide that the world had already embarked on a major energy transition by then—just as, with hindsight, we can say the same about the 1890s. Today, as then, economic, environmental, and social pressures have made the old system unsustainable and obsolete, and the process of change is quietly gathering momentum.
>
> Slowly people and governments are rising to one of the most fundamental challenges humanity has ever faced: passing on to our children a natural environment that has not been substantially degraded by our short term needs or desires.[36]

Like the Lovinses, Flavin has devoted all of his adult life to shaping a sustainable energy future. He is invigorated in his mission by the

---

Mobilizing Principle 5:
Create a New Energy Paradigm

In contrast to the nuclear future initially proposed as a solution to America's energy crisis, both Amory and Hunter Lovins (the "soft energy path") and Christopher Flavin (the "coming energy revolution") have created a positive alternative paradigm of an environmentally sustainable, non-nuclear-energy future and have designed short- and long-term strategies for achieving that future. This alternative global vision of a technologically viable, environmentally benign, and economically competitive safe-energy future has provided a powerful rallying point for mobilizing broad domestic and international support for antinuclear, pro-safe-energy policies.

knowledge that significant progress has been made and will continue to be made. "I feel like we're still in the relatively early stages," he states. "But we definitely have made progress. We're definitely going toward the light at the end of the tunnel." For Flavin, and for all the profiles in power, that light at the end of the tunnel is the aurora of the solar age—the coming age of light.

Chapter Seven

Profiles in Courage

> *A nation which has forgotten the quality of courage which in the past*
> *has been brought into public life is not as likely to insist upon or reward*
> *that quality in its chosen leaders today—and in fact we have forgotten.*
> —*President John F. Kennedy,* Profiles in Courage, *1956*

We are now able to place the antinuclear movement in historical perspective and summarize what we have learned concerning the questions originally posed by this study. First, what factors led to the initial abandonment of nuclear power by the electric utilities? Second, what was the impact of the antinuclear movement? Third, what do these profiles teach us about citizen activism and social movements in general?

To address the first and second questions, we begin this concluding chapter with a "Brief History of the Antinuclear Movement." Then we examine the third question by revisiting our "Mobilizing Principles for Energy Activists" and applying President Kennedy's ideas about the role of "Courage in Democracy" to our profiles in power. We conclude this study by placing the question of the United States' energy future within the broader context of the "climate change" and "sustainable yield threshold" issues that portend "A World at Risk."

In considering the broader public-policy significance of the case studies presented throughout this book, we find that our profiles in power were successful largely because they also became profiles in courage, in President Kennedy's sense of the term.[1] Consequently, our case studies elucidate a set of mobilizing principles for energy activists and a series of insights into the role of courage in democracy.[2] They also indicate the high level of commitment and courage it will take to address the grave environmental problems raised by the fossil fuel era and to make the transition to the solar age.

Brief History of the Antinuclear Movement

The U.S. antinuclear movement first caught the public's attention in 1974 when Sam Lovejoy, an organic farmer in Montague, Massachusetts, single-handedly toppled a 500-foot utility tower to protest the construction of two nuclear power plants. Today, after more than 20 years of protest, the domestic market for nuclear power plants has collapsed in the United States; no new nuclear plants have been ordered by utilities since 1978. In the 1990s, activist attention has focused primarily on the fallout of the nuclear industry—bailout costs for failed plants, monitoring of aging and unsafe plants, and public opposition to radioactive waste storage dumps.

However, the roots of the antinuclear movement reach back half a century. The atomic bombing of Japan in 1945 ushered in the Atomic Age and inextricably linked the public controversies about nuclear power and nuclear weapons. Several studies trace the origins and diffusion of the antinuclear movement from a national debate in the late forties about the control of the atom to an international protest against nuclear power that crested in the late eighties in the wake of Chernobyl.[3] The history of the antinuclear movement can be broadly outlined in four phases: (1) historical roots, 1945 to 1967; (2) scientific dissent, 1968 to 1972; (3) the rise of a national movement, 1973 to 1979; and (4) the decentralization of nuclear power protest, 1980 to 1996.[4]

Historical Roots, 1945–1967   The initial debate focused on nuclear weapons policy. Due to the esoteric nature of the technologies involved, the original parameters of the public debate surrounding nuclear weapons and (eventually) nuclear power were first articulated within the confines of the scientific community. This often acrimonious discourse spanned both the pre-1945 decision to build and drop "the bomb" and the later, post-1945 attempts by scientists to gain international control over atomic weapons. Much of these post–World War II efforts were orchestrated by professional associations such as the Federation of Atomic Scientists and the Pugwash Conference on Science and World Affairs.

During the McCarthy era, even mild demonstrations within the scientific community against military nuclear policy were branded as treason and often stamped out. However, by the late fifties and early sixties, public protest against radioactive fallout from nuclear weapons testing grew. In 1962, Dr. Linus Pauling won the Nobel Peace Prize for his work to stop the atmospheric testing of nuclear weapons, and the "Ban the Bomb" movement spread throughout the United States and Britain. These pressures led to the Atmospheric Test Ban Treaty of 1962 and the Nuclear Nonproliferation Treaty of 1968, which established safeguards on the nuclear power fuel cycle under the supervision of the International Atomic Energy Commission.

Soon after President Eisenhower's call for peaceful uses of the atom, the first civilian reactor was built at Shippingport, Pennsylvania, in 1953. At the same time, initial public concern about nuclear power developed around potential radiation dangers from the proposed Meshoppen plant, also in Pennsylvania. This local concern mirrored the broader national issues of radioactivity and public health raised by weapons testing.

Scientific Dissent, 1968–1972   During this phase, dissent within the scientific community about the health, safety, and environmental impact of nuclear power surfaced in public and was incorporated into citizen legal interventions at specific power plants.[5] In the early seventies, Drs. Gofman, Tamplin, and Sternglass lent their credibility to the nascent antinuclear movement.[6] The three researchers, whose work impacted the emerging field of "health physics," had been censured by the government for releasing studies that warned of the dangers posed by low-level radiation to public health, particularly regarding infant mortality and increased cancer risks.

In 1971, nuclear engineers and physicists from the Union of Concerned Scientists (UCS) began publishing reports that, for the first time, seriously shook public confidence in the safety of nuclear power plants. The UCS released data indicating the inadequacy of the industry's emergency core cooling system (ECCS) tests and demonstrating that dissent on this issue within the AEC had been suppressed.[7] A major environmental group sued the AEC in an attempt to shut down two-thirds of the nation's operating reactors because of faulty safety systems and the risk of a meltdown.

Finally, the discharge of superheated water from reactor cooling systems caused large marine kills in Florida, New Jersey, and New York, creating a new alliance between nuclear critics and the nascent modern environmental movement, which arose after the Santa Barbara oil spill of 1968.[8] Activists realized that they could use the 1969 National Environmental Policy Act (NEPA) to question the impact of nuclear power plants on the local ecology in licensing hearings. This strategy was upheld in the benchmark Calvert Cliffs federal court ruling of 1971, which took the unprecedented step of weakening the absolute authority of the AEC on nuclear matters by ruling that environmental impact studies had to be completed before the agency could issue a construction permit.

The early seventies saw local antinuclear groups, supported by scientific testimony, adopt a strategy of citizen intervention and witnessed the legitimization of nuclear power as a major issue by the emerging environmental movement. Because citizen intervenors before the AEC encountered the "steam-roller of agency arrogance, expert elitism, and stacked-deck proceedings," the interventions were usually ineffective. But the alliance with the environmentalists spread the seeds of a growing national movement.

The Rise of a National Movement, 1973–1979 The first energy crisis of 1973 to 1974 transformed what had been an elite critique of nuclear power into a vigorous nationwide protest movement. The Arab oil embargo that followed the Egyptian-Israeli War marked the first time in modern history that energy supplies had a major impact on international economic stability. These events changed the nature of nuclear politics in the United States forever. First, they placed energy planning on an objective, cost-benefit basis; second, they elevated energy to a major domestic and international policy issue; third, they provided the antinuclear movement with the media attention needed to make it a major voice in the national energy policy debate.

During the second Nixon (1973–1974) and Carter (1977–1980) administrations, energy issues moved to center stage. Under the banner of "Clean Energy," Nixon proposed that nuclear energy be expanded to provide at least 40 percent of U.S. electricity and that the breeder reactor be developed. Calling the energy issue "the moral equivalent of war," Carter outlined a comprehensive energy policy that reversed the Nixon agenda by de-emphasizing nuclear power and promoting renewable energy. Carter made major commitments to coal, synthetic fuels, alternative energy, and conservation. In keeping his campaign promise to avoid a "plutonium economy," he invoked his credentials as a nuclear engineer to justify his veto of the fast breeder reactor at Clinch River and the deferral of the nuclear reprocessing plant at Barnwell.

Between 1974 and 1976, nuclear power and energy policy were ubiquitous issues in American politics. Congress continued to support the industry and to override nuclear critics and empowered a single agency, the Nuclear Regulatory Commission (NRC), both to promote and to police nuclear power. In response, Ralph Nader condemned nuclear power as "technological suicide" and convened the first Critical Mass conference to forge an alliance between consumers and environmentalists. Mainline environmental organizations joined Nader in calling for a moratorium on nuclear power development.

In 1974, Karen Silkwood, a Kerr-McGee plutonium processing plant worker in Oklahoma, became the movement's first martyr when she was mysteriously killed in a car accident while delivering plant documents to a newspaper reporter. Now, as segments of the women's and labor movements raised their voices in opposition to nuclear energy, a broad-based national coalition emerged.

While NRC insiders continued to leak documents showing that nuclear power was unsafe, the government released the Rasmussen Report in 1974, which demonstrated the "one-in-a-million" statistical improbability of a nuclear meltdown causing more than a thousand deaths.[9] In March 1975, a fire broke out at the Browns Ferry reactor in Alabama and burned through the wires controlling the ECCS. As public support wavered, the National Council of Churches denounced the "plutonium economy" required by nuclear power.

In 1976 the Nuclear Safeguards Initiative, the first major public referendum on nuclear power, was put on the California ballot. Similar initiatives were put to the vote in other states. Working through pronuclear organizations such as the Atomic Industrial Forum, Edison Electric Institute, and Citizens for Jobs and Energy, the manufacturers and utilities created an effective countercampaign and showed their ability to defeat nuclear opponents in statewide elections. A pronuclear countermovement was launched.

That same year, four reactor engineers defected from the industry to speak out against nuclear power. As one defector put it, "I thought it was important that someone with more knowledge of reactors than Jane Fonda was talking to the public." In 1977, the protests entered a more militant phase as sit-ins and plant blockades took place at Seabrook in New Hampshire and Diablo Canyon in California.[10] During this period, the nuclear industry came under an extensive attack as diverse groups lent their support to the antinuclear movement.

With the election of President Carter in 1976, it appeared as if the goals of the antinuclear movement had been realized. By 1980, public antinuclear sentiment was so strong that the Democratic Party formally adopted a platform position calling for the phaseout of nuclear power. However, the Democrats did not win the presidency in 1980, and the national policy victories of the antinuclear movement were short-lived.

The Decentralization of Nuclear Power Protest, 1980–1996

During the eighties, three sets of events led to (1) the decline of the national antinuclear movement, (2) the decentralization of nuclear power protest, and (3) the institutionalization of the energy issue. As a result, grassroots antinuclear activists developed new alliances with state and local environmental and consumer groups, as well as with elected officials and regulators. These safe-energy coalitions developed decentralized strategies that focused on local utility issues such as emergency evacuation planning, nuclear waste management, utility regulation, and conservation and renewable-energy programs.

The first set of events involved the near meltdown at Three Mile Island in March 1979 and the Chernobyl disaster of April 1986.[11] These "impossible accidents" led to a credibility meltdown that pushed U.S. public opinion against building more nuclear plants up to nearly 80 percent in 1986 and definitively turned many foreign governments against nuclear technology.[12] Most significantly, these accidents shifted the burden of proof in the safety issue from the "zealots" in the antinuclear movement to the advocates in the nuclear industry.

The second set of events was the "Reagan Revolution" in 1980, which ended the "energy decade" and shifted the national discourse from nuclear power to nuclear war and weapons.[13] In sharp contrast to Carter, Reagan branded antinuclear activists as "modern-day Luddites" and initiated cataclysmic reversals in energy, environmental, and weapons policy. Within a few years, the national antinuclear power movement was in disarray, energy policy had been displaced by weapons policy on the federal level, and major initiatives were launched to revive the nuclear option.

Price summarizes these initiatives, which were carried on throughout the Reagan-Bush years (1980–1992), by pointing out that the Reagan administration drastically cut the budget for alternative energy while increasing nuclear energy funding and restarting work on the breeder reactor.[14] Furthermore, the Reagan administration placed nuclear weapons development under the Department of Energy and introduced (unsuccessful) proposals to obtain weapons-grade plutonium from high-level waste at nuclear power plants. The department initiated steps to limit citizen participation in the reactor-licensing process. It propped up the beleaguered nuclear industry by relaxing nonproliferation policies so that U.S. companies could become major exporters of nuclear technology.

These dramatic changes in national policy brought the antinuclear movement full circle to its historical roots in nuclear disarmament. President Reagan's early anti-Soviet rhetoric, $1.5 trillion military buildup, and Strategic Defense Initiative (Star Wars) caused a major shift in the priorities of the national leadership of the antinuclear movement from nuclear power to nuclear weapons. Ironically, Reagan's efforts to use federal power to preserve the battered nuclear industry were ultimately stymied by his political crusade to establish a "New Federalism" that endorsed free markets, reduced government, and deregulation. Ultimately, these national initiatives could not revive the industry.

As Joppke observes, "The meteoric rise of antinuclear disarmament concerns left no space, and no resources, for sustaining mobilization against nuclear energy. . . . To the degree that an underlying nuclear fear had motivated the opposition to nuclear energy, the latter was simply outflanked by the similar but much more powerful imagery of global annihilation through nuclear war. . . . Deprived of its semantic hegemony, the antinuclear movement was bound to disintegrate."[15] But the antinuclear movement did not disintegrate; it decentralized and survived. Those activists who continued to protest nuclear power refocused their opposition away from national politics and public demonstrations and on the growing economic problems faced by consumers and nuclear utilities in the post-TMI era.

Thus, the third critical set of events involved both the decentralization of nuclear power protest and the institutionalization of the energy issue. Throughout the eighties and into the mid-nineties, nuclear energy continued to be a topic of intense public controversy. During this time, however, antinuclear activists and their allies shifted the locus of that conflict into the more responsive arenas of local, county, and state political structures. There, a significant number of aging, operating, nearly completed, or recently abandoned nuclear plants and projects offered ample targets for local opposition. In addition, a significant number of progressive utilities responded to local campaigns in support of energy efficiency and renewable-energy resources.

In 1983, by unanimously upholding the rights of states to reject new plants—on economic rather than on safety grounds—the United States Supreme Court ratified the decentralization of nuclear policy. By 1984, 11 states had enacted laws restricting or prohibiting new nuclear plant construction. In developing these referenda and other campaigns, local safe-energy groups often received significant legal and technical support from a national network of antinuclear and pro-solar organizations that had crystallized the energy debate during the seventies. This network includes the American Council for an Energy Efficient Economy, Critical Mass Energy Project, Environmental Action Foundation, Environmental Defense Fund, Greenpeace, MHB Technical Associates, Nuclear Information and Resource Service, Safe Energy Communication Council, and the Union of Concerned Scientists. Supported by this network, a decentralized and revitalized safe-energy movement was able to broaden its agenda to encompass both opposition to nuclear power and support for conservation and renewable energy.

Most significantly, as our case studies suggest, all these activities produced the gradual institutionalization of the energy issue. The energy wars of the past two decades have given rise to a new generation of energy activists—*green* utility executives, free-market regulators, independent power producers, demand-side efficiency experts, renewable-energy innovators, and solar technology entrepreneurs. These new energy activists have gradually brought about what Joppke calls the "reassertion of decentralized control" of the energy policy issue and have made it an ongoing concern of established institutions, including electric utilities, independent power producers, and renewable-energy businesses in the economic sphere, as well as of utility regulators, elected officials, and mainline environmental organizations in the political sphere. Thus, the issues of nuclear power originally raised by marginal citizen protesters and professional activists are now being internalized and addressed by mainstream political leaders and business executives.

Impact of the Antinuclear Movement   Sociologist Jerome Price states that "The antinuclear movement is one of the most significant social movements to emerge in the twentieth century."[16] He argues that the movement has crystallized a vital international debate about some of the "gravest problems yet faced by human society." These include how to control the spread of nuclear weapons, how to protect people and the environment from lethal radioactivity, and how to provide sustainable energy sources essential to the prosperity and survival of humanity.

As a social movement, the antinuclear movement has been highly successful. It has pressured the federal government, particularly the U.S. Nuclear Regulatory Commission, to strengthen and enforce the safety regulations for nuclear power plants, making them at the same time more expensive and less desirable. It has also focused intense public scrutiny on critical issues such as methods of forecasting electricity demand, calculation of life cycle power plant costs, the nuclear power–nuclear weapons link, the threat of nuclear terrorism, and the unresolved economic, safety, and waste problems associated with the current generation of aging power plants. Although the antinuclear movement has not substantially changed the U.S. government's pronuclear position, it has materially contributed to the collapse of the commercial nuclear power industry and to the de facto abandonment of the nuclear power option by the nation's utilities.

Some analysts interpret the decline of public protest against nuclear power as evidence of the demise of the antinuclear movement. Not so. What has occurred instead is the *institutionalization* of the antinuclear movement. Certainly, some of the direct-action activists have shifted their attention to nuclear weapons, social justice issues, and even new social movements that combine ecological, peace, and feminist concerns.

Furthermore, one could credibly argue, as Nelkin and Pollak have done for France and Germany and as Price has done for the United States, that groups with a new social movement agenda have played an integral role in the antinuclear movements of these nations.[17] In fact, had we included profiles of the antinuclear struggles by the Mothers for Peace at the Diablo Canyon plant in California or the Clamshell Alliance at the Seabrook site in New Hampshire, we might well have included a case study on radical ecology (i.e., deep ecology, ecofeminism, green politics, spiritual ecology, etc.). However, important as the radical ecology movement is, we chose not to emphasize it here for both factual and theoretical reasons. The main reason is that we disagree with the viewpoint that the antinuclear movement in the United States has been successful, or important, primarily because it is part of—or a harbinger for—an emerging social movement that will serve to bring about larger social and political transformation.

To the contrary, our case studies suggest that the antinuclear movement has thrived by carrying its contests into less visible, and more specialized, institutional arenas—regulatory and licensing hearings, legal and economic challenges, public financing forums, and community and utility renewable-energy projects. As a result, the legitimate issues raised by antinuclear activists have now been taken up (co-opted, if you will) and legitimized by mainstream environmental and scientific organizations, by utility executives and public service commissioners, and by business leaders and public officials.

Mobilizing Principles for Energy Activists

Each of our case studies illustrates an essential mobilizing principle for energy and citizen activists. These principles may be summarized as follows:

Chapter 2: The Reactor Techies:
> Establish truth force.

Chapter 3: The Ratepayers' Revolt:
> Define the issue so as to build broad coalition.

Chapter 4: The Conservation Revolution:
> Demonstrate viable alternative solutions.

Chapter 5: The Energy Entrepreneurs:
> Combine economics and environmentalism.

Chapter 6: The Dawn of the Solar Age:
> Create a new energy paradigm.

This book has documented the success of these principles regarding the antinuclear and pro-safe-energy movement. The broader question is what do these principles tell us about the dynamics of citizen activism and social movements?

From a general perspective, it is clear that the energy policy debate has been played out in both national and local arenas, where antagonistic pro- and antinuclear forces have been competing for the support of key audiences in the energy drama. On the one hand, antinuclear actors attempted to raise and answer questions about nuclear power to produce changes in political power regarding energy policy. On the other hand, institutional elites—in government, science, and industry—attempted to maintain their hegemonic ideology by sustaining their definitions of the situation.

The outcome of such public debates hinges to a great extent on how well social movements—and the citizen activists who lead them as contestants in social conflicts—challenge and sustain interpretations of power relations. In this context, social movements are essentially symbolic social dramas whose goal is the production of "meaning" for participants, antagonists, and observers. Sociologists Snow and Benford refer to this process as "framing," because social movements "assign meaning to and interpret relevant events and conditions in ways that are intended to mobilize potential adherents and constituents, to garner bystander support, and to demobilize antagonists."[18]

Comparative studies of social movements, such as Sidney Tarrow's seminal work *Power in Movement,* argue that the success of these movements is dependent on this framing process.[19] By framing the energy debate around the mobilizing principles we have outlined, the antinuclear movement was able to achieve both the consensus and action mobilization fundamental to the success of social movements in the political arena. We further suggest that all social movements, regardless of whether they promote issues as diverse as civil rights, workers' rights, or the right to life, need to find *relevant* ways to address these mobilizing principles if they are to sustain collective action and achieve political power.

Who Owns the Sun?

All of these mobilizing principles will have to be invoked in order to revitalize the now stagnant solar industry in the United States. Over the past two decades, the promises of energy independence and of a solar energy revolution have been repeatedly derailed in large part by the resistance of most electric utility, fossil fuel, and nuclear power companies.

Today, however, photovoltaics (PVs) hold a special place in the coming solar age. PVs are the first widely applicable electric energy source whose fuel is not a commodity. Decentralized solar electric energy is the first power source since the Industrial Revolution that can break the energy companies' monopoly on power. The big questions are who owns these PV power systems and, more specifically, who owns the electric power these power systems make? Will the energy companies hold on to their power monopoly, or will electric power become something that consumers can generate, own, and control? Authors Daniel Berman and John O'Connor pose the question even more broadly in their recent book *Who Owns the Sun?*[20]

As *Profiles in Power* demonstrates, only when the public ultimately controlled the electric companies, as in the cases of SMUD and WPPSS, did customers have the political ability to reclaim their energy future after expensive nuclear boondoggles. In other cases, such as Turkey Point and Shoreham, the most that organized ratepayers were able to achieve was a risk-sharing compromise in which they had to pay dearly for their utilities' mistakes and mismanagement.

The experience of SMUD shows that democratic empowerment, local decision making, and economic self-sufficiency not only are possible at municipally owned utilities but can be technically and administratively superior to the generation and distribution of electricity by privately owned utilities. Even in areas where electric power is now completely controlled by a private monopoly, the sale price of household-generated solar electricity (and of energy produced by other decentralized power sources) will become a bigger and bigger issue over time—especially as PV system costs become competitive. With large-scale, continuous, and orderly increases in PV purchases, experts believe that the installed price of photovoltaic power systems can come down to $5 to $7 per peak watt by the year 2000 and to $3 to $4 per peak watt by the year 2010.[21]

In this context, citizens who have invested in solar equipment connected to the utility grid will want to know why the utility sells them electricity at 12¢ per kilowatt-hour but credits them at only 4¢ per kilowatt-hour for the rooftop PV power they generate from residential solar power plants. Why not pay a premium to encourage solar electricity, as is done in many cities in Germany and Switzerland? Citizens will want to know why they are not allowed a special nighttime rate to charge up their electric bicycles and cars, when rooftop solar modules generate enough electricity to power both their homes and their vehicles.

Although few people can afford to spend $10,000 or more for the up-front cost of a stand-alone PV system connected to the grid, many people can afford the $150 per month required to purchase such a system over time at home mortgage loan interest rates, particularly when they would own the system free and clear in 15 or 20 years—if such loans were made available by banks or utilities. In the new solar economy, will utilities universally buy back home-generated power at a price that makes investment in PVs worthwhile, or will they pay only a fraction of its true value and try to maintain a monopoly over the generation and transmission equipment—thereby turning consumers into solar sharecroppers instead of solar homesteaders?

In order to resolve these questions in a manner that accelerates the widespread commercialization of solar energy, a central task of a revitalized antinuclear and pro-solar movement in America will be to put the power of grassroots democracy behind PVs and other renewable-energy technologies whose efficacy can no longer be denied on technological grounds.

The authors of *Who Owns the Sun?* argue that public ownership, with local democratic control of utilities, is a necessary (if not a sufficient) condition for the rebirth of the solar industry in the United States for two reasons. First, unlike a large private enterprise, a publicly owned utility is not compelled to constantly increase sales in order to increase profit margins and stock prices. Second, a well-managed public entity can supply electricity more cheaply because it does not have to pay stockholders a percentage of earnings each year in dividends. As competition and restructuring continue to transform the utility industry, municipal control of electricity may become the best way to protect the average citizen's access to affordable, reliable electricity and to ensure continued utility promotion of clean, renewable energy.

Calling for "more democracy" and "more local control" as the keys to solving America's energy problems, Berman and O'Connor propose a new "blueprint for a revitalized solar movement," which advocates the following:

- Public "ownership" of energy—just as with water or schools.
- Access to loans for PVs, other renewables, and other forms of energy- saving technologies, just as people purchasing autos or homes have access to such loans.
- Reinstitution of tax credits and rebates for renewable-energy investments.
- Net metering and rate-based incentives, so that independent home- and business-based electricity producers are paid the same price for the power they generate as they pay for utility-generated grid power.

- Massive public and private-sector investments in renewable-energy technologies and building techniques to reestablish U.S. leadership in this emerging global industry.
- Partnerships between industry, government, and local communities to oversee the new Green industries.
- Scholarships and retraining for displaced fossil fuel workers and small business loans to support new solar tradespeople.
- Congressional hearings to examine why none of the foregoing is federal or state policy.

We do not believe that the energy issue can be fundamentally reduced to a question of public versus private power. Rather, we believe the key to achieving these goals lies in truly leveling the playing field so that viable forms of conservation and renewable energy have an equal opportunity to compete in the marketplace.

However, we do agree with Berman and O'Connor that the ability to translate this blueprint into policy will depend on a revitalized popular mobilization on energy issues not seen since the 1970s-era oil shocks and the battles over nuclear power. In that era, the mass mobilization of energy activism stopped nuclear power plant construction and launched the solar energy and conservation movements. Today, at the dawn of the solar age, the pivotal battles are being fought for the social and economic control of energy and to shape a clean and renewable energy system that will live up to its democratic potential. This renewable-energy system will continue to be opposed by the fossil fuel and nuclear industries, whose long-term strategy is to keep society addicted to natural gas, petroleum, and uranium, delay the solar transition until oil and gas are too expensive to recover, and then burn the coal reserves and put a meter on the sun.

The full potential of political democracy, of social justice, and of sustainable development will never be realized without meaningful public participation in shaping our energy future. The full promise of the solar revolution will occur only at the expense of the private energy monopolies, and this revolution will not take place without a passionate public fight. Because the sun shines everywhere, solar energy is inherently democratic. Therefore, Americans should have an unalienable right to the solar energy they collect on their rooftops. But the battle for a safe and renewable energy future will not be won without the concerted efforts of scores of citizens who step forward once again to become profiles in power.

Courage and Democracy

President Kennedy's book *Profiles in Courage* is a historical study of senators and congressmen who had the courage to defy the majority of voters for the sake of principle and the national interest. They did so despite the "unbounded calumny and vilification" that accompanied their acts of courage.

In his conclusion, Kennedy wrote, "I am persuaded after long study of the record that the national interest, rather than private or political gain, furnished the basic motivation for the actions of those whose deeds are therein described."[22] In each case, these statesmen did not act because they "loved the public better than themselves." On the contrary, they acted precisely because they did love themselves—because each one's love of, and respect for, himself was stronger than the pressures of public disapproval.

Likewise, we cannot say that the profiles in this book do not enjoy personal profit or public acclaim. However, each one became a profile in power because of the firm faith and conviction that his or her course was *the right one*. Whereas Kennedy's statesmen acted in "the national interest," our profiles in power acted in what they perceived to be both the nation's interest and the earth's interest. Perhaps they are representative of a new breed of global citizens who hold themselves to a higher environmental ethic and moral standard.

Whereas Kennedy studied statesmen, only one of our profiles became an elected public figure. In fact, politics furnished them the opportunity structure to become profiles in power precisely because of the lack of leadership by, or the complicity of, regulators and political officials regarding the misrepresentations, lies, and in some cases the worst excesses and cover-ups of the nuclear industry. Kennedy believed that a democracy of the people must and can face its problems, and writing in the mid-1950s, he never imagined that—as has been the case throughout the history of the nuclear industry—the heavy burden of proof would have to be borne by citizen activists engaged in a prolonged struggle against the combined power of industry and government.

Kennedy observed that "The true democracy, living and growing and inspiring, puts its faith in the people . . . faith that the people will not condemn those whose devotion to principle leads them to unpopular courses, but will reward courage, respect honor and ultimately recognize right." He concluded with the following admonition: "For the continued political success of many of those who withstood the pressures of public opinion, and the ultimate vindication of the rest, enables us to maintain our faith in the long-run judgement of the people."[23]

Over the years, each of our energy activists and entrepreneurs has voiced and acted upon unpopular or minority viewpoints, only to have those convictions vindicated by time and events. The antinuclear movement has been successful because these profiles in power—and many others like them—have demonstrated courage in public affairs.

In this study, we have explored 10 profiles. However, it will take a multitude of profiles in power to address meaningfully the grave problems raised by the fossil fuel era and the Industrial Revolution. Over the past 200 years, these problems have created a world at risk.

A World at Risk

Unfortunately, the depletion of the earth's fossil fuel resources in the next century is part of a much larger and more ominous trend: the nearly simultaneous crossing of "sustainable yield thresholds" for the earth's most essential natural resources. In the nineties, this has resulted on a global scale in overfishing, overgrazing, aquifer depletion, deforestation, and soil erosion. As Lester Brown points out in his essay "The Acceleration of History,"

> When a sustainable yield threshold is crossed, it signals a fundamental change in the relationship between the consumer and that which is being consumed. To use an analogy from economics, the distinction is between consuming interest and spending the capital stock itself. . . . The demands of our generation now exceed the income, the sustainable yield of the earth's ecological endowment.[24]

Combined with the climatic impact of rising temperatures (megastorms, intense hot spells, and prolonged droughts), all of these trends are convening to decrease the world food supply dramatically, so that global food scarcity may become the most visible manifestation of continuing population growth and environmental mismanagement.[25] In sounding this alarm, Brown asks, "Can we avoid catastrophe?" and rhetorically answers "not if we keep sleepwalking through history." The only long-term solution to "securing food supplies for the next generation" depends on an all-out effort, a World War II–scale mobilization to stabilize both world population and climate.

Fortunately, there is a precedent for a global response to a tremendous need for change in a relatively short period of time. In 1974, Nobel laureates Sherwood Rowland and Mario Molina published a seminal article describing the threat to the ozone layer from the release of CFCs in the atmosphere. But it was not until two British scientists actually discovered a growing "hole" in the ozone layer over Antarctica that the international movement to ban and phase out CFCs was able to succeed.

According to Lester Brown, the key questions now are "What will be the climatic equivalent of the hole in the ozone layer?" and "What will finally trigger a meaningful response?" Will it be withering heat waves so intense that they create food shortfalls so massive that the resulting food prices destabilize the world economy? We would add, what will be the climatic equivalent of Three Mile Island and Chernobyl?

The answer may be literally blowing in the wind, as 1995 saw the entry of key players from agriculture, banking, and the insurance industry into the international climate change debate. After suffering billions of dollars in losses from exceptionally intense storms and hurricanes in the 1990s, some major insurance companies are urging policies that will slow climate change. They have been joined by financial institutions, which are leery of a future wave of bad debt that could be generated by crop failures due to droughts and the devastation of coastal real estate by the rising sea levels that will accompany global warming.

In March 1975, Arab leaders gathered in Algiers to attend the first summit meeting of the Organization of Petroleum Exporting Countries (OPEC) and to pay homage to the power of oil.[26] Twenty years later, in March 1995, environmental and world leaders gathered in Berlin to review the findings of the United Nations Intergovernmental Panel on Climate Change (IPCC) and to begin to apply the brakes to the fossil fuel era by reducing greenhouse gas concentrations in the atmosphere.[27] In the nineties, environmental issues are supplanting oil issues, and the findings of the IPCC are of greater concern to global leaders than the pronouncements of OPEC. With 13 worldwide weather-related disasters with damages of more than $3 billion occurring between 1989 and 1995, the "Showdown in Berlin . . . may have been a turning point in climate politics."[28]

In the past, it has usually required a major crisis to bring about a global response in both war and peace. Military and diplomatic examples can be found in the Allied effort to defeat Nazi Germany in World War II and the establishment of the Marshall Plan to rebuild Europe as a bulwark against Soviet Communism during the Cold War. Environmental examples can be found in the European response to the "forest death" caused by acid rain, the response of the industrialized nations to ozone depletion, and the widespread international rejection of nuclear power after the Chernobyl catastrophe.

Unfortunately, in the case of the greenhouse effect and the transition to a solar and hydrogen society, time is not on our side. The longer we put off the transition from a fossil fuel to a solar society, the larger the economic and environmental costs and the more difficult the transition will be. If we wait too long, humanity may lose the option to guide the transition intelligently and will face severe consequences, including widespread environmental degradation, worldwide famines, and political anarchy.

The choice is ours. The implementation of an aggressive national program to fully implement energy conservation and the transformation to a solar and hydrogen economy can definitively address many of the United States' most pressing energy-related problems.[29] Among these are the needs to

- reduce the country's huge and rapidly growing oil trade deficit;
- minimize the economic and political threats of continued and increased dependence on Middle Eastern oil supplies;
- limit and eventually prevent further increases in greenhouse gases, thereby reducing pollution and stabilizing the global climate;
- capture a large share of the enormous potential industry for advanced energy and environmental technologies, which could provide one of the largest international markets for high-tech, high-wage jobs in the next century, with annual sales estimated to exceed $800 billion; and
- increase national security and reduce the risks of nuclear theft, sabotage, and terrorism.

As the international environmental movement grows in influence and world petroleum resources begin a slow decline during the next century, the age of oil will come to an end. In the short term, this process may be accelerated by three factors of uncertain global impact: the growth of energy demand in rapidly changing economies such as Eastern Europe, China, India, and the former Soviet Union; the evolution of environmental policies in the West; and the speed of the commercialization of conservation and energy renewable technologies. As energy historian Daniel Yergin suggests, "with the fate of the planet itself seeming to be in question, the hydrocarbon civilization that oil built could be shaken to its foundations."[30]

We stand, therefore, at the gateway to the solar age.

Perhaps, for some, a transition of this magnitude appears to be beyond the realm of possibility, or beyond the scope of government influence or citizen activism. To those people, we point to the successes of the Marshall Plan in rebuilding Europe, the end of the Cold War with the fall of the Soviet Union, and the impact of the antinuclear movement in alerting the world to the dangers of nuclear weapons and in stalemating nuclear power in the United States. Or to the abolition of slavery in the United States, the transformation of apartheid in South Africa, and the nonviolent overthrow of Communism in Eastern Europe.

For others who still remain skeptical, we remind you of the words of Henry Ford, who shrewdly observed that "There are two kinds of people: those who think they can and those who think they can't. And they're both right."

For all who have found hope and inspiration in these profiles in power, we ask you to join with them in fulfilling the promise of the coming planetary transformation and assist them in playing midwife to the birth of the solar age.

Notes and References

Chapter One

1. For a discussion of the decision to drop the bomb, see John W. Dower et al., "The Atomic Age at Fifty," *Technology Review* 98, no. 6 (1995): 48–79. Our introductory remarks are based on this article.

2. Jonathan Schell, *The Fate of the Earth* (New York: Avon Books, 1982).

3. These data are cited from Nicholas Lenssen, "Nuclear Power Flat," in Lester Brown et al., *Vital Signs 1995* (New York: W. W. Norton, 1995), 52–53.

4. John L. Campbell, *Collapse of an Industry: Nuclear Power and the Contradictions of U.S. Policy* (Ithaca, N.Y.: Cornell University Press, 1988), 6.

5. Cited in Jack J. Kraushaar and Robert A. Ristinen, *Energy and Problems of a Technological Society,* 2d ed. (New York: John Wiley and Sons, 1993), 2.

6. Ibid., 40.

7. Daniel Yergin, *The Prize: The Epic Quest for Oil, Money, and Power* (New York: Simon and Schuster, 1991), 11–15.

8. Donella H. Meadows et al., *Beyond the Limits* (Post Mills, Vt.: Chelsea Green Publishing, 1992). Regarding the possible impact of technological advances, Meadows argues that "the more successfully society puts off its limits through economic and technical adaptations, the more likely it is in the future to run into several of them at the same time." She suggests that the wisest use of technology is to "buy time" in order to bring consumption and population down to sustainable levels.

9. Cited in the Frontline television documentary *The Politics of Power* (WGBH Education Foundation and Center for Investigative Reporting, 20 October 1992), 1.

10. Ibid., 3.

11. Ibid., 3.

12. From the United Nations Intergovernmental Panel on Climate Change, *Climate Change 1995: The IPCC Second Assessment,* as cited in Darren Goetze, "The Climes Are a Changing," *Nucleus* 18, no. 1 (Spring 1996). Other estimates of global sea level rise by the year 2100 range from a low of 1.9 feet to a high of 12.1 feet, according to J. S. Hoffman et al., "Future Global Warming and Sea Level Rise," in *Iceland Symposium '85,* ed. Per Brun (Reykjavik: National Energy Authority, 1986), as cited in Jodi L. Jacobson, "Holding Back the Sea," in Lester Brown et al., *State of the World 1990* (New York: W. W. Norton, 1990), 83.

13. Some observers classify the nuclear breeder reactor as a form of "renewable energy." For further discussion, see Kraushaar and Ristinen, "Nuclear Energy" and "Alternative Sources of Energy," in *Energy and Problems of a Technological Society.*

14. See U.S. Congress, Joint Committee on Atomic Energy, *Nuclear Power Economics—1962 through 1967,* 90 Cong., 2 sess. (Washington, D.C.: Government Printing Office, February 1968), 5; I. C. Bupp, "Nuclear Power: The Promise Melts Away," in Robert Stobaugh and Daniel Yergin, *Energy Future,* 3d ed. (1979; reprint, New York: Vintage Books, 1983), 134–72; and Campbell, *Collapse of an Industry.*

15. See figure 1, "Commercial Reactors Ordered in the United States since 1953," in James M. Jasper, *Nuclear Politics: Energy and the State in the United States, Sweden, and France* (Princeton: Princeton University Press, 1990), 47. According to these data, which were derived from the U.S. Department of Energy and the Atomic Industrial Forum, new commercial reactor orders ceased completely in 1979, and plant cancellations that began in 1972 continued through 1984, the last year for which data is presented.

16. Ibid., 41–63.

17. Campbell, *Collapse of an Industry,* 3–10.

18. Ralph Nader and John Abbotts, *The Menace of Atomic Energy* (New York: W. W. Norton, 1979).

19. See John G. Kemeny and other members of the President's Commission on the Accident at Three Mile Island, *The Need for Change: The Legacy of TMI* (Washington, D.C.: Government Printing

Office, 1979); and Mitchell Rogovin, *Three Mile Island: A Report to the Commissioners and the Public* (Washington, D.C.: Nuclear Regulatory Commission, 1980).

20. Jasper, *Nuclear Politics,* 62.

21. U.S. Office of Technology Assessment, *Nuclear Power in an Age of Uncertainty* (Washington, D.C.: Government Printing Office, OTA-E-216, 1984), 58–60.

22. Charles Komanoff, "Ten Blows That Stopped Nuclear Power," *The Electricity Journal* 4, no. 1 (January/February 1991): 18–25.

23. Amory B. Lovins, "Energy Strategy: The Road Not Taken?" *Foreign Affairs,* October 1976, 65–96.

24. For a comprehensive history of the antinuclear movement, see Jerome Price, *The Antinuclear Movement* (Boston: Twayne Publishers, 1990); and for the viewpoints of antinuclear activists, see Harry Wasserman, *Energy War: Reports from the Front* (Westport, Conn.: Lawrence Hill, 1979).

25. For a discussion of the political context of the antinuclear movement, see Christian Joppke, *Mobilizing against Nuclear Energy: A Comparison of Germany and the United States* (Berkeley: University of California Press, 1993); and for an example of the broad variety of arguments marshaled against nuclear power, see Mark Reader, ed., *Atom's Eve: Ending the Nuclear Age* (New York: McGraw-Hill, 1980).

26. Dorothy Nelkin and Michael Pollack, *The Atom Besieged* (Cambridge: MIT Press, 1982), 1.

27. This view is expressed in both Campbell, *Collapse of an Industry,* and Jasper, *Nuclear Politics.*

28. Albert B. Reynolds, "The Return of Nuclear Power: Nuclear Energy Is About to Make a Big Comeback—Just in Time," *Omni* 16, no. 3 (December 1993): 6. For other articles about a possible resurgence of commercial nuclear power, see Matthew Wald, "New Ideas Changing Nuclear Debate," *New York Times,* 22 July 1990, E5; Peter Miller, "A Comeback for Nuclear Power?" *National Geographic* 180, no. 2 (August 1991): 60–73; and Thomas Lippman, "Is Nuclear Power Blooming Again?" *Washington Post,* 26 April 1991, H1.

29. U.S. Council for Energy Awareness, *1990 Annual Report* (Washington, D.C.: USCEA, 1990).

30. Ibid., 1.

31. Charles Komanoff and Cora Roelofs, *Fiscal Fission: the Economic Failure of Nuclear Power: A Report on the Historical Costs of Nu-*

clear Power in the United States (Washington, D.C.: Greenpeace, 1992), 7–8.

32. Mo Ying W. Seto et al., *Nuclear Power: A Current Risk Assessment* (New York: Moody's Investment Service, 1993), 3.

33. Andrew Maykuth, "Industry Looks to New Technology, New Markets," *Philadelphia Inquirer,* 27 March 1994, D1.

34. Margaret L. Ryan, "EEI Studies Warn Many U.S. Utilities Not Producing Competitively," *Nucleonics Week,* 17 March 1994, 1.

35. Washington International Energy Group, *1995 Electric Utility Outlook* (Washington, D.C.: Washington International Energy Group, 1995), 30.

36. U.S. Council for Energy Awareness, *1990 Annual Report,* 2.

37. "Many Chernobyls Just Waiting to Happen," *Business Week,* 16 March 1992, 116.

38. Amory B. Lovins and L. Hunter Lovins, *Brittle Power: Energy Strategy for National Security* (Andover, Mass.: Brick House Publishing, 1982), 142.

39. For an account of the early phase of antinuclear activities, see Richard S. Lewis, *The Nuclear Power Rebellion* (New York: Viking Press, 1972); Abrahamson's review of Lewis's book appeared in *Science and Public Affairs,* May 1973, 43.

40. Komanoff, "Ten Blows That Stopped Nuclear Power," 25.

41. Dorothy Nelkin, *Nuclear Power and Its Critics: The Cayuga Lake Controversy* (Ithaca, N.Y.: Cornell University Press, 1971); Steve Ebbin and Raphael Kasper, *Citizen Groups and the Nuclear Power Controversy* (Cambridge: MIT Press, 1974); and Stephen L. Del Sesto, *Science, Politics, and Controversy: Civilian Nuclear Power in the United States* (Boulder, Colo.: Westview Press, 1979).

42. Edward J. Walsh, *Democracy in the Shadows: Citizen Mobilization in the Wake of the Accident at TMI* (New York: Greenwood Press, 1988).

43. Donald W. Stever Jr., *Seabrook and the Nuclear Regulatory Commission* (Hanover, N.H.: University Press of New England, 1980).

44. For a comparison of antinuclear movements in France and Germany, see Nelkin and Pollak, *The Atom Besieged;* for an analysis of nuclear politics in the United States, Sweden, and France, see Jasper, *Nuclear Politics;* and for a comparative study of citizen mobilization against nuclear energy in Germany and the United States, see Joppke, *Mobilizing against Nuclear Energy.*

45. Dorothy Nelkin, ed., *Controversy: Politics of Technical Decisions* (Newbury Park, Calif.: Sage Publications, 1992).

46. John F. Kennedy, *Profiles in Courage* (1956; reprint, commemorative edition, New York: Harper and Row, 1964), 1.

Chapter Two

1. From the *Wall Street Journal,* 21 February 1980; as cited in Daniel Ford, *Three Mile Island: Thirty Minutes to Meltdown* (New York: Penguin, 1982), 13.

2. These data were collected from various sources and reported in Christopher Flavin, *Reassessing Nuclear Power: The Fallout From Chernobyl,* Worldwatch Paper 75 (Washington, D.C.: Worldwatch Institute, March 1987), 5.

3. Reported by Nicholas Lenssen and Christopher Flavin, "Meltdown," *Worldwatch* 9, no. 3 (1996): 26.

4. A figure of 280,000 worldwide deaths was calculated by nuclear physicist Richard Webb, *Ecologist* 16, no. 4 (1986). A figure of 500,000 fatal malignancies was initially calculated by Dr. John Gofman and presented at the 192d annual meeting of the American Chemical Society in Anaheim, California, 8 September 1986. Some experts in the scientific community argued that these predictions were extreme and condemned them as "irresponsible" and "scaremongering." For example, Dr. Roland Finston, director of health physics at Stanford University, argued in 1986 that Gofman employed "extremely pessimistic assumptions."

Dr. Gofman's most recent calculations for a definitive estimate of 475,500 all-time Chernobyl-induced fatal cancers are reported in "Chernobyl: A Crossroad in the Radiation Health Sciences," chapter 24 in *Radiation-Induced Cancer from Low-Dose Exposure: An Independent Analysis* (San Francisco: Committee for Nuclear Responsibility Book Division, 1990), 24-1–24-20. Also see table 6, ibid., 36–19, "Cancer and Leukemia Tolls from the Chernobyl Nuclear Power Plant Accident," for distribution of cesium 137 and cesium 134 doses by country or region.

5. These data are reported in Flavin, *Reassessing Nuclear Power,* 66–67.

6. For an excellent discussion of the early days of atomic energy, and for the source of all quoted material in this and the following

paragraph, see Daniel Ford, "High Priests," part 1 in *The Cult of the Atom* (New York: Simon and Schuster, 1982), 17–82.

7. Unless otherwise noted, all the quotes and comments by Dr. John Gofman are from an interview with coauthor Jerry Brown in June 1986.

8. For a concise description of the accident, see Flavin, *Reassessing Nuclear Power,* 8–22, on which this description is based in part. For additional descriptions of the Soviet nuclear program and the Chernobyl disaster, see Michelle Carter and Michael Christensen, *Children of Chernobyl* (Minneapolis: Augsburg, 1993); David R. Marples, *The Social Impact of the Chernobyl Disaster* (New York: St. Martin's Press, 1988); Grigori Medvedev, *The Truth about Chernobyl* (New York: Basic Books, 1991); Ellen Bober Moynagh, "The Legacy of Chernobyl: Its Significance for the Ukraine and the World," *Environmental Affairs* (Boston: Boston College Environmental Affairs Law Review, 1994), 709–51; Chris C. Park, *Chernobyl: The Long Shadow* (New York: Routledge, 1989). Mr. Medvedev was the chief engineer at the time of Chernobyl's construction in 1970. He returned to Chernobyl and conducted a complete investigation; his report is considered an accurate unofficial source document on the plant and the accident.

9. From the *Moscow News,* as quoted in *Independent* (16 February 1989).

10. The comments by Olga Korbut, gymnast and Olympic gold medalist, are found in her introduction to Carter and Christensen, *Children of Chernobyl,* xiii–xvi.

11. Serge Schmemann, "Chernobyl within the Barbed Wire: Monument to Innocence and Anguish," *New York Times International,* 23 April 1991.

12. Volodymyr Yavorivsky, "The Poisoned Ukraine," *Wall Street Journal,* 12 December 1989.

13. John W. Gofman, *Radiation and Human Health* (New York: Pantheon Books, 1981). Other relevant publications by Dr. Gofman include *X-Ray: Health Effects of Common Exams* (San Francisco: Sierra Club Books, 1985); *Radiation-Induced Cancer from Low-Dose Exposure: An Independent Analysis* (San Francisco: Committee for Nuclear Responsibility Book Division, 1990); *Chernobyl Accident: Radiation Consequences for This and Future Generations* (in Russian language only), 1994; and *Preventing Breast Cancer* (San Francisco: Committee for Nuclear Responsibility Book Division, 1995).

He is also the author of more than a hundred scientific papers in peer-review journals in the fields of nuclear and physical chemistry, coronary heart disease, ultracentrifugal analysis of the serum lipoproteins, the relationship of human chromosomes to cancer, and the biological effects of ionizing radiation with particular reference to cancer induction. For additional biographical background on Dr. Gofman, see Gofman, *Radiation-Induced Cancer from Low-Dose Exposure,* vii–viii.

14. John W. Gofman and Arthur R. Tamplin, *Poisoned Power* (Emmanus, Pa.: Rodale Press, 1979), 6. These findings were first reported to the IEEE and in a series of 20 papers to the Joint Committee on Atomic Energy of the U.S. Congress.

15. See Gofman and Tamplin, "Introduction: The Nuclear Juggernaut," in *Poisoned Power,* 4–5.

16. Ibid., xv.

17. Ibid., ix.

18. Rachel Carson, *Silent Spring* (Boston: Houghton Mifflin, 1962).

19. Unless otherwise noted, all quotes and comments by Oncavage are from conversations and interviews with coauthor Jerry Brown from 1979 to 1984. During that time, Jerry Brown and Mark Oncavage were cofounders of Floridians United for Safe Energy (FUSE) in Miami, Florida. Brown is the source of much of the information appearing in the section titled "The Green Grunge at Turkey Point."

20. Richard Udell, *Tube Leaks: A Consumer's and Worker's Guide to Steam Generator Problems at Nuclear Plants* (Washington, D.C.: Critical Mass Energy Project, 1982), 36.

21. In spring 1979, Oncavage began to investigate steam generator problems at Turkey Point as a project for an environmental studies course he was taking from coauthor Jerry Brown at Florida International University in Miami.

22. Ellis Berger, "Nader Urges Dade to Fight FP&L Rate Rise," *Miami News,* 5 November 1982, 7A.

23. For documentation of the causes and costs of steam generator problems, see Udell, *Tube Leaks;* James Riccio and Stephanie Murphy, *The Aging of Nuclear Power Plants* (Washington, D.C.: Nuclear Information and Resource Service, 1988); and Jerry Brown and Mark Oncavage, "Steam Generator Degradation and Nuclear Power Costs: A Generic Problem," in *Proceedings of the Fourth International Conference on Alternative Energy Sources* (Ann Arbor: Ann Arbor Publishers, 1981).

24. Cited in *Miami News,* 27 October 1982.

25. "Whistle Blower Accuses Maine Yankee of Falsifying Documents and Jeopardizing Public Safety," *Press Release* (Washington, D.C.: Union of Concerned Scientists, 4 December 1995).

26. Ibid.

27. Ibid.

28. Shearson Lehman Brothers, "Should Investors Be Concerned about Rising Nuclear Decommissioning Costs?" *Electric Utilities Commentary* 3, no. 1 (6 January 1993), Executive Summary.

Chapter Three

1. "Asia's Energy Temptation," *Economist,* 17 October 1995, 17.

2. Safe Energy Communication Council, "Nuclear Power Economics" (Washington, D.C.: SECC, Fall 1995), 1.

3. Bruce Biewald et al., *Need for and Alternatives to Nuclear Plant License Renewal* (Boston: Tellus Institute, 1992), table 2.1. This analysis is based on a U.S. Department of Energy Study, *Analysis of Nuclear Plant Construction Costs* (DOE/EIA-0485, 1986).

4. Margaret L. Ryan, "EEI Studies Warn Many U.S. Units Not Producing Competitively," *Nucleonics Week,* 17 March 1994, 1.

5. Daniel Borson, *Payment Due: A Reactor-by-Reactor Assessment of the Nuclear Industry's $25+ Billion Decommissioning Bill* (Washington, D.C.: Public Citizen, Critical Mass Energy Project, 11 October 1990), 47–48.

6. Charles Komanoff and Cora Roelofs, *Fiscal Fission: The Economic Failure of Nuclear Power: A Report on the Historical Costs of Nuclear Power in the United States* (Washington, D.C.: Greenpeace, 1992), 7–8. Life cycle costs include costs paid to date per kilowatt-hour from 1968 to 1990 by the utility for direct reactor costs (construction, operations and maintenance, fuel)—6.35¢ per kilowatt-hour; indirect reactor costs, including canceled plants, to-date expenditures, and set-asides for decommissioning—0.90¢ per kilowatt-hour; and federal support costs, including research, regulation, and set-asides for the Waste Disposal Fund—1.55¢ per kilowatt-hour. These combined costs total 8.80¢ per kilowatt-hour.

Regarding the cost per kilowatt-hour for new sources of electricity in 1995, Komanoff Energy Associates reported that these were 0–5¢ for energy efficiency, 2–8¢ for hydroelectricity, 3–5¢ for gas, 5–6¢ for coal, 5–8¢ for wind, 6–8¢ for oil, 9¢ for solar thermal, 10–12¢ for nuclear, and 15–20¢ for solar photovoltaic (solar electric).

7. Prepared remarks of Lewis L. Strauss, chairman, United States Atomic Energy Commission, Washington, D.C., 16 September 1954.

8. Karl Grossman, *Power Crazy* (New York: Grove Press, 1986), ix, xiv.

9. See Ibid., ix–xiii, as the source for, and documentation of, these statements about LILCO. These points are elaborated throughout Grossman's book, which provides an authoritative source for the case against Shoreham as presented by Commissioner Bredes and other antinuclear activists and organizations.

10. Ibid., xiii.

11. Unless otherwise noted, all quotes and comments by Nora Bredes are from an interview with coauthor Jerry Brown in April 1994.

12. Grossman, *Power Crazy,* 322.

13. Ibid., 323.

14. Ibid., 354–55.

15. Ibid., 353.

16. For an in-depth discussion of the ratepayers' rebellion in Washington, see especially Richard Rudolph and Scott Ridley, "Warning Signs," and "Citizen Rebellion," chapters 1 and 6 in *Power Struggle: The Hundred-Year War over Electricity* (New York: Harper and Row, 1986). For an analysis of the WPPSS default from the bondholders' viewpoint, see Howard Gleckman, *WPPSS: From Dream to Default* (New York: The Bond Buyer, 1983).

17. Unless otherwise noted, all quotes and comments by Dan Leahy are from an interview with coauthor Jerry Brown in August 1983. As additional background for this case, interviews were also conducted with William Appel, then a Washington bond attorney with Jadine, Foreman, Turner and Appel; and Mark Reis, director of the Northwest Conservation Act Coalition, which prepared the Model Electric Power and Conservation Plan for the Pacific Northwest, 5 May 1982.

18. For this description of electric power in the Pacific Northwest, we have relied extensively on the observations of Ralph Cavanagh, senior staff attorney, Natural Resources Defense Council, made in an interview with coauthor Jerry Brown in December 1992; and on Ralph Cavanagh, "Electrical Energy Futures," *Environmental Law* 14, no. 133 (1983): 133–75.

19. Cited in Cavanagh, "Electrical Energy Futures," 134.

20. Ibid., 136.

21. Ibid., 148.
22. Saul D. Alinsky, *Reveille for Radicals* (New York: Vintage Books, 1969), 132.
23. Cavanagh, "Electrical Energy Futures," 149.
24. Ibid.
25. Rudolph and Ridley, *Power Struggle,* 210. For further discussion, see chapter 8, "Wall Street: The Stall of the Dividend Machines," 210–37.
26. Ibid., 224–25.
27. Cavanagh, "Electrical Energy Futures," 134.

Chapter Four

1. For a brief discussion of the history of the electric power industry, see Christopher Flavin and Nicholas Lenssen, *Powering the Future: Blueprint for a Sustainable Electric Industry,* Worldwatch Paper 119 (Washington, D.C.: Worldwatch Institute, 1994).
2. For a detailed discussion of the "electric utilities at the crossroad" and of the factors causing the evolution of the utility industry, see Edward Kahn, *Electric Utility Planning and Regulation* (Berkeley: American Council for an Energy-Efficient Economy, 1991).
3. Both authors have been involved with Business Executives for National Security. From 1985 to 1986, Jerry Brown was executive director for BENS of northern California. At the same time, Rinaldo Brutoco was a director of BENS of northern California.
4. Harold Willens, *The Trimtab Factor* (New York: William Morrow, 1984), 27.
5. This information on California and its energy supply is derived from the California Energy Commission, *The 1992–1993 California Energy Plan* (Sacramento: California Energy Commission, 1994).
6. Lee Schjipper and James E. McMahon, *Energy Efficiency in California: A Historical Analysis* (Berkeley: American Council for an Energy-Efficient Economy, 1995), 5. This study provides a detailed technical analysis of the impact of energy efficiency in California since the 1970s.
7. Southern California Energy Company, *1994 Annual Report* (Rosemead, Calif.: Southern California Edison, 1995), 1.
8. Unless otherwise noted, all quotes and comments by Bryson are from an interview with coauthor Jerry Brown in December 1992.
9. A utility's "rate base" refers to the value of its capital assets. Most regulatory attention during the declining-cost era was devoted to

determining the value of capital invested (rate base) and fixing the level of reasonable earnings. The utility industry has also developed an accounting practice, the "used and useful" doctrine, to deal with construction financing costs. This practice transforms financing costs into capital costs and incorporates them into the rate base only when the plant comes into service, i.e., becomes "used and useful" to the ratepayer.

10. Cited in Peter Nulty, "Finding a Payoff in Environmentalism," *Fortune,* 21 October 1991, 80.

11. Ibid., 79.

12. David Roe, *Dynamos and Virgins* (New York: Random House, 1984), 12. Roe provides a personal account of the Environmental Defense Fund's early strategies and conflicts with PG&E before the California Public Utilities Commission to establish the principle of least-cost planning, based primarily on energy conservation. The materials for "PG&E versus 'the Greenie' " are taken from Roe's book and his interview with coauthor Jerry Brown in June 1986.

13. Ibid., 3.

14. Ibid., 13.

15. Interview with Jerry Brown, June 1986.

16. Roe, *Dynamos and Virgins,* 16.

17. Interview with Jerry Brown, December 1992.

18. The term "avoided cost" was introduced as a concept distinct from "marginal cost" and "fuel savings" to analyze and describe the pricing of power purchases made under PURPA. For a discussion of marginal and avoided costs, see Kahn, *Electric Utility Planning and Regulation,* 191–98.

19. See discussion on the "Rise of the Independents" in Flavin and Lenssen, *Powering the Future,* 16–24.

20. Unless otherwise indicated, all data on SCE's performance after 1990 are taken from SCEcorp, *1991 Annual Report* (Rosemead, Calif.: SCEcorp, 1992).

21. Southern California Edison, "Energy Mix: March 1995, Resource Projection (GWh), 1995–2005," 24 March 1995.

22. Interview with coauthor Jerry Brown, December 1992.

23. Ibid.

24. SCEcorp, *1991 Annual Report,* 8.

25. Foster Electric Report, 17 April 1996, report no. 84, 26.

26. In return for delaying the implementation of ZEV mandates until 2003, the CARB also required that the big seven automakers

(General Motors, Ford, Chrysler, Toyota, Nissan, Honda, and Mazda) abide by their commitments to build a "cleaner car" by 2001 (a "49-state car") and to participate in California's ZEV Implementation Advisory Committee. These automakers have agreed to pay up to $100 million in penalties and agreed to the reinstatement of the earlier 2 percent ZEV quota if they fail to comply.

In this context of changing regulations, it should be noted that the interviews with John Bryson of SCE and with David Freeman of SMUD took place in 1992, *after* the original LEV/ZEV program was enacted by the state legislature in 1990 and *before* the CARB relaxed the ZEV implementation schedule in 1996. As such, these interviews and profiles reflect the enthusiasm and momentum generated at SCE and SMUD by the initial ZEV implementation schedule.

27. Terry Jackson, "The Electric Car," *Miami Herald,* 24 March 1996, F1. The federal Clean Air Act Amendments (CAAA) of 1990 gave California the authority to set stricter auto emissions standards than the rest of the nation and gave other states the choice between adopting either the California or the federal standards. Although both New York and Massachusetts have passed ZEV mandates, to date the other northeastern states have refused to adopt similar requirements. In March 1997, a federal court invalidated a U.S. Environmental Protection Agency attempt to impose electric vehicle and ZEV standards on northeastern states.

28. Ibid.

29. For a summary discussion of the impact of the conservation revolution at other utilities, see the cover story "Conservation Power—the Payoff in Energy Efficiency," *Business Week,* 16 September 1991, 86–92.

30. For 12 months ended 30 June 1992, see SMUD, Quarterly Report, 2d Quarter, Sacramento, 1992.

31. Interview with coauthor Jerry Brown, December 1992. All of the quotes from David Freeman in this chapter are from this interview, unless otherwise noted. In March 1994, Freeman left SMUD to become the president and chief executive officer of the New York Power Authority.

32. This synopsis of SMUD's history before the shutdown of Rancho Seco in 1989 is based on an interview with Edward A. Smeloff, president, SMUD Board of Directors, conducted by coauthor Jerry Brown in December 1991. Unless otherwise noted, all quotes from Smeloff are from this interview.

33. Ibid.

34. According to SMUD, trees cut cooling costs 20 to 40 percent per year. Savings from shade trees for a 1,600-square-foot Sacramento home are $80 per year. SMUD, *1991 Annual Report,* Sacramento, 1992.

35. Ed Smeloff, "Sacramento Solution: Energy Efficiency" (Washington, D.C.: SECC, 1991).

36. SMUD, *EV Pioneer News* 1 (Summer 1992): 5.

37. Ibid., 4.

38. For a summary of utility and industry conservation initiatives underway during the early 1990s, at the time the interviews with Bryson and Freeman were conducted, see "Conservation Power: the Payoff in Energy Efficiency," *Business Week,* 16 September 1991, 86–91.

39. Ibid., 86.

40. See, for example, "Conservation: The Key Energy Resource," chapter 6 in *Energy Future,* ed. Robert Stobaugh and Daniel Yergin, Report of The Energy Project at the Harvard Business School (New York: Vintage Books, 1979).

41. For a detailed analysis of four energy scenarios, see Alliance to Save Energy et al., *America's Energy Choices* (Cambridge, Mass.: Union of Concerned Scientists, 1991). The data quoted here are derived from the Executive Summary, 1–4.

42. See Flavin and Lenssen, *Powering the Future,* 46. On 24 May 1995, the California Public Utilities Commission recommended a major restructuring of the state's electric service industry, with the ultimate goal of lowering the cost of electricity to customers. This restructuring was the result of the Order Instituting Rulemaking on the Commission's Proposed Policies Governing Restructuring California's Electric Services Industry and Reforming Regulation, Before the Public Utilities Commission of the State of California, filed 20 April 1994.

Central to the commission's recommendation was the establishment of a Power Exchange structure instead of bilateral agreements or contracts for direct delivery of electricity by a power producer to a buyer. In SCE's view, the Power Exchange will ensure fair, open access to the transmission system and suppliers, a market for all power producers and customers, and unbiased administration of a region's electric power needs.

Although the typical California residential bill is 10 percent lower than the national average, the average electric rate of 10.7¢ per kilowatt-hour is about 3¢ above the national average. The 10.7¢ average rate breaks down as follows: generation, 42 percent; government-mandated power purchase contract, 33 percent; transmission and distribution, 20 percent; and demand-side management and other programs, such as low-income rate assistance, 5 percent. SCE's 1996 cost to generate electricity averages 4.8¢ per kilowatt-hour, while the mandatory purchases average 8.9¢ per kilowatt-hour.

It is noteworthy that mandated power purchases made up 33 percent of SCE's total generation in 1994, compared to 6 percent for the national average—or almost six times the national average for more costly renewable and alternative energy sources. In 1995, SCE expected to pay $1.7 billion above market for this power, so that mandated power purchases result in almost 20 percent higher rates for SCE's customers because they have 10-year fixed energy payments based on a 1983 forecast of oil prices escalating to $100 per barrel. In 1996, oil cost about $15 per barrel. For further discussion of SCE's views on the commission's recommendations, see Corporate Communications, SCE, "California's Electric Industry Restructuring—Questions and Answers," July 1995.

Chapter Five

1. Neil Baldwin, *Edison: Inventing the Century* (New York: Hyperion, 1995). The following ideas about Edison's work are derived from a book review on Baldwin's biography by Peter Coy, "Edison: What Made the Lightbulbs Go On?" *Business Week,* 20 February 1995, 17.

2. Baldwin, *Edison,* 103.

3. Ibid.

4. Electric Power Research Institute et al., *Distributed Utility Valuation Project Monograph,* EPRI Report TR-102807 (San Francisco: Quantitative Solutions, 1993).

5. Ibid., vi.

6. Christopher Flavin and Nicholas Lennsen, *Beyond the Petroleum Age,* Worldwatch Paper 100 (Washington, D.C.: Worldwatch Institute, December 1990), 19.

7. Carl J. Weinberg and Robert H. Williams, "Energy from the Sun," *Scientific American,* September 1990. Also see Flavin and Lenssen, *Beyond the Petroleum Age,* 18–19, for projections of renewable electricity costs in the year 2000, in 1988 cents per kilowatt-hour, as follows: 5¢ for wind, 4¢ for geothermal, 10¢ for photovoltaic, 6¢ for

solar thermal troughs with gas assistance. By 2030, photovoltaics could provide a large share of the world's electricity for as little as 4¢ per kilowatt-hour.

8. Nancy Cole and P. J. Skerrett, *Renewables Are Ready: People Creating Renewable Energy Solutions,* Union of Concerned Scientists (White River Junction, Vt.: Chelsea Green Publishing, 1995), 1.

9. Ibid., xi.

10. The Royal Dutch Shell "Energy in Transition" scenario is described in Joseph J. Romm and Charles B. Curtis, "Mideast Oil Forever?" *Atlantic Monthly* 277, no. 4 (April 1996): 57–74.

11. "The Future of Energy," *Economist,* 7 October 1995, 23–26.

12. For an insightful discussion into the dynamics of utility deregulation, see Gregg Easterbrook, "Energy: The Future of Electric Power," *Atlantic Monthly* 272, no. 1 (July 1993): 42–46.

13. Real Goods, "Mission Statement," *1994 Annual Report.*

14. William Irwin Thompson, "The Meta-Industrial Village," chapter 2 in *Darkness and Scattered Light: Speculations on the Future* (Garden City, N.Y.: Anchor Press/Doubleday, 1978), 54–103.

15. Ibid., 80.

16. All of John Schaeffer's comments cited in this chapter were made in an interview with coauthor Jerry Brown in August 1994.

17. Michael Potts, "The Real Goods Story," *Alternative Energy Sourcebook,* 7th ed. (Ukiah, Calif.: Real Goods, 1993), 21.

18. National Photovoltaics Program, U.S. Department of Energy, *Photovoltaics Program Plan, FY 1991—FY 1995* (Golden, Colo.: National Renewable Energy Laboratory, 1991), 4, 31.

19. Gary Beckwith, "Welcome Back, Solar Tax Credits," *Real Goods News,* June 1994, 14.

20. Horace, *Odes,* book III, ode iii, 1, 1.

21. Real Goods, "Mission Statement," *1994 Annual Report.*

22. Michael Brower, *Cool Energy: Renewable Solutions to Environmental Problems* (Cambridge: MIT Press, 1992), 40.

23. Christopher Flavin, "Harnessing the Sun and the Wind," in Lester Brown et al., *State of the World* (New York: W. W. Norton, 1995), 59.

24. Brower, *Cool Energy,* 40.

25. Paul Maycock, "Photovoltaics Are Economical NOW!" *Real Goods News,* 1994, 5.

26. Brower, *Cool Energy,* 39.

27. U.S. Department of Energy, *Photovoltaics Program Plan,* 6.

28. Schaeffer, "Editorial," *Real Goods News,* 1994, 3.

29. Ibid.

30. Ibid.

31. Ibid.

32. Cited in Flavin and Lenssen, *Beyond the Petroleum Age,* 26.

33. Flavin and Lenssen, *Power Surge: Guide to the Coming Energy Revolution* (New York: W. W. Norton, 1994), 160.

34. Schaeffer, "Editorial," *Real Goods News,* 1994, 3.

35. Thompson, *Darkness and Scattered Light,* 77.

36. All quotes from John Perry were taken from an interview conducted with coauthor Jerry Brown in October 1995.

37. Jesse H. Ausubel, "Energy and Environment: The Light Path," in *Energy Systems and Policy* (New York: Rockefeller University, 1991), 184.

38. Robert H. Williams "The Clean Machine," *Technology Review,* April 1994, 21.

39. For an insightful discussion of the physical and philosophical implications of climate change, see Bill McKibben, *The End of Nature* (New York: Anchor Books, 1989).

40. Excerpted from the briefing paper "The Greenhouse Effect" (Cambridge: Union of Concerned Scientists), April 1989. Without this naturally occurring "greenhouse" blanket, the earth's surface would be nearly 35 degrees colder, making it uninhabitable.

41. J. S. Hoffman et al., "Future Global Warming and Sea Level Rise," in Per Brun, ed., *Iceland Symposium '85* (Reykjavik: National Energy Authority, 1986); as cited in Jodi Jacobson, "Holding Back the Sea," *State of the World* (New York: W. W. Norton, 1990), 83.

42. Although the California Zero Emissions Vehicle (ZEV) regulation timetable has been significantly set back during early 1996, when this book was being written, the full implications of this time shift on ZEV production had not yet been established. Therefore, almost all references to the legislation and its implications are reported from articles and data written under the assumption that the legislation would be implemented as originally passed, with the 2 percent sales standards mandated for 1998 increasing to 5 percent in 2001 and to 10 percent in 2003.

43. Jeffrey Zygmont, "Here Comes the Sungo: Solar Cars Juice Up Their Engines and Take to the Road," *Omni* 16, no. 8 (May 1994): 20.

44. David Woodruff, Larry Armstrong, and John Carey, "Electric Cars: Will They Work? And Who Will Buy Them?" *Business Week,* 30 May 1994, 114.

45. Roland J. Hwang, "Say Goodbye to the Gas Pump," *Nucleus* 15, no. 3 (Fall 1993): 1–3. Currently EVs' maximum range per charge is about 100 miles, and recharge times take between 5 and 7 hours. Because of the heavy and expensive battery packs necessary to power them, EVs out-cost their gasoline counterparts by as much as $10,000. Further, though battery technology is giving EVs greater and greater ranges through advances in lead-acid and other electrolyte mediums, the fact remains that a kilogram of batteries contains over 100 times less energy than a kilogram of gasoline, making EVs enormously un-competitive with respect to fuel energy density.

46. Williams, "The Clean Machine," 24.

47. Ibid., 25.

48. U.S. Electricar, "The Drive to Clean Air," *1993 Annual Report,* 7.

49. Peter Hoffman, ed., *The Hydrogen Letter* 8, no. 2 (February 1993): 1.

50. Thomas S. Kuhn, *The Structure of Scientific Revolutions* (Chicago: University of Chicago Press, 1970).

51. Williams, "The Clean Machine," 21.

52. Marshall Miller, "A Fuel for All Reasons," *Nucleus* 16, no. 3 (Fall 1994): 1.

53. David Smith, "Benz, GM Back Ballard Engine," *Vancouver Sun,* 22 April 1994, D5.

54. Williams, "The Clean Machine," 24.

55. Energy Partners, *Total Energy Supply: The "Gas Station" Demonstration Program,* (West Palm Bach, Fla.: Energy Partners, 1993), 1–2.

56. Ibid.

57. Peter Lehman and Christine Parra, "Hydrogen Fuel from the Sun," *Solar Today,* September/October 1994, 21.

58. Smith, "Benz, GM Back Ballard Engine," D5.

59. Ballard Power Systems, Inc., *Annual Report 1993* and *Annual Report 1994* (North Vancouver, British Columbia, Canada).

60. Ibid.

61. Meridian Corporation, *Characterization of U.S. Energy Resources and Reserves,* prepared for Deputy Assistant Secretary for Renewable Energy, U.S. Department of Energy, June 1989, 9.

62. Cole and Skerrett, *Renewables Are Ready,* 4. Federal R&D funding for renewable energy was cut from $667.5 million in fiscal year 1979 to $114.7 million in fiscal year 1989, while nuclear fission re-

ceived $609.1 million in fiscal year 1989. By fiscal 1995, the renewable-energy budget had been increased upward again to approximately $400 million.

63. See Flavin and Lessen, *Beyond the Petroleum Age,* 17; and Cole and Skerrett, *Renewables Are Ready,* 1–4.

64. Dr. Hans Blix, director general of the International Atomic Energy Agency, press release, 4 July 1989.

Chapter Six

1. Joseph Romm and Charles Curtis, "Mideast Oil Forever?" *Atlantic Monthly* 277, no. 4 (April 1996): 57–74.

2. Ibid., 57.

3. Ibid.

4. Amory B. Lovins, "Energy Strategy: The Road Not Taken?" *Foreign Affairs,* October 1976, 65–96. The first scientist to envision a solar economy was Frederick Soddy, *Cartesian Economics* (London: Hendersons, 1922); Soddy was an English chemist who shared the Nobel Prize with Rutherford for introducing isotopes into atomic theory. The first economist to fully understand the coming solar age was Nicholas Georgescu-Rogen, *The Entropy Law and the Economic Process* (1971), as discussed in Hazel Henderson, *The Politics of the Solar Age: Alternatives to Economics* (Indianapolis: Knowledge Systems, 1988), 224–40.

5. Robert A. Nisbet, *Social Change and History: Aspects of the Western Theory of Development* (London: Oxford University Press, 1969), 4.

6. These observations were drawn from Gregg Easterbrook, "Energy: The Future of Electric Power," *Atlantic Monthly,* July 1993, 42–46.

7. Cited in Harlan Clifford, "Power Broker," *Profiles,* December 1992, 49.

8. Amory Lovins, *Soft Energy Paths: Toward a Durable Peace* (New York: Harper and Row, 1979).

9. All comments and quotes from Hunter Lovins are from an interview with coauthor Jerry Brown in August 1991. This profile uses the first names of Hunter and Amory Lovins in order to be able to distinguish their respective comments.

10. Unless otherwise cited, all comments and quotes from Amory Lovins are from his taped remarks on "Building a New Energy Fu-

ture," Conference for a Nuclear-Free 1990s, Washington, D.C., April 1991 (Boulder, Colo.: Sounds True, 1991). For a general list of writings by and about Amory and Hunter Lovins, see the "Publication List and Order Form," Rocky Mountain Institute, Snowmass, Colo.

11. Cited in James R. Udall, "Amory Lovins: Walking the Soft Path," *Sierra,* January/February 1990, 129.

12. Amory Lovins, "Energy Strategy," 95–96.

13. Cited in Andrew D. Basiago, "The House Where the Future Lives," *Calypso Log,* September 1986, 11.

14. The parable of the refrigerator is cited in "The Plowboy Interview," *Mother Earth News,* July/August 1984, 17–18.

15. Ibid., 18. Subsequently, a Danish engineer showed that 260 kilowatt-hours per year would be highly cost-effective; shortly afterward, in 1979, a California engineer built a refrigerator that used 288 kilowatt-hours per year and built a prototype in 1982 that used only 64. At the Rocky Mountain Institute, the zero-energy passive refrigerator will use only about a half a kilowatt per year—to run the light that goes on when you open the door.

16. See the *Visitors' Guide—Rocky Mountain Institute* (Snowmass, Colo., 1991).

17. For other discussions of the emerging water crisis, see Marc Reisner, *Overtapped Oasis: Reform or Revolution for Western Water* (Washington, D.C.: Island Press, 1990); Sandra Postel, *Last Oasis: Facing Water Scarcity* (New York: W. W. Norton, 1992); and Janet N. Abramovitz, *Imperiled Waters, Impoverished Future: The Decline of Freshwater Ecosystem,* Worldwatch Paper 128, (Washington, D.C.: Worldwatch Institute, March 1996).

18. Amory B. Lovins and L. Hunter Lovins, *Brittle Power: Energy Strategy for National Security* (Andover, Mass.: Brick House Publishing, 1982).

19. Ibid., 1–2.

20. L. Hunter Lovins, Amory B. Lovins, and H. Richard Heede, "Energy Policy," in *Changing America: Blueprints for the New Administration,* Citizens Transition Project, ed. Mark Green (New York: New Market Press, 1992), 672.

21. Ibid., 674.

22. Ibid., 676–78.

23. Christopher Flavin and Nicholas Lenssen, *Power Surge: Guide to the Coming Energy Revolution* (New York: W. W. Norton, 1994), 275–76. Unless otherwise noted, all comments and quotations

attributed to Flavin are either cited from *Power Surge* or taken from an interview with coauthor Jerry Brown in May 1995.

24. Ibid., 278.

25. Flavin has written or coauthored many reports for the Worldwatch Institute's Paper Series, including "The Future of Synthetic Materials: The Petroleum Connections," no. 36; "Energy and Architecture," no. 40; "Wind Power: A Turning Point," no. 45; "Electricity from Sunlight: The Future of Photovoltaics," no. 52; "Nuclear Power: The Market Test," no. 57; "Electricity's Future," no. 61; "World Oil," no. 66; "Reassessing Nuclear Power: The Fallout from Chernobyl," no. 75; "Building on Success: The Age of Energy Efficiency," no. 82; "Slowing Global Warming: A Worldwide Strategy," no. 91; "Beyond the Petroleum Age: Designing a Solar Economy," no. 100; and "Powering the Future: Blueprint for a Sustainable Electricity Industry," no. 119. He also regularly contributes chapters on energy-related topics to the annual *State of the World* report. All of these publications are available from the Worldwatch Institute, Washington, D.C.

26. Flavin and Lenssen, *Power Surge*; see throughout for a description of these trends and technologies.

27. Ibid., 29–70; the second and third chapters of *Power Surge* are titled "Oil Shock" and "Eco Shock," respectively. The following sections titled "The Middle East Tinderbox" and "The Greenhouse Effect" are based largely on materials presented in these chapters.

28. Ibid., 59.

29. Darren Goetze, "The Climes They Are a Changing," *Nucleus* 18, no. 1 (Spring 1996): 2; see this article for a summary of the IPCC report.

30. Ibid., 12.

31. Christopher Flavin and Nicholas Lenssen, *Beyond the Petroleum Age: Designing a Solar Economy,* Worldwatch Paper 100 (Washington, D.C.: Worldwatch Institute, December 1990).

32. Ibid., 17.

33. Flavin and Lenssen, *Power Surge,* 280–81.

34. Ibid., 287. See chapter 13, "Through the Looking Glass," for a full discussion of the Worldwatch Sustainable Future and the renewable technologies that are in place to realize this future. The following discussion on wind, natural gas, and solar and hydrogen power systems is based in part on this chapter.

35. Ibid., 289–90.

36. Ibid., 310–11.

Chapter Seven

1. President John F. Kennedy, *Profiles in Courage* (New York: Harper and Row, 1956), 1–31.

2. Ibid., 249–60.

3. See Robert C. Mitchell, "From Elite Quarrel to Mass Movement," *Transaction/Society* 18, no. 5 (July/August 1981): 76–84; Nelkin and Pollak, *The Atom Besieged;* and Joppke, *Mobilizing against Nuclear Energy.*

4. This history relies extensively on, and at times paraphrases, Price, "The Emergence of the Antinuclear Movement," in *The Antinuclear Movement,* 1–37.

5. Steven Ebbin and Raphael Kasper, *Citizens Groups and the Nuclear Power Controversy* (Cambridge: MIT Press, 1974); Stephen Del Sesto, *Science, Politics, and Controversy: Civilian Nuclear Power in the United States, 1946–1974* (Boulder, Colo.: Westview Press, 1979).

6. John Gofman and Arthur Tamplin, *Poisoned Power.*

7. Daniel Ford, *The Cult of the Atom.*

8. For an excellent history that traces the environmental movement back to the founding of the United States, see Stewart L. Udall, *The Quiet Crisis and the Next Generation* (Salt Lake City: Peregrine Smith Books, 1988). For a broad interpretation of the history of the environmental movement in the twentieth century, see Robert Gottlieb, *Forcing the Spring: The Transformation of the American Environmental Movement* (Washington, D.C.: Island Press, 1993).

9. See Union of Concerned Scientists, *The Risks of Nuclear Power Reactors: A Review of the NRC Reactor Safety Study WASH-1400* (Cambridge, Mass.: Union of Concerned Scientists, 1977).

10. Donald W. Stever Jr., *Seabrook and the Nuclear Regulatory Commission* (Hanover, N.H.: University Press of New England, 1980).

11. For excellent documentation and discussion, see Joppke, "Three Mile Island and the Decline of Nuclear Power in the United States," in *Mobilizing against Nuclear Power,* 133–59.

12. Flavin, *Reassessing Nuclear Power.*

13. For an insightful discussion of this shift and its impact on the antinuclear movement, see Joppke, "From Energy to Weapons: The Changing Nuclear Opposition," *Mobilizing against Nuclear Power,* 144–59.

14. For a summary of the Reagan and Bush administrations' nuclear policies, see Price, *The Antinuclear Movement,* 24–27.

15. Joppke, *Mobilizing against Nuclear Power,* 148–49.

16. Price, *The Antinuclear Movement,* 132.

17. See especially Nelkin and Pollak, "Social and Political Significance," chapter 14 in *The Atom Besieged,* 192–99; and Price, "Postscript on Green Politics," in *The Antinuclear Movement* (rev. ed. 1990), 140–41. For a comprehensive discussion of the thinking and movements that encompass radical ecology, see Carolyn Merchant, *Radical Ecology: The Search for a Livable World* (New York: Routledge, 1992).

18. Snow and Benford, "Ideology, Frame Resonance, and Participant Mobilization," *International Social Movement Research* 1 (1988): 198. For a comprehensive discussion of "framing collective action," see Sidney Tarrow, *Power in Movement: Social Movements, Collective Action and Politics* (Cambridge: Cambridge University Press, 1994), 118–34.

19. Tarrow, *Power in Movement.* As Tarrow has argued, to apply usefully to social movements, social theory must be extended beyond the issue of "consensus mobilization" or "consensus framing" to address the question of how resource-poor actors can mount and sustain collective action against powerful opponents. This is particularly true in the case of the antinuclear movement, which began as a contest between marginal protesters and dissident scientists against the then seemingly omnipotent power of the "atomic brotherhood" and its allies in business and government.

Combining the theoretical insights of Snow and Benford, and of Tarrow, we can identify four factors that affected the mobilizing potential of the antinuclear movement. These are the (1) core framing tasks, or consensus mobilization; (2) political opportunity structure; (3) tactics of contention; and (4) cycles of protest. Together, these factors are essential to what Tarrow calls the "construction of movement" and, in the case of the antinuclear movement, to the successful "outcomes of movement."

This is not the appropriate format for exploring these four factors in depth, or for an extensive discussion of the antinuclear movement and social theory. (For a comprehensive discussion of "The Antinuclear Movement and Sociological Theory," see Price, *The Antinuclear Movement,* 143–58.) However, we would note that from a theoretical perspective, the mobilizing principles articulated in this chapter have played an essential role both in shaping the dynamics of each of these four factors and in determining the "construction" and the "outcomes" of the antinuclear movement.

20. Daniel M. Berman and John T. O'Connor, *Who Owns the Sun? People, Politics, and the Struggle for a Solar Economy* (White River Junction, Vt.: Chelsea Green Publishing, 1996). This section draws extensively on the ideas presented in chapter 8, "Fighting for a New Solar Economy," 213–45, and paraphrases the "blueprint for a revitalized solar movement" outlined on page 241.

21. Ibid., 177.

22. Kennedy, *Profiles in Courage,* 250.

23. Ibid., 256–57.

24. Lester R. Brown, "The Acceleration of History," in Lester R. Brown et al., *State of the World 1996* (New York: W. W. Norton, 1996), 4.

25. Ibid., 4–7. L. Brown points out that "in 1996, world carryover stocks of grain—the amount in the bin when the new harvest begins—are projected to drop to 245 million tons, down from 294 million tons in 1995. This third consecutive annual decline will reduce stocks to an estimated 49 days of consumption, the lowest level on record."

26. For a detailed description of this meeting, see Anthony Sampson, *The Seven Sisters: The Great Oil Companies and the World They Shaped* (New York: Bantam Books, 1975), 1–20.

27. For a report on the Berlin Conference, see Christopher Flavin, "Facing Up to the Risks of Climate Change," in L. Brown, *State of the World 1996,* 21–39.

28. Ibid., 33.

29. Romm and Curtis, "Mideast Oil Forever?" 74.

30. Yergin, *The Prize,* 780.

Selected Bibliography

We have included some of the more important books related to the nuclear power controversy and the renewable-energy future, including a few earlier works that are worth reading. Most of these books are cited at some point in the text.

Alliance to Save Energy, et al. *America's Energy Choices*. Cambridge, Mass.: Union of Concerned Scientists, 1991. A detailed analysis of four renewable-energy scenarios, including a climate stabilization case.

Baldwin, Neil. *Edison: Inventing the Century*. New York: Hyperion, 1995. This first biography of Edison chronicles the development of the electric light-bulb and the birth of the electric power industry.

Ballard Power Systems, Inc. *Annual Report 1994*. North Vancouver, British Columbia, Canada. Corporate annual report of North America's largest hydrogen power fuel cell company outlines both current research and commercialization strategies.

Berman, Daniel M., and John T. O'Connor. *Who Owns the Sun? People, Politics, and the Struggle for a Solar Economy*. White River Junction, Vt.: Chelsea Green Publishing, 1996. This book examines the political basis for the failure of once-promising renewable technologies and calls for the public ownership of energy and for renewed citizen activism to revitalize the solar energy industry.

Brower, Michael. *Cool Energy: Renewable Solutions to Environmental Problems*. Cambridge: MIT Press, 1992. Examines technologies and policies needed for a renewable-energy future.

Brown, Lester R. "The Acceleration of History." In Lester R. Brown, et al., *State of the World 1996*. New York: W. W. Norton, 1996. This seminal article outlines an unprecedented acceleration in the crossing of global sustainable yield thresholds, particularly in the areas of food production and greenhouse gas emissions.

Campbell, John L. *Collapse of an Industry: Nuclear Power and the Contradictions of U.S. Policy*. Ithaca: Cornell University Press, 1988. Excellent institutional analysis argues that the nuclear industry died well before the appearance of major accidents, public protests, and energy conservation; focus on unique role of U.S. institutions in nuclear policy failure.

Carter, Michelle, and Michael Christensen. *Children of Chernobyl*. Minneapolis: Augsburg, 1993. Explores the Chernobyl disaster within the context of the collapse of the Soviet Union and the efforts to provide ongoing care to the victims of the world's worst nuclear accident.

Cavanagh, Ralph. "Electrical Energy Futures." *Environmental Law* 14, no. 133 (1983). Excellent historical description of the evolution of electric power in the Pacific Northwest and analysis of the planning errors that led to the WPPSS bond default.

Cole, Nancy, and P. J. Skerrett. *Renewables Are Ready: People Creating Renewable Energy Solutions*. White River Junction, Vt.: Chelsea Green Publishing, 1995. A case study guide to renewable-energy technologies currently being implemented in diverse local communities across the United States.

Flavin, Christopher, and Nicholas Lenssen. *Power Surge: Guide to the Coming Energy Revolution*. New York: W. W. Norton, 1994. Argues that the world energy economy is poised for a major shift from oil and coal to clean, decentralized renewable-energy systems over the next few decades.

———. *Powering the Future: Blueprint for a Sustainable Electric Industry*. Worldwatch Paper 119. Washington, D.C.: Worldwatch Institute, 1994. Outlines the sweeping changes facing the $800-billion global electric power industry and proposes an environmentally sound model for the power industry.

Ford, Daniel. *The Cult of the Atom*. New York: Simon and Schuster, 1982. Exposé based on secret files of the U.S. Atomic Energy Commission. Documents repeated suppression of reports on the real risks of catastrophic nuclear accidents in the early years of nuclear industry.

———. *Three Mile Island: Thirty Minutes to Meltdown*. New York: Penguin, 1982. Traces the development of the Three Mile Island nuclear power plant and explains why the accident occurred, how it was handled, and what it portends for the future.

Gleckman, Howard. *WPPSS: From Dream to Default*. Special Report. New York: The Bond Buyer, 1983. Provides historical and financial analysis of the Washington Public Power Supply System's $2.25 billion default from the bondholders' perspective.

Gofman, John W. *Radiation-Induced Cancer from Low-Dose Exposure: An Independent Analysis*. San Francisco: Committee for Nuclear Responsibility Book Division, 1990. Comprehensive analysis of cancers induced by low-dose radiation exposure, including breast cancer, plus definitive projections of all-time Chernobyl-induced fatal cancers.

Gofman, John W., and Arthur Tamplin. *Poisoned Power.* Emmanus, Pa.: Rodale Press, 1971. Report of pioneering research on the effects of radiation on the environment and human beings, written by scientists whose work was suppressed by the Atomic Energy Commission.

Gottlieb, Robert. *Forcing the Spring: The Transformation of the American Environmental Movement.* Washington, D.C.: Island Press, 1993. Provides a broad interpretation of the history of the environmental movement in the twentieth century, in the context of other social movements that arose over the past century.

Grossman, Karl. *Power Crazy.* New York: Grove Press, 1986. Documents the history of how citizen and legislator opposition to Long Island Light Company's Shoreham power plant ultimately led New York Governor Cuomo to prevent the plant from opening.

Gyorgy, Anna. *No Nukes: Everyone's Guide to Nuclear Power.* 2d ed. Boston: South End Press, 1980. The first edition of this book was the handbook for antinuclear activists in the late 1970s.

Henderson, Hazel. *The Politics of the Solar Age: Alternatives to Economics.* Indianapolis: Knowledge Systems, 1988. This far-reaching work reconceptualizes economics from an ecological perspective and advocates a shift from the present petroleum era to a new solar age.

Hertsgaard, Mark. *Nuclear Inc.* New York: Pantheon, 1983. One of the most incisive analyses of nuclear power during the Reagan era.

Hoyle, Fred. *Energy or Extinction? The Case for Nuclear Energy.* Salem, N.H.: Heinemann Educational Books, 1977. Considered by the nuclear industry to be one of the best explanations of energy and nuclear power.

Jasper, James M. *Nuclear Politics: Energy and the State in the United States, Sweden, and France.* Princeton: Princeton University Press, 1990. Comparative international analysis evaluates the impact of structural, cultural, and biographical influences on nuclear power in three nations.

Joppke, Christian. *Mobilizing against Nuclear Energy: A Comparison of Germany and the United States.* Berkeley: University of California Press, 1993. Insightful cross-national analysis of the origins, courses, and outcomes of the antinuclear movements in West Germany and the United States.

Kahn, Edward. *Electric Utility Planning and Regulation.* Berkeley, Calif.: American Council for an Energy-Efficient Economy, 1991. Provides detailed economic analysis and discussion of the "electric utilities at the crossroads" and of the historical and contemporary factors causing the evolution of the utility industry.

Kemeny, John G., and other members of the President's Commission on the Accident at Three Mile Island. *The Need for Change: The Legacy of TMI.* Washington, D.C.: Government Printing Office, 1979. Official report of the President's Commission on Three Mile Island, whose findings led to increased regulatory oversight and safety retrofitting of nuclear power plants.

Kennedy, John F. *Profiles in Courage.* 1956. Reprint, commemorative edition, New York: Harper and Row, 1964. Kennedy's Pulitzer Prize–winning profiles of eight public figures who had the courage to follow their convictions on matters of principle despite their vilification by the overwhelming majority of voters.

Komanoff, Charles, and Cora Roelofs. *Fiscal Fission: The Economic Failure of Nuclear Power, A Report on the Historical Costs of Nuclear Power in the United States.* Washington, D.C.: Greenpeace, 1992. Only industry-wide study to assemble and evaluate *all* the costs of nuclear power (including capital costs, operating costs, and "back-end" costs such as decommissioning set-asides and waste disposal payments) and combine these with cancellation write-offs and federal subsidies.

Lovins, Amory B. *Soft Energy Paths: Toward a Durable Peace.* New York: Harper and Row, 1979. Expanded analysis of Lovins's seminal 1976 *Foreign Affairs* article "Energy Strategy: The Road Not Taken?" which provided the theoretical and technological underpinnings for the renewable, soft path energy case.

Lovins, Amory B., and L. Hunter Lovins. *Brittle Power: Energy Strategy for National Security.* Andover, Mass.: Brick House Publishing, 1982. Documents the national security implications of a centralized energy system prone to sudden massive failures.

Marples, David R. *The Social Impact of the Chernobyl Disaster.* New York: St. Martin's Press, 1988. Detailed examination of the social and human aftermath of the world's worst nuclear accident, based on a wide variety of Soviet source materials and a fact-finding mission to the Soviet Union in 1987.

McKibben, Bill. *The End of Nature.* New York: Anchor Books, 1989. Insightful discussion of the physical and philosophical implications of climate change.

Meadows, Donella H., et al. *Beyond the Limits.* Post Mills, Vt.: Chelsea Green Publishing, 1992. Argues that the more successfully society delays its limits through economic and technical adaptations, the more likely it is in the future to run into several of those limits at the same time. Suggests that the wisest use of technology is to buy time in order to bring consumption and population down to sustainable levels.

Medvedev, Grigori. *The Truth about Chernobyl.* New York: Basic Books, 1991. Medvedev was the chief engineer at the time of Chernobyl's construction in 1970. He returned to Chernobyl and conducted a complete investigation of the disaster; his report is considered an accurate unofficial source document on the plant and the accident.

Merchant, Carolyn. *Radical Ecology: The Search for a Livable World.* New York: Routledge, 1992. A comprehensive discussion of the thinking and movements that encompass radical ecology.

Nelkin, Dorothy, and Michael Pollack. *The Atom Besieged.* Cambridge: MIT Press, 1982. Comparative analysis of the social and political differences in governmental responses to, and outcomes of, the antinuclear movements in France and Germany.

Price, Jerome. *The Antinuclear Movement.* Rev. ed. Boston: Twayne Publishers, 1990. A comprehensive history and analysis of the antinuclear movement in the United States.

Ramberg, Bennett. *Global Nuclear Energy Risks: The Search for Preventative Medicine.* Boulder, Colo.: Westview Press, 1986. Description of historical international efforts to prevent nuclear proliferation through security measures at nuclear power plants.

Reader, Mark, ed. *Atom's Eve: Ending the Nuclear Age.* New York: McGraw-Hill, 1980. Heralds the end of the nuclear age by compiling the various arguments marshaled against nuclear power.

Roe, David. *Dynamos and Virgins.* New York: Random House, 1984. Roe provides a personal account of the Environmental Defense Fund's early strategies and conflicts with PG&E before the California Public Utilities Commission to establish the principle of least cost planning, based primarily on energy conservation.

Rogovin, Mitchell. *Three Mile Island: A Report to the Commissioners and the Public.* Washington, D.C.: Nuclear Regulatory Commission, 1980. One of several official reports on the Three Mile Island accident; also referred to as the Rogovin Report.

Rudolph, Richard, and Scott Ridley. *Power Struggle: The Hundred-Year War over Electricity.* New York: Harper and Row, 1986. The first book to explore the utility industry's politics and the history of what has been a century-long battle for control of the nation's electric power systems.

Sampson, Anthony. *The Seven Sisters: The Great Oil Companies and the World They Shaped.* New York: Bantam Books, 1975. A brilliant journalistic history of the rise of the great oil companies—the seven sisters—which dominated world economy and diplomacy in the twentieth century.

Schell, Jonathan. *The Fate of the Earth.* New York: Avon Books, 1982. A analysis of the primary and secondary effects of nuclear war and the philosophical issues surrounding our unique ability to end history.

Seto, Mo Ying W., et al. *Nuclear Power: A Current Risk Assessment.* New York: Moody's Investment Service, April 1993. Wall Street analyst's evaluation of investment risks surrounding the nuclear industry.

Stobaugh, Robert, and Daniel Yergin, eds. *Energy Future.* Report of The Energy Project at the Harvard Business School. New York: Vintage Books, 1979. One of several major studies produced in the 1970s to seek policy solutions in the face of the Three Mile Island accident and the oil-based energy crises of the 1970s.

Sugai, Wayne. *Nuclear Power and Ratepayer Protest: The Washington Public Power Supply System Crisis.* Boulder, Colo.: Westview Press, 1987. Describes a model of "mass insurgency" and the ratepayers' revolt as expressed in the Initiative 394 campaign in the state of Washington.

Tarrow, Sidney. *Power in Movement: Social Movements, Collective Action, and Politics.* New York: Cambridge University Press, 1994. Tarrow addresses the question of how resource-poor actors can mount and sustain collective action against powerful opponents. This is particularly significant in the case of the antinuclear movement, which began as a contest of marginal protesters and dissident scientists against the then seemingly omnipotent "atomic brotherhood" and its allies in business and government.

Thomas, Steve D. *The Realities of Nuclear Power: International Economic and Regulatory Experience.* New York: Cambridge University Press, 1988. Describes the international development of nuclear power in major nations.

Udall, Stewart L. *The Quiet Crisis and the Next Generation.* Salt Lake City: Peregrine Smith Books, 1988. An excellent history that traces the environmental movement back to the founding of the republic.

U.S. Council for Energy Awareness. *1990 Annual Report.* Washington, D.C.: USCEA, 1990. Annual report outlines the policies and positions of the nuclear industry and its allies.

Walsh, Edward J. *Democracy in the Shadows: Citizen Mobilization in the Wake of the Accident at TMI.* New York: Greenwood Press, 1988. An examination of the diverse citizens' organizations that arose after the Three Mile Island accident.

Weinberg, Alvin, and Russ Manning. *The Second Nuclear Era: A New Start for Nuclear Power.* New York: Praeger, 1985. An optimistic analysis of the future of nuclear technology.

Willens, Harold. *The Trimtab Factor.* New York: William Morrow, 1984. Personal account of the issues that mobilized business executives to participate in the policy-making arena to end the threat of nuclear war and to change U.S.-Soviet relations.

Yergin, Daniel. *The Prize: The Epic Quest for Oil, Money, and Power.* New York: Simon and Schuster, 1991. Prize-winning historical study of the central role of oil in the economics and politics of the twentieth century.

Index

The Authors

Jerry Brown was born in Paterson, New Jersey. He graduated from Antioch College in 1965 and received his Ph.D. from Cornell University in 1972. He has taught and published in the areas of social movements, energy policy, industrial competitiveness, and environmental technology. During the past 25 years, he has served in executive roles with a variety of public policy organizations, including Cesar Chavez's United Farm Workers (UFW), Floridians United for Safe Energy (FUSE), and Business Executives for National Security (BENS). He is associate professor of environmental studies and sociology/anthropology at Florida International University in Miami. He also serves as an investment-banking consultant to technology companies and is a fellow of the World Business Academy.

Rinaldo Brutoco was born in Toronto, Canada. He received a Juris Doctor degree with highest honors from UCLA School of Law in 1971. While attending UCLA, he founded California's first nonprofit, public-interest law center. Over the past two decades, he has developed a reputation as an innovative and socially conscious business entrepreneur. He is the founder of the World Business Academy and was its president during its first five years; he serves on the boards of the Gorbachev Foundation USA and The Men's Wearhouse. He is the cofounder and CEO of Red Rose Collection, a San Francisco–based catalog company that sells "products for empowering people."

The Editor

Robert D. Benford received his Ph.D. from the University of Texas at Austin in 1987 and is associate professor of sociology at the University of Nebraska–Lincoln. His published works include *The Nuclear Cage* (with Lester Kurtz and Jennifer Turpin) and numerous articles and book chapters on social movements, nuclear politics, war and peace museums, environmental controversies, and qualitative research methods. His current research focuses on the linkages between the social construction of movement discourse, collective identity, and collective memory.